CHILD DEVELOPMENT
AND
BEHAVIORAL PEDIATRICS

CROSSCURRENTS IN CONTEMPORARY PSYCHOLOGY

A series of volumes edited by Marc H. Bornstein

CHILD DEVELOPMENT
AND
BEHAVIORAL PEDIATRICS

Edited by

Marc H. Bornstein
and
Janice L. Genevro

National Institute of Child Health and Human Development

LAWRENCE ERLBAUM ASSOCIATES, PUBLISHERS

1996   Mahwah, New Jersey

Lawrence Erlbaum Associates, Inc., Publishers
10 Industrial Avenue
Mahwah, NJ   07430

Library of Congress Cataloging-in-Publication Data

Child development and behavioral pediatrics / edited by Marc H. Bornstein and Janice L. Genevro.
    p. cm. — (Crosscurrents in contemporary psychology)
Includes bibliographical references and index.
ISBN 0-8058-2364-6 (cloth : alk. paper)
    1. Pediatrics—Psychological aspects. 2. Sick children—Psychology. I. Genevro, Janice L. II. Series.
RJ47.5.C4415 1996
618.92'0001'9—dc20   96-15892
                                                             CIP

Books published by Lawrence Erlbaum Associates are printed on acid-free paper and their bindings are chosen for strength and durability.

Printed in the United States of America
10 9 8 7 6 5 4 3 2 1

In Memoriam

Anita Rose Bornstein

*who dedicated her professional life
to better the lives of young children*

and

E. Beatrice Genevro and George W. Genevro

and *In Memoriam*

Elva B. Dale and F. Cameron Dale

*who have inspired others to follow their examples
as educators, parents, grandparents, and activists
caring for the generations that follow*

Series Prologue

CROSSCURRENTS IN CONTEMPORARY PSYCHOLOGY

Contemporary psychology is increasingly diversified, pluralistic, and specialized, and most psychologists venture beyond the confines of their substantive specialty only rarely. Yet psychologists with different specialties encounter similar problems, ask similar questions, and share similar concerns. Unfortunately, today there are very few arenas available for the expression or exploration of what is common across psychological subdisciplines. The *Crosscurrents in Contemporary Psychology* series is intended to serve as such a forum.

The chief aim of this series is to provide integrated perspectives on supradisciplinary themes in psychology. The first volume in the series was devoted to a consideration of *Psychological Development from Infancy*; the second volume to *Comparative Methods in Psychology*; volumes three, four, and five examined relations between *Psychology and Its Allied Disciplines* in the humanities, the social sciences, and the natural sciences; volume six concerned itself with *Sensitive Periods in Development*; volume seven focused on *Interaction in Human Development*; and volume eight with *Cultural Approaches to Parenting*. This volume examines the intersection of child development and behavioral pediatrics. Future volumes in this series will be devoted to the segmentation of behavior and the role of the nonnormal in understanding the normal.

Each volume in this series treats a different issue and is self-contained, yet the series as a whole endeavors to interrelate psychological subdisciplines by bringing shared perspectives to bear on a variety of concerns common to psychological theory and research. As a consequence of this structure and the flexibility and scope it affords, volumes in the *Crosscurrents in Contemporary Psychology* series will appeal, individually or as a group, to scientists with diverse interests. Reflecting the nature and intent of this series, contributing authors are drawn from a broad spectrum of humanities and sciences—anthropology to zoology—but representational emphasis is placed on active contributing authorities to the contemporary psychological literature.

Crosscurrents in Contemporary Psychology is a series whose explicit intent is to explore a broad range of crossdisciplinary concerns. In its focus on such issues, the series is devoted to promoting interest in the interconnectedness of research and theory in psychological study.

Child Development and Behavioral Pediatrics derives from original presentations given at a workshop of the same name held on March 29, 1995, in Indianapolis, Indiana. The workshop was sponsored by the National Institute of Child Health and Human Development. We are especially grateful to Barbara Wright for her devotion, help, and good cheer during the organization of the workshop and the production of this volume; to Dr. Arthur S. Levine and Dr. Duane F. Alexander of the National Institute of Child Health and Human Development for sponsoring the workshop and for their continuing support of research into all facets of human growth and children's health; and to the production staff at LEA for continuing excellence.

Marc H. Bornstein
Janice L. Genevro

Contents

Contributors to This Volume

Dr. Curt Acredolo   Department of Applied Behavioral Sciences, University of California, Davis, Davis, CA 95616

Dr. Carol Andreassen   Child and Family Research/NICHD, Building 31 Room B2B15, 9000 Rockville Pike, Bethesda, MD 20892-2030

Dr. Marc H. Bornstein   Child and Family Research/NICHD, Building 31 Room B2B15, 9000 Rockville Pike, Bethesda, MD 20892-2030

Dr. W. Thomas Boyce   School of Epidemiology and Child Development, School of Public Health and Institute of Human Development, 570 University Hall #1190, University of California, Berkeley, Berkeley, CA 94720-1190

Dr. Janice L. Genevro   Child and Family Research/NICHD, Building 31 Room B2B15, 9000 Rockville Pike, Bethesda, MD 20892-2030

Dr. Zeev N. Kain   Yale University School of Medicine, Department of Anesthesiology, 333 Cedar Street, New Haven, CT 06510

Dr. Nancy Leffert   Search Institute, Thresher Square West, 700 South Third Street, Suite 210, Minneapolis, MN 55415

Dr. Linda C. Mayes   Yale Child Study Center, 230 S. Frontage Road, New Haven, CT 06510

Dr. Jacqueline O'Connor   Department of Applied Behavioral Sciences, University of California, Davis, Davis, CA 95616

Dr. Hanuš Papoušek   Institut für Soziale Pädiatrie und Jugendmedizin, Universität München, Heiglhofstrasse 63, 8000 Munich 70, Germany

Dr. Mechthild Papoušek   Institut für Soziale Pädiatrie und Jugendmedizin, Universität München, Heiglhofstrasse 63, 8000 Munich 70, Germany

Dr. Arthur H. Parmelee, Jr.   764 Iliff Street, Pacific Palisades, CA 90272

Dr. Anne C. Petersen   National Science Foundation, Room 1205, 4201 Wilson Boulevard, Arlington, VA 22230

Dr. David Steward   687 The Alameda, Berkeley, CA 94707

Dr. Margaret S. Steward   Office of the Dean, School of Medicine, University of California, Davis, Davis, CA 95616

1

Child Development and Behavioral Pediatrics: An Introduction

Marc H. Bornstein
Janice L. Genevro
National Institute of Child Health and Human Development

Being sick is a normal part of childhood, and being seriously ill or a patient is the unfortunate lot of many children. Every child in the United States has some contact with the health care system at some time, and it is estimated that one out of every two children or adolescents is hospitalized as a result of illness or injury. In other words, routine well-child care and medical visits for minor illnesses, injuries, and the like are common experiences in the lives of most children, and many children must face even more serious medical issues. Being injured, undergoing routine medical procedures, getting sick, or being hospitalized all confront children with challenges on many levels—physical, mental, emotional, and social.

This aspect of the normal ecology of childhood involves both child developmentalists and pediatricians. Yet, child development specialists with medical interests are few and far between, and pediatricians normally have so many practical matters, other than the cognitive and social issues of their patients, to address that justifiably developmental concerns, individual differences, and the like are often given short shrift. Such concerns fail to recruit much attention in general pediatrics training, and next to the exigencies of more purely biological and physiological approaches to children's health care, may fall near the bottom of the priority list. This unhappy and unproductive situation is more than unfortunate. Although the

1

pioneers of modern pediatrics recognized child development issues as a major concern, pediatricians' training in the recent past has focused on the biological and biochemical, and on laboratory investigations of the origins and treatment of specific physical disorders. Psychology's interests lie in the social, emotional, and mental aspects of children's development and child health, but psychologists' training has traditionally neglected critical physical health aspects of development in favor of normal ontogeny, except perhaps for health issues in at-risk populations.

It has also been the case that methods for assessing children's trauma and responses to trauma have often been borrowed whole cloth from adult concepts and instruments, and attempts to assess children's understanding and coping with medical events have sometimes rather simplistically adopted adult models, as if children's emotions, cognitions, and behaviors, and approaches to understanding them, were qualitatively the same as those of adults. Reciprocally, adults who observe children's illness or who must administer pain frequently use different criteria for assessing a child's distress than the child would, and they are prone to underestimate children's pain. Clearly, developmental psychology and medical advances are out of sync with one another.

Foresightedly, Abraham Jacobi, the father of pediatrics in the United States, emphasized differences between the medical treatments of children and adults in the late 1800s: The "therapeutics of infancy and childhood are by no means so similar to those of the adult that the rules of the latter can simply be adapted to the former by reducing doses. The differences are many" (U.S. Department of Health, Education, and Welfare, 1976, p. 9). Thus, children exhibit systematic differences in responses to illness and injury, even in the appraisal of threat, based on demographic and developmental characteristics. For example, with development comes an increasing capacity for the cognitive representation of events and a concomitantly increasing capacity for cognitive regulation of the event-response process. Children's representations of themselves, others, and the world around them thus could play a critical role in shaping and facilitating their coping responses to distressing medical experiences.

The premise of this volume is that developmental and psychological factors are central elements in many current problems in child health, including persistent crying in infants, sources of children's injury and respiratory illness, children's coping with medical procedures, childhood trauma, and physical and mental well-being in adolescence. Understanding, promoting, and maintaining children's health, therefore, depend to a great extent—and are likely to depend even more in the future—on elucidating the determinants and consequences of children's and parents' health-related behaviors and attitudes.

Current theories of child development as a continuing transaction between children's inherent characteristics and the multiple environments in which they develop provide a foundation for identifying and understanding the ways in which children's physical health and development are intertwined. Developmental scientists argue that inherited constitution and experienced environments mutually influence one another during the course of development of the individual (see Gottlieb, 1983; Hinde, 1983). This so-called *transactional* model is further articulated by the recognition that inherent characteristics of individuals are shaped by experience and vice versa, and that a constant process of mutual influence between heredity and experience continues throughout childhood, and, indeed, the life span (Sameroff, 1983; Sameroff & Chandler, 1975). The transactional view holds that the effects of an experience depend on the nature of the specific experience and the constitutional endowment of/interpretation by the child. Similarly, the individual's contribution to his or her own development at any point reflects endogenous characteristics in combination with aspects of that individual's life history. If a particular child's early experiences were pathogenic, a positive new experience may be able to reverse some adverse effects, but the child may still be worse off than another child whose early experiences were benign and who later encountered the same positive new experience.

This perspective emphasizes the ways in which biologically based propensities and individual experiences mutually influence development. Neither biological predispositions nor experiences alone determine the course, direction, termination, or final resting level of development; rather, these life forces influence one another as development proceeds. The transactional model of development applies to the analysis and understanding of medical problems in children. From child development comes the view that maturational status, developmental level, experiential history, and individual differences factors (like intelligence, gender, temperament, and so forth) coordinate to engender differential reactions and responses to everyday as well as severe medical challenges. From behavioral pediatrics comes the view that biological, physical, and epidemiological factors converge to challenge the child medically. It is the task of child development and behavioral pediatrics to coordinate these joint perspectives on children's health problems.

This approach is also consonant with models that highlight the systemic nature of development, and take "an integrative approach to the multiple levels of organization presumed to comprise the nature of human life"

(Lerner, Castellino, Terry, Villarruel, & McKinney, 1995, p. 286). Development is thus a process in which the child as a multidimensional biological, cognitive, social, and emotional being engages in transactions with multi-layered environments, including parents (with their own biological, cognitive, social, and emotional characteristics) and larger networks, including siblings and family, peers, school, culture, and of primary import for this discussion, the health care system.

Applying a transactional systems approach to understanding children's health and illness experiences is demonstrated, for example, in recognizing the ineluctable role parents play in their children's wellness and illness. Children are not alone in becoming ill or getting well. Children do not make their own health care decisions; other people usually do, and the people most likely to be involved are parents and doctors (Hickson & Clayton, 1995). As medical ethics today increasingly rejects a paternalistic model of medical decision making, parents are brought even more into that decision making. Therefore, parents' concerns regarding pediatric practice are of substantial import. Hickson, Altemeier, and O'Connor (1983) interviewed a large number of mothers whose children were waiting to be seen in group pediatrics practices. Parents were asked to indicate all the concerns they had for their children and their single greatest concern. Fully 70% of parents' greatest concerns related to behavior, development, adjustment to life changes (divorce, moving, death of a family member), and the transition to adolescence, and not to issues concerning physical health. Yet, only 30% of those parents with psychosocial concerns indicated that they had ever brought, or intended to bring, those same concerns to the attention of their children's doctors, even though many parents indicated that these problems were disruptive to their households. When asked why, some parents stated that there was simply no time in the confines of a pediatric visit to deal with such issues. Others believed that physicians were not interested in providing such assistance, and many indicated that they never recognized that a pediatrician might be a source of help. The parent–physician relationship represents a dialogue of critical importance to the child and exemplifies the multidimensional, systemic nature of care in children's health.

The contributors to this volume include physicians and psychologists who apply principles of developmental and social psychology to their research on specific problems in children's health. These chapters therefore delineate current areas of collaboration between developmental psychology and behavioral pediatrics. We hope that these perspectives will prompt researchers and practitioners to explore additional ways in which more extensive endeavors at the interface of these two disciplines will facilitate efforts to understand children's health behaviors and foster children's well-being.

Following this Introduction, in chapter 2, Mechthild and Hanuš Papoušek address "Infantile Persistent Crying, State Regulation, and Interaction With Parents: A Systems View." The Papoušeks decompose sources of infant persistent crying, a common problem in pediatric practice and a major cause of new parents' distress. They examine the etiology and pathophysiology of infantile persistent crying from a dynamic systems perspective and identify regulatory failures in the organization of infants' sleep–wake cycles. In addition, they evaluate constitutional variation in babies in conjunction with a revealing analysis of everyday contexts and consequences of parent–infant interaction style. Their approach portends new kinds of remediation and therapeutic intervention in families in which persistent infant crying is a concern.

Chapter 3 addresses relations of "Biobehavioral Reactivity and Injuries in Children and Adolescents." In a set of complementary studies, W. Thomas Boyce underscores the role played by individual variability in cardiovascular and immune reactivity to environmental stress in the incidence of childhood injury and illness. Individual differences factors in children, as he shows, are keys to understanding relations between stress and specific child health outcomes: The incidence of injury and illness relates to an interaction between stress and individual variation in reactivity in children.

Janice L. Genevro, Carol J. Andreassen, and Marc H. Bornstein present two studies of "Young Children's Understanding of Routine Medical Care and Strategies for Coping With Stressful Medical Experiences." They have found, in evaluations of children's everyday knowledge of pediatric care and adjustment to hospitalization and surgery, that developmental processes and individual differences are reflected in children's understanding and in the coping resources children bring with them to these challenging, and potentially threatening, circumstances. Age, gender, and specific cognitive capabilities relate to children's coping knowledge and preferences, for example.

Zeev N. Kain and Linda C. Mayes, in chapter 5 on "Anxiety in Children During the Perioperative Period," address concerns regarding preoperative anxiety in children, especially as it modifies children's responses to preparation for elective surgery. Contrary to common belief—and unfortunately—children whose parents are present exhibit more anxiety at the time of anesthesia administration, and mothers who receive a preparation program appear more anxious, leading to a reevaluation of the role of parents in the perioperative period and their influences on their children's adjustment to potentially distressing medical situations.

Margaret S. Steward, Jacqueline O'Connor, Curt Acredolo, and David S. Steward then present a theoretical model to guide the longitudinal study of survivors of cancer across the transition from middle childhood to adolescence in chapter 6, "The Trauma and Memory of Cancer Treatment in Children." Their specific interests focus on investigating links between children's trauma during cancer treatment and children's memories as survivors. Steward et al. review theory and empirical advances in the study of cognitions related to childhood trauma, as well as the methodological possibility of assessing the impact of traumatic events—and survivors' memories and reappraisals of those events—on the development of children's health behavior patterns and developing personality characteristics.

Nancy Leffert and Anne C. Petersen address "Biology, Challenge, and Coping in Adolescence: Effects on Physical and Mental Health" in chapter 7. Adolescence is a time of multiple changes and challenges, telescoped to a brief period. As a major developmental transition, adolescence is characterized by significant alterations: The physical changes of puberty are dramatic, and social changes occur in multiple settings, such as school transitions, peer relations, and family interactions. Adolescents are especially likely to find themselves in new and challenging situations, and they are particularly vulnerable to impulsive behaviors, which contribute to special health risks. The amount of change experienced by young people may be so stressful as to sometimes tax their capacity to cope.

In a concluding commentary, Arthur H. Parmelee, Jr. offers observations about all these contributions. In the main, he points out that children's health and illness experiences are a part of the larger stream of their psychological and physical development, and of their acquisition of vital social knowledge. Parmelee emphasizes well-child visits as important opportunities for education and pediatric intervention with families. Such visits may represent the only chance many parents have to speak with professionals about their concerns about their children's developmental and psychological well-being.

A set of common themes emerges out of the substantive topical variety that constitutes the local foci of chapters in this volume. Commonalities are especially noteworthy in the study of adjustment and development in children. Age, gender, cognitive, emotional, and social capabilities, as well as biological substrates, and how these individual differences factors in children interact with parental beliefs and behaviors to affect pediatric health care utilization and children's own health-related behaviors and cognitions also show commonalities. For example, Boyce demonstrates that individual differences in biobehavioral reactivity moderate associations between psychological stress and the incidence of certain kinds of injuries and illnesses. Kain and Mayes show that contemporary preparation strategies for children's surgery, however advanced and well intended, may be ineffective for certain children and in some children may even provoke anxiety.

Where associations between behavioral predictions and child development have been explored, they have produced increasingly sophisticated approaches to and analyses of medical problems. This observation is illustrated by elaborating on the roles of central individual differences factors and the developmental function in children for several health-related issues that are discussed in this volume. For example, Genevro et al. point out how children's age relates positively to their knowledge of coping (especially cognitive distraction) strategies. Steward and colleagues indicate, and Leffert and Petersen echo, that, although adolescence should be a very healthy stage in the life cycle, it may be the most risky: The leading causes of morbidity and mortality in adolescence relate to risk decisions made by adolescents themselves. Further, Kain and Mayes identify differential concerns of younger versus older surgical patients, and report that younger patients are more anxious with preoperative preparation. Regarding gender, Genevro and colleagues point to subtle but significant gender effects, and Leffert and Petersen indicate higher rates of clinical risk for early developing girls. In the cognitive domain, Genevro et al. report on the role of problem-solving differences in children's understanding of medical procedures and coping. Likewise, Steward and colleagues underscore the mediating role of memory in relation to adolescent outcomes in survivors of childhood cancer.

By far the most consistent theme, however, concerns the intersection of temperament, personality, and social styles. The Papoušeks reference the critical importance of variation in parental interactional styles. Kain and Mayes point to the compound of trauma by parents' distress responses in children's anesthesia administration. Steward et al. describe how some children, having survived a life-threatening event, respond by becoming conservative in regard to risky behaviors, whereas others respond with either an increased attitude of invulnerability or an increased sense of external control (or both), leading to more liberal attitudes toward risky behavior.

In addition, other biological and physiological individual differences factors arise in these discussions, including the Papoušeks on individual differences in sleep–wake regulation in infants; Boyce on individual differences in cardiovascular and immune reactivity in young children; and

Leffert and Petersen on individual differences in iron deficiency in adolescents.

An inevitable consequence of these developments in the discrimination of individual and family adaptation is a tailoring of intervention, remediation, and therapeutic programs. Closer behavioral analysis and application mean more complexity and subtlety, but also, presumably, efforts that promise enhanced effectiveness in medical treatment of the young.

We would add several further observations to this discussion. The first (inevitably) concerns future research. There are many leads to pursue, but the following spring directly from the intersection of issues captured in these chapters: On the individual differences question, for example, what factors render some children and adolescents vulnerable and others seemingly resilient to the potentially traumatizing effects of diverse medical interventions—some to develop effective coping styles, and others, less fortunately, to develop ineffective coping styles that may become lifelong patterns? We think these are especially fruitful preventive and therapeutic questions for pediatric psychology. Also, an interesting empirical conundrum arises with respect to the sequelae of childhood medical experience: Childhood trauma has been assumed by some to have a lifelong influence on personality and behavior. However, the nature and magnitude of the effects of trauma on children, as well as on adults and the family around them, and the factors that determine the qualitative nature or accentuate or diminish the influence of childhood trauma, are ambiguous and certainly merit the future attention of researchers.

Second, we think the work included in this volume reinforces the value of dynamical systems views of development for psychological and pediatric research and further promotes the significance of specificity in research. This body of work invites exploration of joint, interactive effects of multiple environmental and biological factors on the incidence and treatment of illness and injury in children. Leffert and Petersen, for example, show how the confluence of physiological, cognitive, psychosocial, and parenting changes combine to influence the nature of children's coping with the challenge of adolescence. And, as the Papoušeks show at the start, pediatric approaches and psychological approaches—when implemented alone—proved insufficient and unsuccessful in attacking a model problem of infant persistent crying; however, joined together they provided some greater success and relief for children and parents. Similarly, as Genevro et al. propose, children's coping with medical treatments designed to benefit them, and their subsequent adaptation, may be facilitated by assisting children in appraising and making sense of the experiences and the resources they themselves bring to these specific and troubling situations.

We hope that these chapters foster further interdisciplinary collaborations, where "the action" in the future of pediatric psychology research and practice may be. Attention to this work should also lead to more direct clinical applicability, and translation for preventive policy strategies and therapeutic interventions.

Medical and psychological research together can better address questions about optimal diagnosis and programs, the child populations that are likely to benefit from different types of services, and the increasingly sophisticated and comprehensive training of professionals in clinical health care. Promoting collaboration among pediatricians and psychologists can only result in the better treatment of all aspects of children's growth and development.

REFERENCES

Gottlieb, G. (1983). The psychobiological approach to developmental issues. In P. H. Mussen (Series Ed.) and M. M. Haith & J. J. Campos (Eds.), *Handbook of child psychology: Vol. 2. Infancy and developmental psychobiology* (pp. 1–26). New York: Wiley.

Hickson, G. B., Altemeier, W. A., & O'Connor, S. (1983). Concerns of mothers seeking care in private pediatric offices: Opportunities for expanding services. *Pediatrics, 72,* 619–624.

Hickson, G. B., & Clayton, E. W. (1995). Parents and their children's doctors. In M. H. Bornstein (Ed.), *Handbook of parenting: Vol. 4, Applied and practical parenting* (pp. 163–185). Mahwah, NJ: Lawrence Erlbaum Associates.

Hinde, R. A. (1983). Ethology and child development. In P. Mussen (Series Ed.) and M. M. Haith & J. J. Campos (Eds.), *Handbook of child psychology: Vol. 2. Infancy and developmental psychobiology* (pp. 27–94). New York: Wiley.

Lerner, R. M., Castellino, D. R., Terry, P. A., Villarruel, F. A., & McKinney, M. H. (1995). Developmental contextual perspective on parenting. In M. H. Bornstein (Ed.), *Handbook of parenting: Vol. 2. Biology and ecology of parenting* (pp. 285–309). Mahwah, NJ: Lawrence Erlbaum Associates.

Sameroff, A. J. (1983). Developmental systems: Contexts and evolution. In P. H. Mussen (Series Ed.) & W. Kessen (Ed.), *Handbook of child psychology: Vol. 1. History, theory, and methods* (pp. 237–294). New York: Wiley.

Sameroff, A. J., & Chandler, M. J. (1975). Reproductive risk and the continuum of caretaking casualty. In F. D. Horowitz (Ed.), *Review of child development research* (Vol. 4, pp. 187–244). Chicago: University of Chicago Press.

United States Department of Health, Education, & Welfare. (1976). *Child health in America.* Rockville, MD: Author.

2

Infantile Persistent Crying, State Regulation, and Interaction With Parents: A Systems View

Mechthild Papoušek
Hanuš Papoušek
Institute for Social Pediatrics and Youth Medicine
University of Munich

During the first postpartum months of life, 15% to 25% of otherwise healthy infants spend up to one half of their waking time in states of unexplained fussiness and inconsolable crying. This condition, often referred to as *persistent crying* or *infantile colic*, is among the most common problems encountered in pediatric practice and it constitutes a major source of parental distress and concern. Yet its etiology, pathophysiology, and risks are not well understood.

The normal developmental course of crying and fussing in early infancy reaches an average peak of 2½ hours per day at about 6 weeks of age (Alvarez, 1994; Brazelton, 1962; St. James-Roberts & Halil, 1991). Individual variability in both the amount and intensity of cry and fuss behavior is remarkably high. In the highest one quarter of the distribution, infants cry and fuss for more than 3 hours a day, for more than 3 days a week, for more than 3 consecutive weeks (Wessel, Cobb, Jackson, Harris, & Detwiler, 1954). These limits have been commonly accepted as diagnostic criteria of infant persistent crying or colic (see Barr, 1990; St. James-Roberts, 1993; St. James-Roberts, Conroy, Wilsher, & Barker, 1994).

11

Persistent crying episodes have been characterized by paroxysms of intense, high-pitched crying; physical signs of hypertonia; back arching, flexed knees, and flushed face; abdominal distention; and inconsolability (Lester, Boukydis, Garcia-Coll, Hole, & Peucker, 1992). Moreover, infant behavior appears frantic and out of control. Because of these features, persistent crying episodes have typically been perceived as signs of abdominal pain. In a community sample of infants with persistent crying (St. James-Roberts et al., 1994), the largest proportions of crying and fussing episodes were found to occur during states of unsettled, irritable fussiness (59%) or states of sustained unexplained crying (31%); only a small proportion could be assessed as a true colic state (8%). Although infrequent in individual infants in samples drawn from the community, colic states seem to have a particularly strong impact on parents and clinicians, and they predominate in clinical samples of infants whose parents seek professional help.

For decades, the salience of the "colic pain" syndrome prompted research into pediatric causes, with a major focus on symptoms of gastrointestinal immaturity and protein intolerance. However, convincing empirical support has been demonstrated for none of these competing explanatory hypotheses (Miller & Barr, 1991). The findings are either contradictory or limited to small subgroups of infants suffering from esophageal reflux or specific protein intolerance. Psychologists have been similarly unsuccessful in identifying psychosocial causes of persistent crying except in small subgroups. Various studies have reported reliable associations between persistent crying and parental factors, such as maternal responsiveness (Bell & Ainsworth, 1972; Hubbard & van IJzendoorn, 1991), prenatal anxiety (Zuckerman, Bauchner, Parker, & Cabral, 1990), postpartum depression (Cutrona & Troutman, 1986; Miller, Barr, & Eaton, 1993), or even infant neglect or abuse (Frodi, 1985). However, the direction and functional mechanisms of causal effects or potential interactions among psychosocial and pediatric factors are still insufficiently understood.

One common limitation of pediatric and psychological findings to date is their exclusive reliance on measures of amount and intensity of crying and fussing behavior. Other striking characteristics of the condition have not attracted sufficient scientific attention, although they may shed new light on the nature and origins of infantile persistent crying:

1. Persistent crying typically follows a diurnal pattern clustering in the evening hours (St. James-Roberts & Halil, 1991). It is associated with prolonged periods of wake–sleep transitions in which infants may be overtired.

2. Episodes of persistent crying typically follow a statelike dynamic pattern and are characterized by a paroxysmal onset, a self-maintaining equilibrium, and resistance to external soothing interventions (inconsolability; Lester et al., 1992; Wolff, 1987).

3. The acoustic features of colic cries point to particularly high levels of autonomic arousal, suggesting an imbalance of relatively high levels of sympathetic arousal and low vagal tone (Fuller, Keefe, & Curtin, 1994; Lester et al., 1992).

4. Infantile persistent crying, colic, and irritability are terms often used interchangeably in the literature—a circumstance indicating potential links to constitutional or temperamental variations along the dimensions of soothability, hyperperceptivity, hyperreactivity, adaptability, predictability, and overall motility (Bates, 1987; Carey, 1984; Lester et al., 1992; Lounsbury & Bates, 1982).

5. The developmental course of persistent crying seems to parallel the development of circadian sleep–wake organization (Hurry, Bowyer, & St. James-Roberts, 1991; Papoušek, 1984; Parmelee, Wenner, & Schulz, 1964).

6. Persistent crying peaks at around 6 weeks of age; that is, at a period of "peculiar immaturity in the behavioral make-up of the human infant" (Prechtl, 1993, p. 47). This period is characterized by processes of intense growth and maturation, by rapid improvement of learning abilities and postnatal adaptation, and thus also by a particular vulnerability to environmental risks and dependency on environmental support (Papoušek & Papoušek, 1984). The level of behavioral regulation seems to be particularly problematic in relation to sleep–wake organization, state transitions, and regulation of arousal and attention during coping with environmental stimulation.

7. Persistent crying is commonly considered to reflect a self-limiting condition. It typically subsides by the end of 3 months during a period of major neural and behavioral shifting when new behavioral qualities and coping capacities emerge and constitute a new level of behavioral organization (Emde, Gaensbauer, & Harmon, 1976; Parmelee & Stern, 1972; Prechtl, 1984).

All of the aforementioned characteristics of infantile persistent crying have led us to hypothesize that persistent crying is closely interlinked with regulatory difficulties in the organization of sleep and waking states (Papoušek, 1984; Papoušek & Papoušek, 1990). Rather than searching for a new causal explanation of persistent crying in the realm of sleep–wake organization, however, we wish to take a detailed look at some developmental processes that may be related to persistent crying. We do so from a dynamic systems perspective with a major focus on regulatory processes that are involved in everyday parent–infant interactions (Papoušek & Papoušek, 1990; Papoušek & von Hofacker, 1995). Our approach is based on previous analyses of the infant's integrative and regulatory capacities (Papoušek, 1969; Papoušek & Papoušek, 1979) and the parent's intuitive support of the infant's integration of biological and social experiences (Papoušek, 1994b; Papoušek & Papoušek, 1987).

SLEEP–WAKE CYCLES

The developmental curve of crying and fussing closely parallels a period of dramatic changes in the temporal organization of sleep–wake states. A wealth of elaborate studies has portrayed the development of sleep states in term and preterm infants with the help of actograms (Kleitman & Engelmann, 1953), polygraphic recordings (Emde & Walker, 1976; Parmelee et al., 1964; Paul & Dittrichová, 1974), and videosomnography in the home (Anders & Keener, 1985; Anders, Keener, Kraemer, 1985). Active sleep can be clearly defined from 32 to 34 weeks gestational age; it occupies 50% of the newborn's sleep and shows a slight proportional decline thereafter (Parmelee et al., 1964). Indeterminate or unclassifiable sleep is considered to reflect poorly organized, immature sleeping states; depending on the rigor of the scoring criteria, it may initially reach high proportions (Paul & Dittrichová, 1974), but shows a steady decline from birth to 16 weeks in favor of quiet sleep (Parmelee et al., 1964). The longest sleep period increases from 4 hours at 2 weeks to 5 to 6 hours by 6 weeks and 8 hours by 16 weeks (Parmelee et al., 1964). Total sleep time decreases from 16½ hours in the newborn to 15 hours at 16 weeks.

The chronobiological organization of sleep and waking is determined by interactions of three major periodicities (see Stratton, 1982, for a review). A 50- to 60-minute basic rest–activity cycle governing the cyclic alternation of quiet and active sleep is present at birth and does not change its periodicity throughout the first year (Stern, Parmelee, & Harris, 1973). A 4-hour sleep–wake cycle dominating at birth is considered to be under the control of a gastrointestinal feeding cycle. Circadian sleep–wake periodicity of about 24 hours begins soon after birth to shift the longest sustained sleep period to nighttime. By 3 months, the intrinsic circadian organization of sleep–wake states is well established and synchronized with environmental day–night periodicity, and daytime sleep is consolidated into well-defined naps (Bornstein & Lamb, 1992; Hellbrügge, 1960; Kleitman & Engelmann, 1953; Papoušek, 1984). Interestingly, the circadian sleep rhythm has its peak between 1 a.m. and 3 a.m., and its trough between 6 p.m. and 8 p.m.; that is, the time of the evening crying peak.

According to Parmelee and Stern (1972), fundamental biological rhythms become evident very early in life and remain relatively invariant while the behavioral patterns of sleep and wakefulness change dramatically in relation to the rapid maturation of CNS processes. The two major maturational changes concern (a) an increasing proportion of quiescent periods in each state parameter, and (b) an increasing association of state parameters proceeding from an almost complete dissociation in the fetus at 24 gestational weeks to a close coherence and rhythmic cycling by 3 months past term.

The ontogeny of quiet sleep deserves particular attention because each of its parameters (EEG, EOG, EMG) shows evidence of the maturation of inhibitory processes and feedback control mechanisms in the brain (Emde & Walker, 1976; Parmelee & Stern, 1972). Quiet sleep is viewed as a highly controlled state that presumably involves coordination of complex interactions between the brain stem and higher inhibitory centers in the forebrain. It also includes inhibitory control over motor activity and muscle tone.

Much less attention has been paid to the development of waking states (Becker & Thoman, 1982), on account of methodological difficulties in capturing the growing complexity of wakefulness beyond the newborn age. A variety of taxonomies has been proposed, but none has found general acceptance (e.g., Papoušek, 1969; Prechtl, 1974; Thoman, Korner, & Kraemer, 1975; Wolff, 1987). Yet, the concept of states as mutually exclusive self-regulating dispositions of the organism has helped in understanding not only sleep–wake organization, but also systematic changes in the organism's input–output relations (Wolff, 1987) and reciprocities between integrative processes and behavioral regulation (Papoušek, 1969). The concept of mutually exclusive states also has facilitated predictions of later behavioral and medical dysfunctions (Thoman, Denenberg, Sievel, Zeidner, & Becker, 1981).

The states of wakefulness undergo rapid changes during the early postpartum months. Newborn infants awaken about every 4 hours and stay awake for 1 to 2 hours (Parmelee & Stern, 1972). The longest sustained wakeful period increases slowly from 2 to 3 hours to 4 hours at 16 weeks. Among the newborn's states of wakefulness—such as alert inactivity, waking activity, fussing, and crying—the alert inactivity state is particularly interesting because attentional processes seem to mature simultaneously with the development of quiet sleep and sustained sleep. Alert inactivity as described by Wolff (1984) is the primary state in which the young infant is attentive in the sense of selective looking and visual pursuit. However, during the first postpartum weeks, wakefulness exhibits few of the self-regulatory properties that characterize sleep states. Alert waking (Wolff, 1987) slowly develops from brief episodes of transient alertness to stable periods of uninterrupted waking, and critically depends on environmental stimulation. In fact, wakefulness does not seem to emerge as a stable state until sometime between 2 and 3 months.

After 6 weeks post term, crying and fussing begin to decrease, and exploratory manipulation of toys and noncry vocalizations increase (Dittrichová & Lapáčková, 1964). Alert inactivity is replaced around 8 weeks with a new state of alert activity: Infants begin to combine rhythmic limb activity with visual pursuit and spontaneously initiate and coordinate newly acquired motor patterns (Wolff, 1984). The new level of self-initiated goal-directed action maintains the infant in a stable waking state "as if the acquisition of these movements buffered the system against the potentially disruptive effects of hunger, cold, wet diapers and the like" (Wolff, 1984, p. 154), and perhaps against persistent crying.

In agreement with current knowledge on sleep–wake organization, one could speculate that the regulatory dysfunction of sleep–wake organization in infants with persistent crying results from a maturational delay, particularly in relation to the most highly organized states of quiet sleep and sustained alert activity. The typical time course of infantile persistent crying supports such a view. However, the ontogeny of sleep–wake organization and the reciprocities between conditions of sleep and wakefulness can only be properly understood if other sources of interindividual variability are taken into account, as for example, the infant's general self-regulatory competence and the parent's intuitive support of that competence. Such factors may help to explain why infantile colic often does not subside by 3 months, and why many infants continue to present symptoms of fussiness, crying, and sleep problems up to 6 months of age or older.

One source of individual variability in infant crying and fussing has been found to result from intricate reciprocal relations between regulation of behavioral states and the course of integrative processes. This was observed in some of the earliest studies on infant learning or problem solving (Papoušek, 1969) and summarized in the concept of infants' "fundamental adaptive response system" (Papoušek & Papoušek, 1979). In young infants, integrative processes such as sensory perception, learning, cognition, and motor adaptation are closely related to the regulation of behavioral states as observable in concomitant changes of autonomic functions, general motor activity, arousal or attention, and social signaling. On the one hand, the course of integrative processes depends on the preceding infant state: Integration functions optimally in states of alert waking and becomes impaired in states of fussiness or crying. On the other hand, focusing attention on some distracting stimulus during fussiness or crying may function as an efficient self-regulatory mechanism in young infants (Bornstein et al., 1992; Wolff, 1987). Likewise, successful learning and coping with environmental demands may stabilize and maintain alert active waking states (Papoušek, 1969) and preclude fussiness and crying.

Stable individual differences in state organization have been reported in the newborn (Thoman, et al., 1975), in 1- to 5-week-olds (Thoman et al., 1981), or in 2- to 20-week-olds (Dittrichová, Paul, & Vondráček, 1976; Tautermannová, 1973); it has been suggested that the degree of stability reflects the functioning of the central nervous system and predicts developmental outcome (Thoman et al., 1981). Among the infant's states, quiet sleep and alert wakefulness seem to be interrelated as the most highly organized and stable, whereas active sleep, nonalert waking activity, and crying are more variable and associated with high levels of arousal. Similarly, individual variation is evident in learning and other integrative processes from the newborn age (Papoušek, 1969, 1977). Stable dyadic profiles of mother–infant interactions in the home have been found in the percentage of time allocated to four interactional contexts—feeding, changing and bathing, social attention, and baby alone (Acebo & Thoman, 1992; Thoman, Acebo, & Becker, 1983). Interestingly, low interactional consistency seems to relate to high amounts of infant crying in the mother's presence.

INFANT PERSISTENT CRYING, TEMPERAMENT, AND PARENT–INFANT COMMUNICATION

Infant crying and fussiness have often been associated with individual temperamental differences in soothability, irritability, adaptability, predictability, proneness to fear, and activity level; in other words, with different aspects of self-regulatory competence. According to definitions provided by Rothbart and Derryberry (1981), temperament is primarily based on stable, biologically determined individual differences in reactivity (arousability of the individual's response system) and self-regulation. Self-regulation in this case refers to processes that modulate the organism's reactivity through approach or avoidance, attentional processes or inhibition, under the influence of specifiable neurophysiological, endocrinological, and/or behavioral processes.

Not enough is known about potential interrelations between infantile persistent crying as a self-limiting condition of the first postpartum months and as a temperamental variation with presumed long-term stability. Recent concepts of infant temperament that attempt to account for interactions of temperament with environmental and maturational factors seem to be particularly relevant in this respect:

> Although most theorists agree that temperament attributes tend to be stable over time, they also appreciate how much the expression of temperament individuality . . . may change as a result of development and maturation, experiential influence, the contexts in which temperament is expressed, and the integration of temperament into an emerging personality organization. (Bornstein & Lamb, 1992, pp. 402–403)

From a psychobiological perspective, communication may be the most significant means of evolutionary adaptation in humans; as such, it seems to be connected with important self-regulatory functions on the one hand, and with risk of pathogenetic deviations in behavioral regulation on the other (Papoušek & Papoušek, 1992). Consequently, interactions with the social environment include numerous situations in which the regulation of state and behavioral/emotional coping may be favorably or unfavorably affected by qualities of communication processes engaged in by caregivers and infants.

During interactions with their preverbal infants, parents intuitively respond to infants' behavioral cues indicating current levels of arousal, attention, readiness to interact, integrative processes, fatigue, and pleasure or displeasure (Papoušek & Papoušek, 1987, 1995). Under favorable conditions, parents tend not only to intervene when infants fuss or cry, but they respond to precursors of crying, such as nondistress cues in the infants' hand gestures, muscle tone, noncry vocalization, and facial displays. Parents respond with behavioral patterns affecting infant arousal and attention, and use feedback cues to calibrate and fine-tune the intensity and timing of their interventions. Thus, the parent's intuitive behavior compensates for the infant's initial maturational constraints in self-regulatory competence: Parents facilitate and support infants' regulation of affective arousal and attention, quality of alert waking states, self-soothing, and transition to sleep (Papoušek, 1984; Papoušek, Papoušek, & Symmes, 1991). Consequently, preverbal communication may play a pivotal role in the regulation of infant states and in the prevention of infant crying and its causes.

Although preverbal communication may typically be considered a buffering system enabling the parent–infant dyad to cope successfully with minor maturational or temperamental constraints in infants' regulatory capacities (Papoušek & Papoušek, 1990), it may fail under unfavorable conditions. Persistent infant crying can drain parental resources; it may cause or worsen maternal states of postpartum depression, exhaustion, or ambivalence; it also may activate latent neurotic conflicts in parents, and inhibit intuitive parenting capacities. Consequently, a lack of adequate parental support may maintain or exacerbate regulatory dysfunction in infants and thus lead to a vicious circle of negative reciprocity in the parent–infant relationship (Papoušek & Papoušek, 1990; Papoušek & von Hofacker, 1995).

THE MUNICH INTERDISCIPLINARY RESEARCH AND INTERVENTION PROGRAM FOR FUSSY BABIES

In order to investigate the clinical relevance of these concepts, the Munich Interdisciplinary Research and Intervention Program for Fussy Babies was designed to serve two integrated goals: (a) to offer interdisciplinary diagnostic and intervention services for infants suffering from persistent crying, and (b) to collect standardized diagnostic information and comprehensive audiovisual documentation for scientific analyses. The program has profited from creative cooperation among specialists in pediatrics, developmental neurology, psychiatry, developmental psychology, and developmental psychobiology.

Infants are referred to the program because of persistent crying. Surprisingly, only a small proportion of referrals concern infants under 3 months of age; most referrals are of older children up to the age of 24 months. In the majority of cases, the condition did not subside by 3 months, but the peak of regulatory dysfunctions shifted to the nighttime. This chapter examines the hypothesis that infantile persistent crying results from some regulatory dysfunction in the organization of sleeping and waking. The data presented were obtained from the youngest group of infants with symptoms of infantile persistent crying.

Sample

A total of 112 1- to 6-month-old infants, including 61 infants with persistent crying referred to the Munich Fussy Baby Program (Mean age = 3.6 months, $SD = 1.4$) and 51 age-matched controls from the local community (Mean age = 3.6, $SD = 1.2$), were assigned to one of three groups depending on (a) whether or not the mother perceived a cry problem, and (b) whether or not the infant met Wessel's criteria of persistent crying (Wessel et al., 1954).

In the community sample (a random group of healthy infants recruited through birth records in the local newspaper), 28% of mothers also reported a condition of infantile persistent crying, and, with the exception of two subjects, they reported only moderate amounts of crying and fussing and did not seek professional help. The average daily amounts of crying and fussing were used for reassignment of infants from the pooled clinical and community samples. A slight modification of Wessel et al.'s (1954) criterion of infantile persistent crying (more than 3 hours of crying and fussing per 24 hours on average during the past 5-day period) was met by 35 referred infants (58%) and by two community infants (4%), that is by a total of 37 (Wessel group). The less frequently crying infants (non-Wessel group) included 26 referred infants (42%) and 12 community infants (24%), that is a total of 38; they presented a cry problem to the mother, but cried and fussed for less than 3 hours per day on average. The remaining 37 community infants (73%) represented the control group.

Procedures and Methods of Study

The same sequence of standardized diagnostic procedures was applied to examine infants and their families from both the clinical and community samples. First, the average daily amounts of crying, fussing, and sleeping per 24 hours and per morning, afternoon, evening, and nighttime hours were extracted from 5-day, 24-hour protocols that mothers prepared prior to the first session. Semistructured neuropediatric and psychological diagnostic interviews provided information about symptoms of regulatory behavioral dysfunction; about biological and psychosocial risk factors related to pregnancy, birth, and postnatal adaptation; and about parents' current psychological state, current family relationships, and support systems. The infant's health state and neuromotor maturity were assessed in pediatric examinations including detailed neurological assessments. Standardized questionnaires were then used to assess infant temperament (*Infant Characteristics Questionnaire* by Bates, Freeland, & Lounsbury, 1979) and to provide information on maternal feelings of self-efficacy, depressed mood, maternal child-care attitudes and feelings, marital satisfaction, and perceived social support. The parent's intuitive competence and the infant's self-regulatory competence were analyzed from videotapes of face-to-face mother–infant interactions.

Our analysis of these features of study focuses on those data that may elucidate early regulatory functioning in infants with persistent crying, which include data on sleep–wake organization, infant temperament, and neuromotor regulation. Other data, such as on biological and psychosocial risk factors, on mothers' psychological condition and resources, and on mother–infant interactions have been reported elsewhere (Papoušek & von Hofacker, 1995).

Findings About Babies Who Cry Persistently

Table 2.1 compares crying, sleeping, and temperament in 1- to 3-month-old infants across three groups: high amounts of crying (Wessel), moderate amounts (non-Wessel), and low amounts (control). The total duration of crying and fussing per 24 hours averaged more than 5 hours in the Wessel group, 2 hours in the non-Wessel group, and 1 hour in the control group. Even more pronounced were the group differences in the total duration of crying proper. Wessel infants spent 50% of cry and fuss duration (2½ hours) in actual crying states, as compared to non-Wessel infants (31% or 40 minutes) and control infants (18% or 15 minutes). As shown in Figure 2.1, Wessel infants fussed and cried significantly more during all parts of the day, with a distinct evening peak between 6 p.m. and midnight (Figure 2.1).

The three groups differed significantly in the majority of sleep measures (Table 2.1): As compared to controls, Wessel infants slept 1½ hours less per 24 hours, and their longest sustained sleep period averaged 5 hours, that is 2½ hours less than controls. They fell asleep 1 hour later in the evening. During nighttime sleep, they awoke twice as often and for periods that were twice as long. The most pronounced sleep disturbance co-occurred with the evening crying peak. As shown in Figure 2.1, the diurnal curve of crying and fussing was an exact mirror image of the diurnal curve of sleeping.

Strikingly similar results were obtained for the respective groups of 4- to 6-month-old infants (Figure 2.2), with only a few deviations: Total sleep time showed a small overall decline and more distinct diurnal patterning; and the number of nighttime awakenings increased by one in all groups. As compared to the 1-to 3-month-olds, the older Wessel infants showed a significant decrease in crying in the evening hours, concomitant with a diurnal shift of daytime sleep to the evening hours (6 p.m. to midnight); a shift of the most pronounced sleep disturbance from the first to the second half of the night (Figure 2.2); and a shift of the cry and fuss peak into the afternoon.

Thus, the protocol data reveal distinct signs of dysregulated sleep–wake organization, including overall sleep deprivation, problems in wake–sleep transitions and in sustaining prolonged episodes of uninterrupted sleep, and a failure or developmental delay in diurnal sleep–wake organization.

The evidence of dysregulated sleep–wake organization was supported and complemented by parental reports of infants' behavioral functioning in

TABLE 2.1
Infants' Sleep–Wake Organization and Temperament in Three Groups
Differing in the Amount of Crying and Fussing (1 to 3 Months)

	Control	Non-Wessel	Wessel	One-way ANOVA		Posthoc Duncan*
	$n = 18$	$n = 16$	$n = 21$	$F, df\,2$	p	$p < .05$
Cry/fuss per 24 h (min)	56	121	312			
Fuss per 24 h (min)	45	83	155	8.8	.0005	W > N,C
Cry per 24 h (min)	10	38	156	73.9	.0000	W > N,C
Number of cry episodes	0.5	1.6	4.8	52.6	.0000	W > N > C
Sleep per 24 h (min)	837	817	743	6.2	.0039	W < N,C
Sleep 18.00 to 24.00 (min)	209	203	148	6.1	.0043	W < N,C
Sleep 0.00 to 6.00 (min)	338	326	291	5.6	.0063	W < N > C
Longest sleep episode (min)	467	366	310	7.2	.0018	W, N < C
Nighttime waking (min)	24	44	51	4.2	.0218	W > N > C
Number of nighttime awakenings	0.9	1.3	2.0	3.0	.0500	W > C
Latency to fall asleep (min)	14	30	46	5.9	.0067	W > C
Time at falling asleep (hour)	20.54	20.42	21.48	3.4	.0424	W > N,C
Time in parents' bed (min)	79	121	204	1.7	ns	
Temperament						
Difficulty	19.1	28.5	37.5	33.5	.0000	W > N > C
Unpredictability	8.1	9.9	14.9	2.2	.0001	W > N,C
Unadaptability	8.7	11.4	12.0	2.4	ns	

Note. W = Wessel, N = Non-Wessel, C = Control

states of wakefulness. Mothers of infants in the Wessel group described their infants as "hyperperceptive" or "hyperreactive" and as easily aroused but difficult to calm down. The mothers reported that their infants had considerable difficulties in settling to sleep, and, during the day, evidenced a lack of sustained sleep episodes for more than 10 to 30 minutes. Putting the infant to sleep often required inventive soothing techniques, including car driving, machine noises, or jumping with the infant on a gymnastics ball. These mothers perceived their infants as in need of particularly intense and endless soothing interventions, such as intense forms of vestibular stimulation, continuous carrying in close body contact, or hourly feedings. They typically described afternoon or evening crescendos of an unpleasant transitional state of infantile hyperarousal, exhaustion, and fatigue leading to an evening peak in crying. These build-ups typically included the risk of vicious cycles: The hyperaroused infant signalled a need for continuous intense stimulation, and, in turn, the stimulation increased the level of arousal and fatigue and counteracted transition to sleep.

Mothers of Wessel babies reported a lack of sustained alert waking states in infants during the daytime. Infants signaled an almost continuous need of entertainment, resistance to prone or supine horizontal positions, and a strong preference for being picked up and carried around in a vertical position. Only intense forms of distracting stimulation seemed to prevent or suppress fussing and crying states. Mothers often considered immediate responsiveness to the first signs of fussiness decisive for preventing sudden transition to inconsolable colic states, but

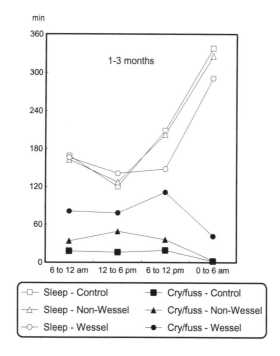

FIGURE 2.1.   Diurnal distribution of crying and fussing and sleeping in 1- to 3-month-old infants: Average duration (min) per time of day.

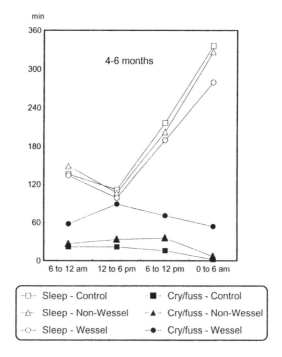

FIGURE 2.2.   Diurnal distribution of crying and fussing and sleeping in 4- to 6-month-old infants: Average duration (min) per time of day.

admitted substantial inconsistency in many cases. They often needed a "time-out" for their own recovery on account of a build-up of tension, exhaustion, and irritability, and they left the infant "to cry it out" for prolonged periods of time. Moreover, they tended to take time-outs when infants were awake and quiet.

Mothers' reports were reflected in the summary scores from standardized questionnaires on infant temperament. As shown in Table 2.1 for the 1- to 3-month-olds, the three groups differed significantly along the dimensions of difficultness and predictability. The younger Wessel infants were perceived as significantly more difficult and less predictable than infants from the other age-matched groups. The older Wessel infants were perceived as more difficult and less adaptable than the other groups.

The neuropediatric physical examination revealed mild to moderate neurological problems indicative of mild delay in neuromotor maturation in more than 50% of infants in both the Wessel and non-Wessel groups as compared to 18% in the control group.

As reported elsewhere (Papoušek & von Hofacker, 1995), neither intestinal problems, nor any other single causal factor could be identified to account for persistent crying. In contrast, the condition was significantly associated with multiple biological and psychosocial risk factors on both sides of the parent–infant system. According to the questionnaire data, the mothers of Wessel infants were significantly more depressed than the mothers of non-Wessel and control babies; they were more exhausted, more frustrated, and more anxious. They obtained lower scores on self-esteem and self-efficacy, and higher scores on marital dissatisfaction. Failures of mother–infant communication in contexts of face-to-face interactions in the laboratory were found in one half of the mother–infant pairs in the Wessel group (Papoušek, 1994a).

Comment: The Picture of "Colic"

These protocol data confirm the assumed association between amounts of crying and fussing and sleeping in terms of total duration per 24 hours, diurnal patterns, and age-related changes. Crying and fussing and sleeping were inversely related, as recently reported in the only other study to examine both crying and fussing and sleeping in the same subjects (Hurry, et al., 1991).

The data suggest that infantile persistent crying is associated with the following symptoms of disturbance in sleep–wake organization: problems in settling to sleep, lack of sustained uninterrupted sleep episodes; an average deprivation of 1½ hours of total sleep; restriction of daytime sleep to brief naps; and low-quality waking states with a high proportion of transitional states of fatigue, hyperarousal, irritability, fussiness, or crying, presumably in lieu of sustained states of alert waking. The sleep disturbance in this sample is of a higher magnitude than that reported in a London study by Hurry et al. (1991), probably due to age differences of the samples. Although sleep disturbance is most evident in the first half of the night (at the time of the evening crying peak), signs of dysfunctional sleep–wake organization are evident throughout the day.

This association does not imply causal relations between crying and dysfunctional sleep–wake organization in one or the other direction. However, the findings raise questions about the nature of the relation and about common underlying processes. For instance, the data may reflect a delay of the diurnal shift of sustained sleep to the nighttime hours in the Wessel group. They may also result from an imbalance in homeostatic control of autonomic arousal, with a prevalence of excitatory sympathetic mechanisms over parasympathetic inhibitory mechanisms as suggested by Lester et al. (1992). Moreover, the poor quality of sleep with frequent awakenings, restlessness, and high levels of motor activity suggest that "colicky" infants may have particularly low levels of quiet sleep. Until recently, sleep–wake state organization has not been studied in infants with high levels of persistent crying. However, indirect evidence of common underlying processes comes from studies on the ontogeny of sleep and waking.

PERSISTENT CRYING AND PARENTING

Another key source of individual variation in fussing and crying has been found in patterns of everyday parent–infant interactions. Persistent crying culminates in infants at a time when parents undergo a remarkable psychological and sociocultural adaptation to their new roles and thus may be particularly vulnerable to psychophysiological effects of inconsolable crying (Boukydis & Burgess, 1982; Donovan, 1981). Persistent infant crying has been shown to elicit sympathetic arousal and irritability in adult listeners, as well as feelings of inefficacy, helplessness, and depression. The signalling of infants during states of persistent crying challenges parents' intuitive competence, and calls on their intuitive soothing or cry-preventing repertoire and nonconscious propensities to provide support to infant behavioral self-regulation.

Our observations confirm the assumption that persistent crying has a strong impact on a mother's psychological condition and may rapidly drain her physical and psychological resources, particularly in cases of prenatal anxiety, depression, marital conflict, postpartum depression, and other psychosocial risks (Papoušek & von Hofacker, in press). The infant's uncontrollable and unexplainable crying elicits maternal feelings of inefficacy or incompetence in soothing, feeding, or otherwise satisfying her baby. If several or all interactional domains are affected, maternal feelings of helplessness and loss of control often become pervasive and promote reliance on rational advice rather than on intuitive competence. Such feelings may even inhibit intuitive parenting. Inhibition of intuitive parenting may result in a number of observable signs of interactional failures such as avoidance of playful interchanges when the infant is alert and ready to interact; low-keyed, stereotyped, or missing patterns of typical intuitive parenting; unresponsiveness to the infant's feedback signals of self-regulatory processes; or unpredictable, inadequate, or inefficient parental responses, often with delayed latencies (Papoušek & von Hofacker, 1995).

A close look at the patterns of soothing or cry-preventing interventions in these cases often reveals serious failures in parent–infant communication.

Behavioral observations of normal infants in the home point to nonlinear relations between the amount of crying and fussing while being held by the mother and maternal responsiveness (Acebo & Thoman, 1992):

> Up to a certain point, increased crying . . . was associated with a general increase in attention to and stimulation of the infant, however, the highest level of crying in this context was associated with a further increase in physical stimulation but with apparent distancing from the infant in other ways. (p. 79)

This was demonstrated, for instance, in decreased rates of maternal looking and talking, in less face-to-face communication, and in more ignoring of cries.

In our infants with persistent crying, the majority of mothers perceived their infants as signaling peculiar needs of body contact and continuous carrying, of intense vestibular stimulation, or of intense forms of distracting stimulation. For most of the 24-hour day, mothers invested considerable effort in facilitating their infant's transition to sleep or, during fussy states, in preventing a sudden build-up of arousal to inconsolable states of persistent crying. But they also often felt unable to engage in stress-free, playful face-to-face interchanges when the infant was quiet: Thus, mothers failed to provide the infant with the support necessary to coordinate alert waking activities and attentional processes.

Unhappily, the resulting imbalance of undifferentiated immediate responsiveness to the first signs of distress (Bernal, 1973) and lack of responsiveness to signals of interactional readiness may lead to unfavorable consequences: First, the infant's contingency learning during interactions with parents predominantly concerns effects of cry and fuss signals on maternal attention and thus promotes instrumental crying at an early age. Second, infants are deprived of everyday practice of self-soothing capacities. Third, infants keep eliciting intense forms of soothing or cry-preventing interventions when they are already in states of hyperarousal and overtiredness; parental intuitive support becomes dysfunctional and may fail, particularly if parents themselves become tense and irritable. Thus, interaction with an inconsolable infant often leads to vicious cycles of reciprocal spirals of hyperarousal, hyperstimulation, and exhaustion (Papoušek, 1985; Papoušek & Papoušek, 1990).

Although further research on the biological basis of persistent crying is clearly warranted, it has become evident that this condition may be a matter of a general regulatory dysfunction that concerns the states of alert wakefulness and sleep as well as sleep–wake transitions. The condition seems to result from dynamic interactions among maturation, temperament, disturbances of central nervous system integrity due to environmental risk, and learning experiences in everyday contexts of parent–infant communication.

A crucial test of these concepts may lie in the clinical applicability of preventive and therapeutic interventions in families with a persistently crying infant. Better understanding of parental intuitive support of infant integrative competence and behavioral regulation allowed us to design adequate diagnostic as well as preventive and therapeutic methods for cases of failures in parent–infant interactions. Intuitive interventions that support sustained alert waking in infants, facilitate transitions to sleep, and reduce the duration of fussiness occupy a significant proportion of parental care of young infants; failures in them seem to cause or to worsen infant colic (Papoušek & Papoušek, 1987, 1990; Papoušek & von Hofacker, 1995).

A valuable basis for designs of diagnostic and therapeutic measures was derived from experience with residential care for infants with mothers at a special research unit (Papoušek, 1967). Adequate caregiving with respect to the regulation of infant behavioral and emotional states and consultative support to mothers with various social, psychological, or medical problems entirely excluded excessive crying in infants and generally reduced fussing and crying to very low levels in a sample of more than 300 infants (Dittrichová & Papoušek, 1992).

Correspondingly, in the Munich Fussy Baby Program, adequate attention to daily routines and sleep–wake cycles throughout the day and reduction of parental hyperstimulation during transitional states of fussiness, crying, and fatigue, together with organization of short periods of physical recovery and psychological relaxation for the parent, have proven effective in interrupting cycles of communicative failures. In addition, mothers' differential responsiveness to signals of distress may be improved according to pediatric suggestions by Taubman (1984). Overall amounts of crying have been effectively reduced by counselling parents of "colicky" infants on how to correctly interpret and answer infant cries. The keys to successful interventions seem, however, to lie in the encouragement of mutually rewarding parent–infant interchanges and in the disinhibition and reactivation of intuitive competencies in parents. The latter forms of intervention seem to raise the interactional system to a higher level of regulatory functioning and promote sustained states of alert waking activities in infants with new contingencies between noncry means of infant signaling and parental responses, and with concomitant positive feelings of self-efficacy in parents. Such improvements in the quality of waking through playful interchanges have often shown striking and immediate effects on infants' settling to sleep as well as on their quality of sleep.

ACKNOWLEDGEMENTS

The authors owe special thanks to the clinical and research staff of the Munich Fussy Baby Program, N. von Hofacker, T. Jacubeit, M. Malinowski, and B. Cosmovici. The reported sleep diary data were analyzed in collaboration with Anja Boehm.

REFERENCES

Acebo, C., & Thoman, E. B. (1992). Crying as social behavior. *Infant Mental Health Journal, 13,* 67–82.

Alvarez, M. (1994). Perceived infant fussing and crying patterns in the first year of life in an urban community in Denmark. *Infant Behavior and Development, 17,* 495.

Anders, T. F., & Keener, M. A. (1985). Developmental course of nighttime sleep-wake patterns in full-term and premature infants during the first year of life. I. *Sleep, 8,* 173–192.

Anders, T. F., Keener, M. A., & Kraemer, H. (1985). Sleep-wake state organization, neonatal assessment and development of premature infants during the first year of life. II. *Sleep, 8,* 193–206.

Barr, R. G. (1990). The normal crying curve: What do we really know? *Developmental Medicine and Child Neurology, 32,* 356–362.

Bates, J. E. (1987). Temperament in infancy. In J. D. Osofsky (Ed.), *Handbook of infant development* (pp. 1101–1149). New York: Wiley.

Bates, J. E., Freeland, C. A. B., & Lounsbury, M. L. (1979). Measurement of infant difficultness. *Child Development, 50,* 794–803.

Becker, P. T., & Thoman, E. B. (1982). 'Waking activity': The neglected state of infancy. *Developmental Brain Research, 4,* 395–400.

Bell, S. M., & Ainsworth, M. D. S. (1972). Infant crying and maternal responsiveness. *Child Development, 43,* 1171–1190.

Bernal, J. F. (1973). Night waking in infants during the first 14 months. *Developmental Medicine and Child Neurology, 15,* 760–769.

Bornstein, M. H., & Lamb, M. E. (1992). *Development in infancy: An introduction* (3rd ed.). New York: McGraw-Hill.

Bornstein, M. H., Tamis-LeMonda, C. S., Tal, J., Ludemann, P., Toda, S., Rahn, C. W., Pecheux, M., Azuma, H., & Vardia, D. (1992). Maternal responsiveness to infants in three societies: The United States, France, and Japan. *Child Development, 63,* 808–821.

Boukydis, C. F. Z., & Burgess, R. L. (1982). Adult physiological response to infant cries: Effects of temperament of infant, parental status, and gender. *Child Development, 53,* 1291–1298.

Brazelton, T. B. (1962). Crying in infancy. *Pediatrics, 29,* 579–588.

Carey, W. B. (1984). "Colic": Primary excessive crying as an infant-environment interaction. *Pediatric Clinics of North America, 31*, 993–1005.

Cutrona, C. E., & Troutman, B. R. (1986). Social support, infant temperament, and parenting self-efficacy: A mediational model of postpartum depression. *Child Development, 57*, 1507–1518.

Dittrichová, J., & Lapáčková, V. (1964). Development of the waking state in young infants. *Child Development, 35*, 365–370.

Dittrichová, J., & Papoušek, H. (1992, July). *Middle European population without infant colic: Difficult to believe or difficult to breed?* Presentation at the Internal Conference on Infant Cry Research: Clinical Implications and Applications, Munich, Germany.

Dittrichová, J., Paul, K., & Vondrácek, J. (1976). Individual differences in infants' sleep. *Developmental Medicine and Child Neurology, 18*, 182–188.

Donovan, W. L. (1981). Maternal learned helplessness and physiologic response to infant crying. *Journal of Personality and Social Psychology, 40*, 919–926.

Emde, R. N., Gaensbauer, T. J., & Harmon, R. J. (Eds.). (1976). Emotional expression in infancy: A biobehavioral study. *Psychological Issues, 10* (Monograph No. 37).

Emde, R. N., & Walker, S. (1976). Longitudinal study of infant sleep: Results of 14 subjects studied at monthly intervals. *Psychophysiology, 13*, 456–461.

Frodi, A. (1985). Variations in parental and nonparental response to early infant communication. In M. Reite & T. M. Field (Eds.), *The psychobiology of attachment and separation* (pp. 351–367). New York: Academic Press.

Fuller, B. F., Keefe, M. R., & Curtin, M. (1994). Acoustic analysis of cries from "normal" and "irritable" infants. *Western Journal of Nursing Research, 16*, 243–251.

Hellbrügge, T. (1960). The development of circadian rhythms in infants. *Cold Spring Harbor Symposia on Quantitative Biology, 25*, 311–323.

Hubbard, F. O. A., & van IJzendoorn, M. H. (1991). Maternal unresponsiveness and infant crying across the first 9 months: A natural longitudinal study. *Infant Behavior and Development, 14*, 299–312.

Hurry, J., Bowyer, J., & St. James-Roberts, I. (1991, April). *The development of infant crying and its relationship to sleep-waking organisation.* Presentation at the Biennial Meeting of the Society for Research in Child Development, Seattle, WA.

Kleitman, N., & Engelmann, T. G. (1953). Sleep characteristics of infants. *Journal of Applied Physiology, 6*, 269–282.

Korner, A. F., & Thoman, E. B. (1972). The relative efficacy of contact and vestibular-proprioceptive stimulation in soothing neonates. *Child Development, 43*, 443–453.

Lester, B. M., Boukydis, Z. F., Garcia-Coll, C. T., Hole, W., & Peucker, M. (1992). Infantile colic: Acoustic cry characteristics, maternal perception of cry, and temperament. *Infant Behavior and Development, 15*, 15–26.

Lounsbury, M. L., & Bates, J. E. (1982). The cries of infants with differing levels of perceived temperamental difficultness: Acoustic properties and effects on listeners. *Child Development, 53*, 677–686.

Miller, A. R., & Barr, R. G. (1991). Infantile colic: Is it a gut issue? *Pediatric Clinics of North America, 38*, 1407–1423.

Miller, A. R., Barr, R. G., & Eaton, W. O. (1993). Crying and motor behavior of six-week-old infants and postpartum maternal mood. *Pediatrics, 92*, 551–558.

Papoušek, H. (1969). Individual variability in learned responses during early post-natal development. In R. J. Robinson (Ed.), *Brain and early behavior. Development in the fetus and infant* (pp. 229–252). London: Academic.

Papoušek, H. (1977). Individual differences in adaptive processes of infants. In A. Oliverio (Ed.), *Genetics, environment and intelligence* (pp. 269–283). Amsterdam: Elsevier.

Papoušek, H., & Papoušek, M. (1979). The infant's fundamental adaptive response system in social interaction. In E. B. Thoman (Ed.), *Origins of the infant's social responsiveness* (pp. 175–208). Hillsdale, NJ: Lawrence Erlbaum Associates.

Papoušek, H., & Papoušek, M. (1984). Qualitative transitions in integrative processes during the first trimester of human postpartum life. In H. F. R. Prechtl (Ed.), *Continuity of neural functions from prenatal to postnatal life* (pp. 220–244). London: Spastics International.

Papoušek, H., & Papoušek, M. (1987). Intuitive parenting: A dialectic counterpart to the infant's integrative competence. In J. D. Osofsky (Ed.), *Handbook of infant development*, (2nd ed., pp. 669–720). New York: Wiley.

Papoušek, H. (1967). Conditioning during early post-natal development. In Y. Brackbill & G. G. Thompson (Eds.), Behavior in infancy and early childhood (pp. 259–274). New York: The Free Press.

Papoušek, H., & Papoušek, M. (1992). Beyond emotional bonding: The role of preverbal communication in mental growth and health. *Infant Mental Health Journal, 13*, 43–53.

Papoušek, H., & Papoušek, M. (1995). Intuitive parenting. In M. H. Bornstein (Ed.), *Handbook of parenting, Vol. 2: Ecology and biology of parenting* (pp. 117–136). Mahwah, NJ: Lawrence Erlbaum Associates.

Papoušek, M. (1984). Beobachtungen zur Ausloesung von Schreiepisoden im fruehen Saeuglingsalter [Observations on eliciting cry episodes in early infancy]. *Sozialpaediatrie in Praxis und Klinik, 7*, 86–92.

Papoušek, M. (1985). Umgang mit dem schreienden Saeugling und sozialpaediatrische Beratung [How to cope with a screaming baby and social-pediatric counseling]. *Sozialpaediatrie in Praxis und Klinik, 7*, 294–300, 352–357.

Papoušek, M. (1994a, June). *Failures of mother-infant communication in families with a screaming baby.* Presentation at the 13th Biennial Meetings of the International Society for the Study of Behavioral Development, Amsterdam.

Papoušek, M. (1994b). *Vom ersten Schrei zum ersten Wort: Anfaenge der Sprachentwicklung in der vorsprachlichen Kommunikation* [From first cry to the first word: Language development in the context of preverbal communication]. Bern: Huber.

Papoušek, M., & Papoušek, H. (1990). Excessive infant crying and intuitive parental care: Buffering support and its failures in parent-infant interaction. *Early Child Development and Care, 65*, 117–126.

Papoušek, M., Papoušek, H., & Symmes, D. (1991). The meanings of melodies in motherese in tone and stress languages. *Infant Behavior and Development, 14*, 415–440.

Papoušek, M., & von Hofacker, N. (1995) Persistent crying and parenting: Search for a butterfly in a dynamic system. *Early Development and Parenting, 4*, 209–224.

Parmelee, A. H., & Stern, E. (1972). Development of states in infants. In C. B. Clemente, D. P. Purpura, & F. E. Mayer (Eds.), *Sleep and the maturing nervous system* (pp. 199–228). New York: Academic Press.

Parmelee, A. H., Wenner, W., & Schulz, H. (1964). Infant sleep patters from birth to 16 weeks of age. *Journal of Pediatrics, 65*, 576–582.

Paul, K., & Dittrichová, J. (1974). Development of quiet sleep in infancy. *Physiologia Bohemoslovaca, 23,* 11–18.

Prechtl, H. F. R. (1974). The behavioral states of the newborn infant. *Brain Research, 76,* 185–212.

Prechtl, H. F. R. (Ed.). (1984). *Continuity of neural functions from prenatal to postnatal life.* Oxford, UK: Blackwell Scientific.

Prechtl, H. F. R. (1993). Principles of early motor development in the human. In A. F. Kalverboer, B. Hopkins, & R. Geuze (Eds.), *Motor development in early and later childhood: Longitudinal approaches* (pp. 35–50). Cambridge, UK: Cambridge University Press.

Rothbart, M. K., & Derryberry, D. (1981). Development of individual differences in temperament. In M. E. Lamb & A. Brown (Eds.), *Advances in developmental psychology Vol. 1* (pp. 37–86). Hillsdale, NJ: Lawrence Erlbaum Associates.

Stern, E., Parmelee, A. H., & Harris, M. (1973). Sleep state periodicity in prematures and young infants. *Developmental Psychobiology, 6,* 357–365.

St. James-Roberts, I. (1993). Infant crying: Normal development and persistent crying. In I. St. James-Roberts, G. Harris, & D. Messer (Eds.), *Infant crying, feeding and sleeping. Development, problems and treatments* (pp. 7–25). New York: Harvester.

St. James-Roberts, I., Conroy, S., Wilsher, K., & Barker, S. (1994, June). *Distinguishing between infant crying, fussing and colic behavior.* Presentation at the 13th Biennial Meetings of the International Society for the Study of Behavioral Development, Amsterdam.

St. James-Roberts, I., & Halil, T. (1991). Infant crying patterns in the first year: Normative and clinical findings. *Journal of Child Psychology and Psychiatry, 32,* 951–968.

Stratton, P. (1982). Rhythmic functions in the newborn. In P. Stratton (Ed.), *Psychobiology of the newborn* (pp. 119–145). Chichester, UK: Wiley.

Taubman, B. (1984). Clinical trial of the treatment of colic by modification of parent-infant interaction. *Pediatrics, 74,* 998–1003.

Tautermannová, M. (1973). Individual differences in waking time and some patterns of behavior in infants. *Activitas nervosa superior, 15,* 257–262.

Thoman, E. B., Acebo, C., & Becker, P. (1983). Infant crying and stability in the mother-infant relationship. *Child Development, 54,* 653–659.

Thoman, E. B., Denenberg, V. H., Sievel, J., Zeidner, L. P., & Becker, P. (1981). State organization in neonates: Developmental inconsistency indicates risk for developmental dysfunction. *Neuropediatrics, 12,* 45–54.

Thoman, E. B., Davis, D. H., & Denenberg, V. H. (1987). The sleeping and waking states of infants: Correlations across time and person. *Physiology and Behavior, 41,* 531–537.

Thoman, E. B., Korner, A. F., & Kraemer, H. C. (1975). Individual consistency in behavioral states in neonates. *Developmental Psychobiology, 9,* 271–283.

Wessel, M. A., Cobb, J. C., Jackson, E. B., Harris, G. S., & Detwiler, A. C. (1954). Paroxyxmal fussing in infancy, sometimes called "colic." *Pediatrics, 14,* 421–435.

Wolff, P. H. (1984). Discontinuous changes in human wakefulness around the end of the second month of life: A developmental perspective. In H. F. R. Prechtl (Ed.), *Continuity of neural functions from prenatal to postnatal life* (pp. 144–158). Oxford, UK: Blackwell Scientific.

Wolff, P. H. (1987). *The development of behavioral states and the expression of emotions in early infancy: New proposals for investigation.* Chicago: The University of Chicago Press.

Zuckerman, B., Bauchner, H., Parker, S., & Cabral, H. (1990). Maternal depressive symptoms during pregnancy, and newborn irritability. *Developmental and Behavioral Pediatrics, 11*, 190–194.

3

Biobehavioral Reactivity and Injuries in Children and Adolescents

W. Thomas Boyce
University of California, Berkeley

Research in child development has remained largely uninformed by new knowledge of the biological substrates of behavior, and pediatric research has explored behavioral effects of chronic and acute medical conditions without the conceptual infrastructure of developmental psychology. Because each discipline has an urgent need for the insights of the other, this chapter represents an attempt to explore a *common ground* between behavioral pediatrics and child development by examining, as a single exemplar, the problem of childhood injuries. Accidental injuries, the most prevalent source of morbidity and mortality between infancy and adulthood, are events for which etiology cannot be adequately understood from a single frame of reference, whether biomedical or developmental. Recent advances in injury prevention have been centered strongly within an epidemiological framework, which regards injuries as having etiologic and distributive features not unlike those of other medical diagnoses and events. Injuries occur with both seasonal and geographic variations in incidence, proliferate in point epidemics, involve both environmental and host-related etiologic factors, and require the action of an agent that allows energy transfer and tissue damage to occur (Gordon, 1949; Rivara, 1982). The efficacy of preventive interventions developed in recent decades has been due principally to this epidemiological vision of injuries as events that are not random accidents, but determined, etiologically explicable occurrences involving aspects of a host, an environment, and a physical agent.

Often overlooked in this epidemiological approach, however, are the developmental and psychosocial aspects of injury etiology, which are typically ignored within a biomedical orientation. The medical-epidemiologic view of injuries has stressed environmentally based causes, with typical neglect for the role of individual development and behavior. Appropriately shunning accounts that would blame the victim for injury occurrences (Ryan, 1976), the mainline view of injury epidemiology has doggedly ignored the possibly substantive position of individual characteristics in the sequence of events and processes leading to injury. Indeed, a refusal to consider organismic, individual factors in injury etiology has become nearly an article of faith in the prevailing epidemiologic wisdom. In direct response to such conventions, an alternative view is that injury events are addressed effectively and instructively only through the binocularity of combined biomedical and developmental perspectives. The joint views of both behavioral pediatrics and child development, concurrently examining environmental and organismic etiologies, will ultimately offer the most useful, robust, and heuristic account for injuries to children.

THE EPIDEMIOLOGY OF CHILDHOOD INJURIES

The National Academy of Sciences (1988) described injuries as the most underrecognized major public health problem facing the nation today. Each year in the United States, 23,000 children die following injuries, an annual death rate exceeding that for all childhood diseases combined (Centers for Disease Control and Prevention, 1990).[1] Injury deaths are only the most visible peak, however, of a much larger, underlying mountain of morbidity: An estimated 600,000 U.S. children are hospitalized, and 16 million require emergency medical treatment (Guyer & Elers, 1990; Hazinski, Francescutti, Lapidus, Micik, & Rivara, 1993) following injuries every year. Approximately one in four U.S. children experiences a medically attended injury each year, with boys, poor children, and adolescents sustaining disproportionate shares of the collective injury experience (Scheidt et al., 1995). Further, it is estimated that the direct and indirect costs of pediatric injuries in the United States exceed $7.5 billion annually (Centers for Disease Control and Prevention, 1990).

---

[1]Although not a focus of this chapter, injury is a major cause of death and disability in the developing world, as well. Indeed, rates of injury-related deaths are often higher there than those in industrialized nations.

The major categories of injury events responsible for this extraordinary national burden of childhood mortality and morbidity are quite diverse. Motor vehicle injuries, including occupant, pedestrian, and bicycle-related injuries, account for 48% of injury deaths among children (Hazinski et al., 1993). A virtual epidemic of firearm injuries in the United States has killed more than 4,000 children and adolescents per year since 1989 (Fingerhut, Kleinman, & Godfrey, 1991). Homicides and suicides by firearms have become the second and third most common causes of fatal injuries in children (Hazinski et al., 1993), and murder with a handgun is now the leading cause of death among young African-American males (Fingerhut et al., 1991). Finally, deaths due to drowning have become, especially in California, Arizona, and Florida, a third major, highly preventable source of injury mortality in childhood, with over 2,000 children lost each year (Kallas & O'Rourke, 1993).

Taken together, this carnage of fatal and nonfatal injuries in U.S. children results in over 1 million years of potential life lost annually (Rivara, 1992), produces 44 million days of restricted activity (Dawson & Adams, 1987), and causes profound intellectual and developmental impairments that can change forever the lives of thousands of children (Centers for Disease Control and Prevention, 1990). In the words of a 1990 report from the Centers for Disease Control and Prevention, every year "injuries destroy the health, lives, and livelihoods of millions of people."

Important and impressive progress has been made in the implementation of epidemiologically based injury prevention strategies, both in the United States (National Research Council, 1985) and in other nations of the developed world (Bergman & Rivara, 1991). Despite this progress, injuries have remained etiologically complex and elusive events, only partially responsive to the legislative interventions, technological developments, and health education programs assembled to prevent them (Bass et al., 1993). In part, the unresponsiveness of the nation's injury problem to preventive intercessions may reflect simply the brevity of the period during which injury epidemiology has been a serious focus of public health discourse. From this perspective, perhaps all that is needed to complete the effort is simply a longer journey in the same direction. An alternative view, however, is the possibility that something has been missed in the formulation of the problem, and that a deeper, more elaborated, and more eclectic theory of injury etiology will be required. Largely missing from national deliberations on injury prevention to date has been a serious and continuing attempt to illuminate injury epidemiology from the vantage point of the developmental and behavioral sciences.

THE NONRANDOM DISTRIBUTION
OF INJURY INCIDENCE

Figure 3.1 displays a graphic representation of the single most robust and well-replicated finding in child health services research (Boyce, 1992). In multiple and broadly diverse groups, it has been shown that approximately 15% of children sustain over one half of the population's morbidity experience and are responsible for the majority of the accumulated health care visits. Although most children have infrequent illnesses and injuries, a small group sustains a disproportionate share and utilizes health services at a rate out of keeping with its size. Starfield et al. (1984), for example, showed that acute and recurring medical conditions among children enrolled in a health maintenance organization were non-normally distributed, and that a small subgroup sustained the majority of illnesses and injuries, at a rate that persisted over years of time. In a study of school-related injuries, Boyce, Sobolewski, and Schaefer (1989) similarly showed that 1% of 55,000 primary and secondary school children sustained nearly 20% of the total injuries in a 3-year period. As shown in Figure 3.2, the largest proportion of injured children sustained only a single injury over the 3 study years, whereas a small subset of 573 experienced 1,405 injuries, a number significantly greater than could be predicted by chance alone.

Finally, it appears that even in the absence of parental influences on medical careseeking (Hickson & Clayton, 1995), children's morbidity experience and illness behavior are nonrandomly distributed. Lewis and colleagues, in a series of studies based in a university-affiliated elementary

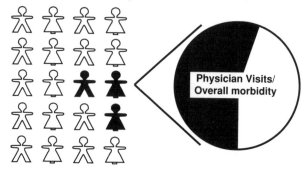

FIGURE 3.1.   The nonrandom distribution of childhood morbidity and health care utilization.

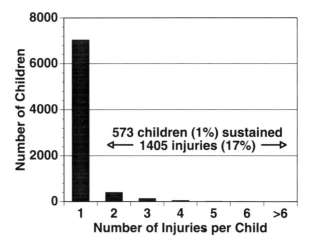

FIGURE 3.2.   School-related injuries in 55,000 students over 3 academic years.

school (Lewis & Lewis, 1983; Lewis & Lewis, 1985), showed that students in an adult-free system of school health care still displayed a marked unevenness in their utilization of school nurse services for injuries and other complaints. Again, approximately 15% of the children, even when empowered to make their own decisions regarding solicitations of care, made over one half of the overall health room visits. In a long-term follow-up of this study, the same investigators showed that children who were consistently high utilizers of nursing care in their elementary school years maintained the same pattern of care-seeking behavior into early adulthood (Lewis & Lewis, 1989).

Some of the children who bear a disproportionate share of injuries and illnesses within a given population are undoubtedly those with chronic diseases (Stein, 1989) or those with high rates of spurious morbidities due to exaggerated pediatric care seeking by anxious parents. In the vulnerable child syndrome, first described by Green and Solnit (1964), high rates of pediatric health service utilization for some children were traceable to parental anxiety surrounding a child's prior life-threatening illness, a resemblance to a loved one who died, or symbolic association with some other painful or threatened loss. On the other hand, neither children with chronic illnesses nor those misperceived as exceptionally vulnerable constitute a group of sufficient size to account for the number who carry inordinate rates of pediatric morbidity and health care utilization (Boyce, 1992). The remaining children in the high morbidity subset appear to be illness and injury prone, and they utilize physician and nursing services at an excessive rate due to true morbidities that are unrelated to known risk factors (Green, 1986). Some have suggested that psychological stress may play a role in generating this predisposition to injury or illness (Green, 1986), whereas others hypothesize a progressive weakening of host resistance due to a positive feedback in which illness begets more illness (Starfield et al., 1984). This debate has not been resolved, however, and the characteristic and marked unevenness of injury distributions in samples of children has remained largely unexplained.

Not surprisingly, efforts to account for disproportionate injury rates in small subsets of children have fallen generally into two categories of explanation: accounts centering on environmental risk factors, and accounts derived from a biological-genetic perspective on individual injury risk. Indeed, the impetus driving all of human development and presumably much of early morbidity experience is the mutual interaction or interplay between aspects of the physical or social environment and characteristic features of the individual child. As promulgated in the work of Sameroff and Chandler (1975), what is critical to developmental processes is not simply the joint features of child and environment, but the transactional, fluid character of the interchange between child and setting.

In the field of injury epidemiology, the perspective of environmental determinism must be credited with a productive focus on injurious physical settings and with an understanding of violence and aggression as products of blighted and unsupportive social contexts (Hiday, 1995). Major advances in childhood injury prevention have been derived from the attention paid by the public health community to unsafe features of children's home and school environments (Grossman & Rivara, 1992). A more biological orientation, on the other hand, has also called attention to constitutionally based differences in *behavior* as risk factors for serious injuries. From this frame of reference, it is not only unsafe contexts that augment injury incidences, but also the stable, injury-promoting characteristics of individual children.

Examples of excellent epidemiological research can be found in both environmental and biological-genetic accounts. A study by Horwitz, Morgenstern, DiPietro, and Morrison (1988), for example, examined family environmental factors that were associated with medically attended injuries in 532 children in a prepaid group practice affiliated with Yale University. Controlling for the confounding effects of sociodemographic factors, health attitudes, and beliefs, the presence of a serious injury over a 1-year follow-up period was best predicted by a combination of a past injury, a mother working more than 15 hours per week, a high rate of noninjury health care utilization, and an accumulation of stressful family life events in the recent past. Other investigators have confirmed prospective associations between structural characteristics of the family environment and the incidence of injuries in childhood (Bijur, Golding, & Kurzon, 1988; Larson & Pless, 1988; Peterson, Ewigman, & Kivlahan, 1993), and still others have compared injury rates in different physical and social contexts of young children, such as homes and group child-care settings (Rivara, DiGuiseppi, Thompson, & Calonge, 1989). There is thus extensive evidence that aspects of a child's family and social environments are linked to risks of medically attended and serious injuries.

By contrast, the work of Bijur, Stewart-Brown, and Butler (1986) on data from the British Births Survey provides equally credible support for the role of individual behavioral factors in injury etiology. In one analysis, reports of injuries between birth and 5 years were ascertained for nearly 12,000 British children born during a single week in April 1970. Occurrences of medically attended injuries were associated with aggressive behavior, even after adjustment for psychosocial variables that included social class, residential crowding, marital status, and the child's gender. In addition, an interaction effect was identified in which hospitalized injuries, the most serious of the reported injury events, were significantly more likely in children showing hyperactive behavior and a proclivity to aggression. Although the weight of current evidence would dispel the simplistic and outdated concept of an injury-prone child, recent investigation does suggest that certain behavioral characteristics are associated with a higher likelihood of injury (Bijur, Golding, & Haslum, 1988; Davidson, Hughes, & O'Connor, 1988; Langley, Silva, & Williams, 1980; Scheidt, 1988). Furthermore, such characteristics appear to be, at least in part, genetically derived and heritable (Bouchard, 1994; Plomin, Owen, & McGuffin, 1994; Plomin & Rende, 1991).

Risk-taking behavior may be one such component of a child's constitutionally based temperament profile (Nyman, 1987). Risk taking is an individual difference in behavior that persists into adolescence, when the consequences of risk taking become considerably increased (Baumrind, 1987; Irwin & Millstein, 1986). Other biologically driven behavioral characteristics may explain gender differences in injury rates by accounting, in part, for the gender-specific, injury-relevant behaviors of children and adolescents (Rivara, Bergman, LoGerfo, & Weiss, 1982). Especially prominent and important in adolescence may be interactions between physiology and behavior during periods of naturally occurring psychological stress (Leffert & Petersen, chapter 7, this volume).

Sound investigation has produced evidence of *both* environmental and individual influences on injury rates, but largely missing from past research have been studies concurrently addressing both sets of influences within a single design. Over the past several years, work in the laboratory of the Division of Behavioral and Developmental Pediatrics at the University of California, San Francisco, has pursued a series of such studies that examine joint and interactive effects of psychological stressors and psychobiologic reactivity to stress as predictors of injury incidence and risk-taking behavior.

PSYCHOBIOLOGIC REACTIVITY AND INJURIES

There is indirect evidence for the role of individual level factors in the relation between psychological stressors and child morbidity. Figure 3.3 summarizes results from four early representative studies that examined prospective associations between stressful life events and various measures of childhood health and illness outcomes. Three important findings are derived from the similarities inherent in the results of these studies. First, there is extraordinary diversity in the outcome measures that are related to stressful events; such outcomes range from streptococcal disease incidence to injury incidence to all-cause illnesses and hospitalizations. Other work suggests that childhood mental health, in addition to the physical health outcomes represented in Figure 3.3, is similarly linked to the occurrence of stressful life events (Jensen, Richters, Ussery, Bloedau, & Davis, 1991).

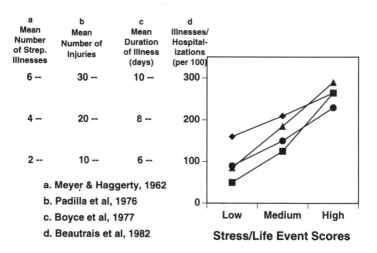

FIGURE 3.3.   Associations between psychologically stressful events and childhood morbidities in four representative studies (Beautrais, Fergusson, & Shannon, 1982; Boyce et al., 1977; Meyer & Haggerty, 1962; Padilla, Rohsenow, & Bergman, 1976).

Second, there is a striking concordance among the four studies in the positive, monotonic, and linear associations consistently found between stressful events and the various health endpoints. In each case, an accumulation of stressors over a relatively short period of time was associated with a significant acceleration in the rate or severity of health conditions. Finally, and not shown in Figure 3.3, the actual data points for each study reflected great variability in the linkage between stressors and outcomes, consistent with associations of limited magnitude. In general, research on stressful life events, in both children and adults, has been characterized by statistically significant but modest associations that rarely account for more than 10% of the variance in illnesses or injuries (Boyce & Jemerin, 1990; Rabkin & Struening, 1976). These findings—that stress and morbidity associations appear reliable and significant and that such associations are almost universally diminutive in scope—raise serious questions about the role of stressful events in the injury and illness experience of most individuals. The findings further suggest the possibility that both environmental factors and organismic factors are involved in the pathogenic effects of psychological stressors. In practical terms, the findings indicate that something about children's *responses* to stressors, either internal, physiologic reactivity or outward, visible behavior, determines the level of impact that a given stressor will have on an individual child. In other words, the results imply that, although environmental stressors may be an important part of the story, unevenness in injury distributions is more likely attributable to the joint interactive influences of stressors and stress reactivity.

Cardiovascular Reactivity and Injuries in Preschool Children

In 1990, our laboratory at the University of California began a study of stress and health in four urban, university-affiliated preschools in San Francisco and Berkeley, California. The principal study objectives were: (a) to develop methods for measuring day-to-day stressors in child care and for ascertaining individual differences in cardiovascular responses to stress in young children, and (b) to examine prospectively the joint contributions of child care stressors and cardiovascular reactivity to preschool morbidity experiences. The two most prevalent health problems in preschool-age children, injuries and respiratory illnesses, were chosen as dependent measures, and a sample of 144 3- to 5-year-old children was assembled.

Child-care stressors were measured using a new instrument, the Child-care Events Questionnaire (CEQ; Kaiser, 1992). Using preschool teachers and child-care providers as informants, a large number of items was generated by asking providers to generate lists of events in child care that challenge the adaptive capacity of children. The 293 items nominated by informants were winnowed and consolidated using informal focus groups of child-care workers, and a final 21-item scale was constructed. Child-care events represented on the final scale were generally mundane, low-intensity stressors that occur with regularity in the lives of young children in group child care. These included events such as change in daily schedule or routine; child's clothing, toy, or project got lost; and self-dressing difficulties. The internal consistency of this scale was high, with a Cronbach's alpha of .82. In questionnaire format, the instrument was completed 1 day every other week by the principal preschool teacher for each study child. The frequency of child-care events was then calculated by summing the number of events during a 6-month period of time and dividing by the number of days the child was present in the center when the CEQ was completed. In addition to the CEQ, an ecologically based estimate of the stressfulness of each child-care center was based on a five-component scale assessing the teacher–child ratio, rate of staff turnovers, proportion of full-time versus part-time teachers, average education level of the teachers, and overall classroom quality. Classroom quality was measured with the Harms (Harms & Clifford, 1980) Early Childhood Environment Rating Scale.

As reported in detail elsewhere (Boyce, Alkon, Tschann, Chesney, & Alpert, 1995), cardiovascular reactivity to stress was assessed using a standardized, 20-minute laboratory protocol designed to evoke measurable blood pressure and heart rate responses in 3- to 5-year-old children. Seven tasks, presented in a standard sequence, were used as the mildly stressful challenges: (a) a child interview, (b) a hidden block construction in which the child was asked to replicate a block structure demonstrated by the examiner, (c) number recall, involving recitation of a digit series, (d) a gestalt closure task, in which the child was asked to identify a familiar object within an incomplete picture, (e) a hypothetical social problem-solving task, (f) a blinded object identification, and (g) a task involving the verbal description of an emotional event. Immediately before and after the presentation of the seven tasks, a calming story was read to the child to allow collection of resting cardiovascular data. During each task and resting period, and at standardized points in time, mean arterial pressure (MAP) and heart rate (HR) were measured. In order to reduce the aversiveness of the monitoring equipment itself, laboratory evaluation sessions were preceded, in each child-care center, by a health fair in which children were shown and allowed to operate the equipment.

Outcome variables, the 6-month incidences of injuries and respiratory illnesses, were ascertained using teacher reports of injuries meeting stand-

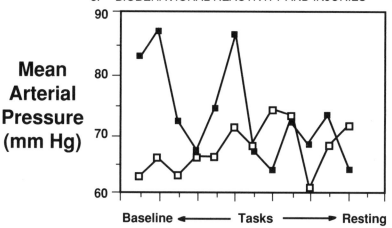

FIGURE 3.4.   MAP data points for two protypical preschool children during cardiovascular reactivity testing.

ardized criteria and biweekly respiratory tract examinations by pediatric nurse practitioners. Both teachers and nurse practitioners were blinded to the cardiovascular reactivity status of the children on which they reported. Reportable injuries were defined for the purposes of the study as events that resulted in bodily harm, as reflected by a physical mark or by a child's sustained complaint of pain for more than 5 consecutive minutes. A respiratory illness was also defined using standardized physical findings from the nurse practitioners' examinations of a child's eyes, ears, nose, throat, and lungs.

Figure 3.4 displays the actual MAP data for two prototypical children, one with a high level of cardiovascular reactivity and the other with low reactivity. The latter child, represented by the open data points, showed relatively low blood pressure levels throughout the protocol and notably little variability. In contrast, the high-reactivity child represented by the closed data points demonstrated several striking MAP elevations during the stressful tasks and marked variability in overall response. These two cases have been selected to emphasize and highlight opposite profiles of cardiovascular responses; reactivity as scored in the study was a continuous, interval-level variable with subgroups of children occupying both ends of the distribution.

When examined in relation to the outcome measure of injury incidence, a set of both predictable and unforeseen results emerged (Barr, Boyce, & Zeltzer, 1994; Liang & Boyce, 1993). As expected on the basis of past findings, child-care stressors were significantly but marginally associated with injury incidence. That is, children whose teachers reported higher rates of day-to-day stressful child-care events had significantly higher incidences of accidental injuries meeting standard criteria. As in past studies of stressful events and health outcomes, the stress–injury association was modest in size and accounted for only about 9% of the variance in injury rates. No significant main effects on injury incidence were found for cardiovascular reactivity.

When the data were examined for possible interactions between environmental stressors and reactivity, however, several interesting and salient findings were revealed. Significant interactions were identified between child-care stressful events and HR reactivity and between ecologic stress and MAP reactivity in the prediction of injury incidence (ß = .38 and .43, respectively, $p < .01$). Moreover, the complete regression model accounted for nearly 30% of the total variation in injury incidence ($F = 2.91, p < .001$).

Figures 3.5a and 3.5b display the character of these significant interaction effects. For purposes of illustration, injury incidence, adjusted for age, gender, child-care stress, and reactivity, is shown as a function of low versus high environmental stress, within the low (one standard deviation below the mean) and high (one standard deviation above the mean) reactivity subgroups of study children. In Figure 3.5a, the interaction of child-care

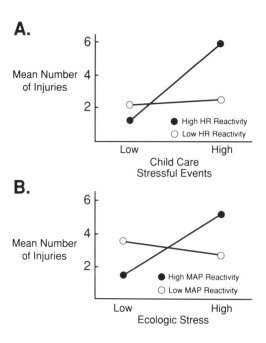

FIGURE 3.5.   Interaction between child-care stressful events and HR reactivity (—O— low reactivity; —●— = high reactivity). Interaction between ecologic stress and MAP reactivity in the prediction of injury incidence ($N = 82$; Boyce, 1991; Liang & Boyce, 1993).

stressful events with HR reactivity is shown, whereas Figure 3.5b displays the homologous interaction of ecological stress and MAP reactivity. The highest numbers of injuries over the study period were sustained by those high-reactivity children who also experienced high levels of child-care stress. Low-reactivity children, on the other hand, sustained similar numbers of injuries regardless of stressor level.

Also shown in Figures 3.5a and 3.5b is the unanticipated observation that the *lowest* injury rates in the study sample were found among high-reactivity children in low-stress environments. Although the difference between high- and low-reactivity subjects in low-stress settings was not as large as that noted in high-stress settings, it is consistent in direction across both of the interactions. That is, in both of the interactions, high-reactivity children in low-stress environments sustained lower adjusted rates of injury than those sustained by the other three subgroups of subjects.

Based on these results, the following preliminary conclusions were formulated. First, psychological stressors are associated with increased rates of pediatric morbidities, but only among the minority of children predisposed to exaggerated psychobiologic responses. This may account for the well-replicated observation that stress and morbidity are significantly but marginally associated at the population level. Second, high-reactivity children are at risk for higher rates of injury and infection in high-stress settings or periods, but are at *lower* risk of such morbidity in predictable low-stress settings or periods. Low-reactivity children, on the other hand, show similar and moderate rates of morbidity in both low- and high-stress conditions. Third, the strong linkage between context and health outcomes in high-reactivity children might plausibly be due to an exquisite sensitivity in such children to the character of the social environment. If reactive children are more sensitive to environmental cues of all sorts, they may absorb more readily or be more subject to the pathogenic and *protective* influences of childhood contexts.

A weakness in the study of reactivity and injuries in preschool children, however, was the fact that cardiovascular responses to laboratory stressors are clearly not themselves involved etiologically in the genesis of either injuries or illnesses. There are no known mechanisms through which an acute and evanescent rise in blood pressure, for example, might escalate a child's risk of injuring himself or herself being injured by another child. Instead, it seems likely that high cardiovascular reactivity serves as a marker or proxy for some other physiologic or behavioral characteristic that might be more directly implicated in an injury event. We thus next turned to an examination of a more proximal factor, risk-taking behavior, that might plausibly constitute the link between reactivity and injuries.

Cardiovascular Reactivity and Risk Behavior in Adolescents

Noting the interactive relations among stress, cardiovascular reactivity, and injuries in our preschool data, Liang et al. (1995) undertook a cross-sectional study of reactivity and risk-taking behavior in a sample of adolescent boys. Risk-taking behavior is known to account, at least in part, for the acceleration in injury rates found during the teenage years (Evans & Waisielewski, 1983; Grossman & Rivara, 1992). It is known, for example, that reduced seat belt use (Williams, Wells, & Lund, 1987), drinking alcohol (National Highway Traffic Safety Administration, 1991), and risky driving behavior (Jonah, 1986) are all more prevalent in adolescents.

A sample of twenty-four 14- to 16-year-old boys underwent a laboratory protocol measuring MAP and HR reactivity to standardized psychological and physical stressors. In addition, the boys completed self-report questionnaire measures of positive and negative life events and recent risk behaviors. The objective of the study was to examine the possibility that the interactive effects of environmental conditions and reactivity on injury incidence are attributable to more proximal influences on risk-taking behaviors.

Cardiovascular reactivity testing was carried out in a manner analogous to that employed for preschool children, but tasks and procedures were chosen appropriate to the age of study subjects. Procedures were also chosen to minimize the possible cardiovascular influences of speech and motor movement. During the resting periods that preceded each of three tasks, subjects were requested to read from mail-order catalogs as a means of achieving a relaxed but alert state. The three challenging tasks were: (a) the Scanning Task, a computer game in which subjects duplicate target shooting sequences (Kamarck et al., 1992); (b) a Social Competence Interview, in which subjects were asked to recall and describe a recent stressful experience (Ewart & Kolodner, 1991); and (c) the cold pressor test, in which subjects submerged the right hand in ice water for a period of 90 seconds. As with the preschool subjects, a Dinamap monitor was used to measure and record MAP and HR at 2-minute intervals throughout the 20-minute protocol.

Positive and negative life events were reported using the Adolescent Perceived Events Scale (Compas, Davis, Forsythe, & Wagner, 1987), an instrument that measures exposure to minor and major life events and assesses subjects' perceptions of events as positive or negative. The outcome variable, risk-taking behavior, was evaluated with the Adolescent Risk Behavior Survey (Millstein et al., 1992), which quantifies 10 adolescent risk activities: skateboarding/rollerblading, bicycling, motorcycling, fighting, driving, riding in a car with a driver younger than 24 years, cigarette smoking, marijuana smoking, drinking, and using illicit drugs.

Data analyses showed that neither life events nor cardiovascular reactivity was independently associated with risk behaviors. As shown in Figure 3.6, a significant interaction was found, however, between positive life events and MAP reactivity in predicting risk behaviors (ß = -2.1, *p* < .01), and the regression model that included the interaction term accounted for nearly 40% of the variance in risk taking.

On first inspection, the character of the interaction in Figure 3.6 appears different from that previously identified for injury incidence among preschool children (Figures 3.5a and 3.5b). On closer scrutiny, however, and taking into account the component of *positive* rather than negative life events, the interaction may be interpreted as closely homologous to that found in the preschool cohort. Note that, as with injuries in the preschool sample, the level of risk behavior among low-reactivity individuals appears relatively unresponsive to the number of positive events. Among high-reactivity subjects, however, there is a marked change in risk behavior, depending on the level of positive life experiences. High-reactivity subjects with few positive events reported high numbers of risk-taking behaviors, whereas those with many positive events reported exceptionally low risk behaviors. This finding suggests that highly reactive children in social environments characterized by an abundance of positive, beneficial events may be protected from injury through a reduction in risk-taking behavior.

The results may account, at least in part, for relations among social environmental conditions, psychobiologic reactivity, and injury experience. High-reactivity children may respond to negative life circumstances (or the

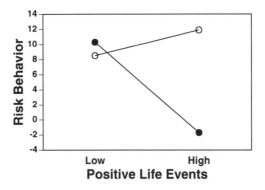

FIGURE 3.6.   Interaction between positive life events and cardiovascular reactivity (–O–— = low reactivity; —●— = high reactivity) in the prediction of high-risk behaviors (N = 24; Liang et al., 1995).

lack of positive, supportive experiences) with an escalation in risk-taking behavior, which could lead acutely to an increased likelihood of serious injury or chronically to a debilitating physical or emotional disorder. Not examined in this current research is the additional, alternative hypothesis that reactive children may be at greater injury risk in high-stress settings by being targeted for aggressive, hostile behavior by other children. It is also conceivable that the apparent protection enjoyed by reactive children in low-stress conditions is attributable to an exceptional interpersonal sensitivity, allowing conflict resolution before injury occurs. However interpreted in terms of the specific behavioral mechanisms, our results suggest that, if heightened injury risks among reactive children are confirmed in future research, preventive interventions directed specifically toward the high-reactivity subpopulation might have dramatic effects on pediatric injuries in general.

Origins of Psychobiologic Reactivity to Stressors

A critical issue in the development of intervention strategies for reactive, high-risk children is the question of the origins of psychobiologic reactivity. Do highly reactive children acquire their physiologic vulnerability through postnatal experiences, or are they born with high reactivity, as a consequence of a specific genetic legacy? Very different approaches to prevention would likely be constructed if high reactivity were a product of constitutional, genetic factors, than might be contemplated if reactivity were derived from environmental learning. Although it is clear that differences in reactivity appear very early in development, at present there is evidence for *both* genetic and environmental determinants.

Programs of research in progress in the laboratories of Kagan (Kagan, 1994; Kagan, Reznick, & Snidman, 1988; Kagan & Snidman, 1991) and Suomi (Higley et al., 1993; Suomi, 1988; Suomi, Rasmussen, & Higley, 1992) and their colleagues provide evidence for heritable, biologically driven reactivity to stress in a subset of both humans and nonhuman primates. Kagan's work offers a longitudinal view, beginning in infancy, of extremely shy and inhibited children who show marked behavioral and autonomic arousal under conditions of challenge and appear to bear an elevated long-term risk of anxiety disorders and perhaps other psychiatric conditions (Hirshfeld et al., 1992). Suomi further demonstrated heritable predispositions to reactive phenotypes in rhesus macaques, and Boyce and Suomi (Boyce, O'Neill-Wagner, Price, Haines, & Suomi, 1994) showed a link between biobehavioral reactivity in monkeys and injury incidence during periods of unusual environmental stress.

On the other hand, a series of studies from the primate laboratory of Schneider and colleagues (Clarke & Schneider, 1993; Clarke, Wittwer, Abbott, & Schneider, 1994; Schneider, 1992) has produced evidence for both short- and long-term increases in postnatal reactivity among rhesus monkey infants exposed to unpredictable noise stress in intrauterine life. This experientially based augmentation in reactivity appears to affect both *physiologic* responses, such as the immunogenicity of pathogenic agents and neoantigens, and *behavioral* responses, such as disturbance behaviors and mutual clinging. The work offers clear evidence that exaggerated biobehavioral reactivity to stress can also have environmental origins, a conclusion with important implications for the design of preventive interventions.

BEHAVIORAL-DEVELOPMENTAL APPROACHES TO INJURY PREVENTION

Research in injury prevention has begun to acknowledge and, to some extent, utilize findings from more basic behavioral and developmental studies of relevance to the injury process (Grossman & Rivara, 1992; Hazinski et al., 1993; Scheidt, 1988). Recognition of injury morbidity and mortality as a major public health problem was followed initially by straightforward efforts to ensure safer environments and products for children through legislation and regulation. There is evidence, moreover, from other industrial nations that such approaches are capable of effecting an initial substantive reduction in serious injury incidence (Bergman & Rivara, 1991). There is also evidence that counseling by primary care physicians can be an effective means of injury prevention (Bass et al., 1993). Many of the more prevalent sources of injury in the United States today, however, involve complex and, at times, subtle patterns of interpersonal behavior that will not be amenable to simplistic epidemiologic manipulations. Aggressive, injurious behavior by young children, homicidal anger in adolescents, intentional physical abuse of children, and stress-related injuries are all examples of complicated social and psychological processes that will require equally complex behavioral solutions.

Such solutions first demand recognition that both environmental and personal factors contribute to injury events. Smith, Smoll, and Ptacek (1990) showed, for example, that the association between stress and athletic injuries in adolescents is moderated by a combination of social support and coping skills. Only athletes low in both coping skills (a personal individual-level variable) and support (a social environmental variable) showed a significant association between stressors and injuries. Others have shown that witnessing interpersonal violence, either on television (Sege & Dietz, 1994) or in the community (DuRant, Cadenhead, Pendergrast, Slavens, & Linder, 1994), promotes the personal commission of violent acts, especially in individuals who are depressed or lacking in a sense of purpose. Installing energy-absorbing materials under climbing structures is undeniably important as a means of preventing injuries in the school yard, but falls from heights must be understood within a more elaborate matrix of causal elements that may include one child pushing another, problems with inattention or impulsivity, difficulties with a specific developmental transition, or stress-related augmentations in risk-taking behavior. A thorough and broadly effective approach to childhood injury prevention must include, by necessity, a more sophisticated appreciation of the developmental and behavioral processes involved in injury occurrence.

CONCLUSIONS

How do the studies, findings, and reflections summarized in this chapter help us in our efforts to think more carefully and creatively about a developmental perspective on childhood injuries (and other biomedical morbidities in children)? First, they compel us to examine *both* personal/organismic *and* environmental/contextual factors in our thinking about injury etiology. In the studies from our laboratory, the highest injury rates were found not simply in reactive subjects, and not simply in the highest stress environments. Rather, the highest injury incidences were found among reactive individuals in contexts characterized by high psychological stress. Neither reactivity nor environmental stress was sufficient in isolation to raise the rates of injury, but the confluence of both produced a reliably higher injury incidence. As suggested in the work of Reiss, Plomin, and Hetherington (1991) and Baumrind (1993), a richer, more elegant approach to the complex, multifactorial disorders of contemporary life will undoubtedly await a more differentiated, and yet integrated, view of the interplay between genetic and contextual forces.

Second, the research reviewed here suggests that the community of behavioral and developmental investigators should consider ways in which personal and environmental factors may *either* augment *or* reduce injury risks. Paradoxically, our findings indicate that, in both monkeys and human children, stress reactivity can serve as either a risk factor or a protective factor, *depending on the context in which the reactive individual is placed* (Bornstein, 1995). Biobehavioral reactivity appears alternately to raise or lower injury risks in a manner contingent on the ambient level of environmental stress. It is important to recognize the ways in which this rather curious perspective on vulnerability and resilience represents a departure from the more conventional view that vulnerability and protection are the negative and positive poles of the same concept (Rutter, 1987). Our observations certainly affirm Rutter's assertion that resilience cannot be seen as a fixed attribute of the individual, but they also move the observer further into a paradoxical orientation in which resilience and vulnerability are regarded as complementary, almost chimeric features of a single reactive individual. Much of the past literature tacitly promulgates a view of vulnerability and resilience as distinctive, irreconcilable attributes of different sets of individuals. Our results challenge such a view, and raise the possibility that both extreme vulnerability and uncommon resilience can be found in the same highly reactive children depending on the basic stressfulness or supportiveness of the surrounding social context.

Finally, the findings of these studies move us beyond the examination of *statistical* interactions to study the transactions *per se* between children and their environments. It will thus be important in future work not simply to examine the concurrent and statistically interactive effects of child and context, but to assess, and measure with precision, the *actual interactions* between children and their psychosocial environments. Perhaps through such future research we can begin to illuminate with greater clarity the complexities involved in the developmental determinants of serious childhood injury.

Future research on injuries and other complex, multiply determined morbidities in children will be best accomplished, beyond any doubt, by new and more effective alliances between pediatric and developmental investigators. Behavioral pediatrics has pursued an agenda for research largely unencumbered by the basic and vast theoretical contributions of developmental psychology, whereas the field of child development has failed to address, with serious intent, the implications of its observations for the physical and mental health of children. From these perspectives, the historical split between behavioral pediatrics and developmental psychology is simply a special case of the more pervasive, insidious, and seemingly lawful division between *psyche* and *soma* that has characterized Western medicine since the dawn of the post-Enlightenment period. We must now be fiercely concerned about the business of putting minds and bodies back together. We must find the breadth of vision, the conceptual courage, and the professional audacity to look past disciplinary borders, and into a new and fertile territory where pediatricians and developmentalists forge singular and creative efforts on behalf of children everywhere.

ACKNOWLEDGMENTS

Preparation of this chapter and the research it summarizes were supported by grants from the National Institute of Child Health and Human Development (1R01 HD 24718) and the William T. Grant Foundation (90-1306-89). Dr. Boyce is also supported by the MacArthur Foundation Research Network on Psychopathology and development.

REFERENCES

Barr, R. G., Boyce, W. T., & Zeltzer, L. (1994). The stress-illness association in children: A perspective from the biobehavioral interface. In R. J. Haggerty, L. R. Sherrod, N. Garmezy, & M. Rutter (Eds.), *Stress, risk, and resilience in children and adolescents: Processes, mechanisms, and interventions* (pp. 182–224). New York: Cambridge University Press.

Bass, J. L., Christoffel, K. K., Widome, M., Boyle, W., Scheidt, P., Stanwick, R., & Roberts, K. (1993). Childhood injury prevention counseling in primary care settings: A critical review of the literature. *Pediatrics, 92*(4), 544–550.

Baumrind, D. (1987). A developmental perspective on adolescent risk taking in contemporary America. In C. E. Irwin (Ed.), *Adolescent social behavior and health* (Vol. 37, pp. 93–125). San Francisco: Jossey-Bass.

Baumrind, D. (1993). The average expectable environment is not good enough: A response to Scarr. *Child Development, 64*, 1299–1317.

Beautrais, A., Fergusson, D., & Shannon, F. (1982). Life events and childhood morbidity: A prospective study. *Pediatrics, 70*, 935–940.

Bergman, A. B., & Rivara, F. P. (1991). Sweden's experience in reducing childhood injuries. *Pediatrics, 88*(1), 69–74.

Bijur, P., Golding, J., & Haslum, M. (1988). Behavioral predictors of injury in school-aged children. *American Journal of Diseases of Children, 142*, 1307–1312.

Bijur, P. E., Golding, J., & Kurzon, M. (1988). Childhood accidents, family size, and birth order. *Social Science and Medicine, 26*(8), 839–843.

Bijur, P. E., Stewart-Brown, S., & Butler, N. (1986). Child behavior and accidental injury in 11,966 preschool children. *American Journal of Diseases of Children, 140*, 487–492.

Bornstein, M. H. (1995). Form and function: Implications for studies of culture and human development. *Culture Psychology, 1*, 123–137.

Bouchard, T. J. (1994). Genes, environment, and personality. *Science, 264*, 1700–1701.

Boyce, W. T. (1991, March). *Stress reactivity and injuries in preschool children.* Paper presented at the Childhood Injury Research and Prevention Strategies for the 1990s meeting, Rockville, MD.

Boyce, W. T. (1992). The vulnerable child: New evidence, new approaches. *Advanced Pediatrics, 39*, 1–33.

Boyce, W. T., Alkon, A., Tschann, J. M., Chesney, M. A., & Alpert, B. S. (In press). Dimensions of psychobiologic reactivity: Cardiovascular responses to laboratory stressors in preschool children. *Annals of Behavioral Medicine.*

Boyce, W. T., & Jemerin, J. J. (1990). Psychobiological differences in childhood stress response: I. Patterns of illness and susceptibility. *Journal of Developmental Behavioral Pediatrics, 11,* 86–94.

Boyce, W. T., Jensen, E. W., Cassel, J. C., Collier, A. M., Smith, A. H., & Ramey, C. T. (1977). Influence of life events and family routines on childhood respiratory tract illness. *Pediatrics, 60,* 609–615.

Boyce, W. T., O'Neill-Wagner, P., Price, C. S., Haines, M., & Suomi, S. J. (1994). *Stress reactivity and violent injuries in free-ranging rhesus monkeys. Pediatric Research, 35*(4), 19A.

Boyce, W. T., Sobolewski, S., & Schaefer, C. (1989). Recurrent injuries in school-age children. *American Journal of Diseases of Children, 143,* 338–342.

Centers for Disease Control and Prevention, Division of Injury Control. (1990). Childhood injuries in the United States. *American Journal of Diseases of Children, 144,* 627–646.

Clarke, A. S., & Schneider, M. L. (1993). Prenatal stress has long-term effects on behavioral responses to stress in juvenile rhesus monkeys. *Developmental Psychobiology, 26*(5), 293–304.

Clarke, A. S., Wittwer, D. J., Abbott, D. H., & Schneider, M. L. (1994). Long-term effects of prenatal stress on HPA axis activity in juvenile rhesus monkeys. *Developmental Psychobiology, 27,* 257–270.

Compas, B. E., Davis, G. E., Forsythe, C. J., & Wagner, B. M. (1987). Assessment of major and daily stressful events during adolescence: The Adolescent Perceived Events Scale. *Journal of Consulting and Clinical Psychology, 55*(4), 534–541.

Davidson, L. L., Hughes, S. J., & O'Connor, P. A. (1988). Preschool behavior problems and subsequent risk of injury. *Pediatrics, 82,* 644–651.

Dawson, D. A., & Adams, P. F. (1987). *Current estimates from the National Health Interview Survey, United States, 1986* (Vital Health Statistics 10). Washington, DC: National Center for Health Statistics.

DuRant, R. H., Cadenhead, C., Pendergrast, R. A., Slavens, G., & Linder, C. W. (1994). Factors associated with the use of violence among urban black adolescents. *American Journal of Public Health, 84*(4), 612–617.

Evans, L., & Waisielewski, P. (1983). Risky driving related to driver and vehicle characteristics. *Accident Analysis and Prevention, 15,* 121–136.

Ewart, C. K., & Kolodner, K. B. (1991). Social competence interview for assessing physiologic reactivity in adolescents. *Psychosomatic Medicine, 53,* 289–304.

Fingerhut, L. A., Kleinman, J. C., & Godfrey, E. (1991). *Firearm mortality among children, youth, and young adults, 1–34 years of age: Trends and current status, United States, 1979–1988* (Monthly vital statistics report 39, No. 11). Washington, DC: National Center for Health Statistics.

Gordon, J. E. (1949). The epidemiology of accidents. *American Journal of Public Health, 39,* 504–515.

Green, M. (1986). Vulnerable child syndrome and its variants. *Pediatrics in Review, 8*(3), 75–80.

Green, M., & Solnit, A. (1964). Reactions to the threatened loss of a child: A vulnerable child syndrome. *Pediatrics, 34,* 58–66.

Grossman, D. C., & Rivara, F. P. (1992). Injury control in childhood. *Pediatric Clinics of North America, 39*(3), 471–485.

Guyer, B., & Elers, B. (1990). The causes, impact, and preventability of childhood injuries in the United States: The magnitude of the problem—An overview. *American Journal of Diseases of Children, 144,* 649–652.

Harms, T., & Clifford, R. M. (1980). *Early childhood environment rating scale.* New York: Teachers College Press.

Hazinski, M. F., Francescutti, L. H., Lapidus, G. D., Micik, S., & Rivara, F. P. (1993). Pediatric injury prevention. *Annals of Emergency Medicine, 22*(2), 456–467.

Hickson, G. B., & Clayton, E. W. (1995). Parents and their children's doctors. In M. H. Bornstein (Ed.), *Handbook of parenting:* Vol. 4. *Applied and practical parenting* (pp. 163–185). Mahwah, NJ: Lawrence Erlbaum Associates.

Hiday, V. A. (1995). The social context of mental illness and violence. *Journal of Health and Social Behavior, 36,* 122–137.

Higley, J. D., Thompson, W. W., Champoux, M., Goldman, D., Hasert, M. F., Kraemer, G. W., Scanlan, J. M., Suomi, S. J., & Linnoila, M. (1993). Paternal and maternal genetic and environmental contributions to cerebrospinal fluid monoamine metabolites in rhesus monkeys (*Macaca mulatta*). *Archives of General Psychiatry, 50,* 615–623.

Hirshfeld, D. R., Rosenbaum, J. F., Biederman, J., Bolduc, E. A., Faraone, S. V., Snidman, N., Reznick, J. S., & Kagan, J. (1992). Stable behavioral inhibition and its association with anxiety disorder. *Journal of the American Academy of Child and Adolescent Psychiatry, 31*(1), 103–111.

Horwitz, S. M., Morgenstern, H., DiPietro, L., & Morrison, C. L. (1988). Determinants of pediatric injuries. *American Journal of Diseases of Children, 142,* 605–611.

Irwin, C. E., & Millstein, S. G. (1986). Biopsychosocial correlates of risk-taking behaviors during adolescence. *Journal of Adolescent Health Care, 7,* 82S–96S.

Jensen, P. S., Richters, J., Ussery, T., Bloedau, L., & Davis, H. (1991). Child psychopathology and environmental influences: Discrete life events versus ongoing adversity. *Journal of the American Academy of Child and Adolescent Psychiatry, 30,* 303–309.

Jonah, B. A. (1986). Accident risk and risk-taking behavior among young drivers. *Accident Analysis and Prevention, 18,* 255–271.

Kagan, J. (1994). *Galen's prophecy.* New York: Basic Books.

Kagan, J., Reznick, J. S., & Snidman, N. (1988). Biological bases of childhood shyness. *Science, 240,* 167–171.

Kagan, J., & Snidman, N. (1991). Infant predictors of inhibited and uninhibited profiles. *Psychological Science, 2*(1), 40–44.

Kaiser, P. (1992). *The influence of temperament and stress on preschoolers' social competence in child care centers.* Unpublished doctoral dissertation, Pacific Graduate School of Psychology, Palo Alto, CA.

Kallas, H. J., & O'Rourke, P. P. (1993). Drowning and immersion injuries in children. *Current Opinions in Pediatrics, 5*(3), 295–302.

Kamarck, T. W., Jennings, J. R., Debski, T. T., Glickman-Weiss, E., Johnson, P. S., Eddy, M. J., & Manuck, S. B. (1992). Reliable measures of behaviorally-evoked cardiovascular reactivity from a PC-based test battery: Results from student and community samples. *Psychophysiology, 29*(1), 17–28.

Langley, J., Silva, P. A., & Williams, S. (1980). A study of the relationship of ninety background, developmental, behavioral and medical factors to childhood accidents. *Australian Paediatrics, 16*, 244–247.

Larson, C. P., & Pless, I. B. (1988). Risk factors for injury in a 3-year-old birth cohort. *American Journal of Diseases of Children, 142* 1052–1057.

Lewis, C. E., & Lewis, M. A. (1983). Improving the health of children: Must the children be involved? *Annual Review of Public Health, 4*, 259–283.

Lewis, C. E., & Lewis, M. A. (1989). Educational outcomes and illness behaviors of participants in a child-initiated care system: A 12-year follow-up study. *Pediatrics, 84*(5), 845–850.

Lewis, M. A., & Lewis, C. E. (1985). Psychological distress and children's use of health services. *Pediatric Annals, 14*, 555–560.

Liang, S. W., & Boyce, W. T. (1993). The psychobiology of childhood stress. *Current Opinion in Pediatrics, 5*, 545–551.

Liang, S. W., Jemerin, J. J., Tschann, J. M., Irwin, C. E., Wara, D. W., & Boyce, W. T. (1995). Life events, cardiovascular reactivity, and risk behavior in adolescent boys. *Pediatrics, 96*, 1101–1105.

Meyer, R. J., & Haggerty, R. J. (1962). Streptococcal infections in families: Factors altering individual susceptibility. *Pediatrics, 29*, 539–549.

Millstein, S. G., Irwin, C. E., Adler, N. E., Cohn, L. D., Kegeles, S. M., & Dolcini, M. M. (1992). Health-risk behaviors and health concerns among young adolescents. *Pediatrics, 89*, 422–428.

National Academy of Sciences. (1988). *Injury control.* Washington, DC: National Academy Press.

National Highway Traffic Safety Administration. (1991). *Fatal accident reporting system, 1989* (DOT HS 807693). Washington, DC: Author.

National Research Council. (1985). *Injury in America.* Washington, DC: National Academy of Sciences.

Nyman, G. (1987). Infant temperament, childhood accidents, and hospitalization. *Clinical Pediatrics, 8*, 398–404.

Padilla, E. R., Rohsenow, D. J., & Bergman, A. B. (1976). Predicting accident frequency in children. *Pediatrics, 58*, 223–226.

Peterson, L., Ewigman, B., & Kivlahan, C. (1993). Judgments regarding appropriate child supervision to prevent injury: The role of environmental risk and child age. *Child Development, 64*, 934–950.

Plomin, R., Owen, M. J., & McGuffin, P. (1994). The genetic basis of complex human behaviors. *Science, 264*, 1733–1739.

Plomin, R., & Rende, R. (1991). Human behavioral genetics. *Annual Review of Psychology, 42*, 161–190.

Rabkin, J. G., & Struening, E. L. (1976). Life events, stress and illness. *Science, 194*, 1013–1020.

Reiss, D., Plomin, R., & Hetherington, E. M. (1991). Genetics and psychiatry: An unheralded window on the environment. *American Journal of Psychiatry, 148*, 283–291.

Rivara, F. P. (1982). Epidemiology of childhood injuries: I. Review of current research and presentation of conceptual framework. *American Journal of Diseases of Children, 136,* 399–405.

Rivara, F. P. (1992). Injury control: Issues and methods for the 1990s. *Pediatric Annals, 21,* 411–413.

Rivara, F. P., Bergman, A. B., LoGerfo, J. P., & Weiss, N. S. (1982). Epidemiology of childhood injuries: II. Sex differences in injury rates. *American Journal of Diseases of Children, 136,* 502–506.

Rivara, F. P., DiGuiseppi, C., Thompson, R. S., & Calonge, N. (1989). Risk of injury to children less than 5 years of age in day care vs. home care settings. *Pediatrics, 84,* 1011–1016.

Rutter, M. (1987). Psychosocial resilience and protective mechanisms. *American Journal of Orthopsychiatry, 57*(3), 316–331.

Ryan, W. (1976). *Blaming the victim.* New York: Vintage Books.

Sameroff, A. J., & Chandler, M. J. (1975). Reproductive risk and the continuum of caretaking casualty. In F. D. Horowitz, M. Hetherington, S. Scarr-Salapatek, & G. Siegel (Eds.), *Review of child development research* (Vol. 4, pp. 187–243). Chicago: University of Chicago Press.

Scheidt, M. D. (1988). Behavioral research toward prevention of childhood injury. *American Journal of Diseases of Children, 142,* 612–617.

Scheidt, P. C., Harel, Y., Trumble, A. C., Jones, D. H., Overpeck, M. D., & Bijur, P. E. (1995). The epidemiology of nonfatal injuries among US children and youth. *American Journal of Public Health, 85*(7), 932–938.

Schneider, M. L. (1992). Prenatal stress exposure alters postnatal behavioral expression under conditions of novelty challenge in rhesus monkey infants. *Developmental Psychobiology, 25*(7), 529–540.

Sege, R., & Dietz, W. (1994). Television viewing and violence in children: The pediatrician as agent for change. *Pediatrics, 94*(4), 600–607.

Smith, R. E., Smoll, F. L., & Ptacek, J. T. (1990). Conjunctive moderator variables in vulnerability and resiliency research: Life stress, social support and coping skills, and adolescent sport injuries. *Journal of Personality and Social Psychology, 58*(3), 360–370.

Starfield, B., Katz, H., Gabriel, A., Livingston, G., Benson, P., Hankin, J., Horn, S., & Steinwachs, D. (1984). Morbidity in childhood: A longitudinal view. *New England Journal of Medicine, 310,* 824–829.

Stein, R. E. K. (1989). *Caring for children with chronic illness: Issues and strategies.* New York: Springer.

Suomi, S. J. (1988). Genetic and maternal contributions to individual differences in Rhesus monkey biobehavioral development. In N. Krasnagor (Ed.), *Psychobiological aspects of behavioral development* (pp. 397–419). New York: Academic Press.

Suomi, S. J., Rasmussen, K. L. R., & Higley, J. D. (1992). Primate models of behavioral and physiologic change in adolescence. In P. W. McAnarney (Ed.), *Biology and behavior.*

Williams, A. F., Wells, J. K., & Lund, A. K. (1987). Voluntary seat belt use among high school students. *Accident Analysis and Prevention, 19,* 251–260.

4

Young Children's Understanding
of Routine Medical Care
and Strategies for Coping
With Stressful Medical Experiences

Janice L. Genevro
Carol J. Andreassen
Marc H. Bornstein
National Institute of Child Health and Human Development

A shared, fundamental concern among parents, pediatricians, and child developmentalists is how best to protect children's well-being, given that minor illnesses and injuries are part of the everyday lives of most families with young children, and hospitalization, surgery, and other types of more extensive medical interventions are not uncommon occurrences (e.g., Boyce, chapter 3, this volume; Bush, Melamed, Sheras, & Greenbaum, 1986; Parmelee, 1986, chapter 8, this volume; Steward, 1988). Normally, medical interventions to promote, maintain, or restore children's physical health are unquestionably in the child's best interest. It is also the case, as Parmelee (1986, 1992, chapter 8, this volume) proposed, that children's experiences with their own illnesses (and those of others) may sometimes actually have salutary effects on select aspects of their own social and emotional development. In addition, as a context in which children may feel challenged and threatened, illness or hospitalization can provide a counterintuitive opportunity in which the development of mastery and control may be fostered (Melamed & Bush, 1985).

Investigating how children comprehend their pediatric care experiences may enlighten parents, pediatricians, and developmentalists regarding children's perceptions and expectations of medical care. Such investigations may also contribute to refining efforts to foster children's development and coping when health problems occur.

An unfortunate paradox exists, however, such that medical interventions can lead to unwanted negative effects on children's short- and long-term psychological development and adaptation, resulting in emotional and behavioral problems or other sequelae (see also Kain & Mayes, chapter 5, this volume; Steward, O'Connor, Acredolo, & Steward, chapter 6, this volume). Children's medical experiences can also negatively affect their families, creating anxiety and challenging the coping skills not only of child patients themselves, but also of parents and siblings. These realities have led to the development and widespread implementation of a variety of programs to prepare children and their families for potentially distressing medical experiences (e.g., Gaynard et al., 1990).

In this chapter, we focus on children's understanding of routine medical care and strategies for coping with more challenging medical experiences. We believe that children's understanding is a critical conduit by which factors such as age, developmental level, individual differences, and previous experiences influence their reactions to medical experiences and hospitalization (see also Rudolph, Dennig, & Weisz, 1995). These psychological and developmental factors, which have been identified as potentially important modifiers of children's responses to programs designed to prepare them and their parents for diverse medical procedures, are also likely to influence children's understanding of their medical experiences and the resources—both internal and external—available to them for coping with those experiences.

To begin to address these issues, we present data from two investigations, one of children's understanding of routine medical experiences and one of their understanding and evaluation of strategies for coping with potentially painful and distressing medical procedures. The first project, which is ongoing, focuses on 4-year-olds' general understanding of routine medical care as reflected in their mental representations of the normative event of "going to the doctor". We are especially interested in how children's mental representations of routine pediatric care integrate the affects and cognitions related to that care with mothers' concerns about their children's health.

The second project, which comprised a comprehensive examination of stress, coping, and development in a sample of school-aged children who were hospitalized for elective surgery, was conducted with colleagues from New York University (Altshuler, Genevro, Ruble, & Bornstein, 1995;

Genevro, Bornstein, Ruble, & Altshuler, 1995). This research focuses on hospitalization for surgery (and associated procedures) as pediatric medical experiences that are fairly common but potentially more challenging and threatening than routine pediatric care.

Before presenting the methods and findings of these studies, we briefly detail the theoretical framework within which we interpret children's understanding of medical care, and their understanding of coping strategies and resources, in relation to their responses to potentially challenging or threatening medical experiences.

CHILDREN'S UNDERSTANDING AS A LINK BETWEEN THEIR PREVIOUS MEDICAL EXPERIENCES AND THEIR CURRENT RESPONSES

In the hospital, a child's *physical* well-being can easily be threatened by such things as painful procedures, unfamiliar and unpleasant sensory stimulation, and curtailment of developmentally appropriate activities. The child's *psychological* well-being can be threatened if the child suffers significant losses. These might include the losses of parental support, perceived control or autonomy, relative autonomy, self-esteem, or sense of security. (Gaynard et al., 1990, p. 16)

Over the past 30 years, a variety of programs has been developed and widely implemented to prepare children for hospitalization, surgery, and other potentially distressing medical experiences because of concerns about the possible deleterious effects of such experiences on the psychological well-being and health of children and their families. These programs utilize diverse techniques—such as the provision of information about hospital and surgical procedures, modeling of coping strategies, and play with medically related toys—to help children and parents prepare for and cope successfully with hospitalization and associated medical procedures (e.g., Gaynard et al., 1990). However, as several investigators have observed (e.g., Kain & Mayes, chapter 5, this volume; Melamed & Bush, 1985; Peterson, Mori, & Carter, 1985), not all children benefit from the preparation strategies utilized in such programs, and under some circumstances preparation programs may even exacerbate children's (and their parents') problematic coping. Multiple factors, including children's age and previous experience with medical care, the timing of interventions, and parental involvement, appear to affect—both singly and in combination—the outcome of efforts to prepare children for potentially distressing medical experiences.

Evidence of differential effects of interventions to prepare children for hospitalization suggests that further clarification is needed of the roles played by age, developmental level, individual differences factors, and prior experiences in children's responses to medical treatment and hospitalization. A more thorough understanding of these issues might also lead to improvements in interventions designed to promote the psychological and physical well-being of children undergoing potentially distressing or painful medical treatments (see also Peterson, 1989).

Many programs designed to prepare children for hospitalization and other potentially aversive medical experiences have been based on the model of stress and coping developed by Lazarus and colleagues (e.g., Lazarus & Folkman, 1984). In this model, coping is defined as "constantly changing cognitive and behavioral efforts to manage specific external and/or internal demands that are appraised as taxing or exceeding the resources of the person" (p. 141). One particularly important premise of this model is that the individual's appraisal of a situation, to a greater extent than objective circumstance, determines perceptions of threat (see also Compas, Worsham, & Ey, 1992). Thus, events (or specific characteristics of events) may be perceived or appraised as particularly stressful by a given individual but not by others. Appraisal of the threat constituted by an event or stimulus is considered *primary appraisal*. Individuals also appraise "whether and how the[y] . . . can cope with the threat or harm" (Gaynard et al., 1990, p. 16); this appraisal of the resources—both external and internal—the individual perceives to be available to him or her to manage a specific threat constitutes *secondary appraisal*.

Peterson (1989) proposed that:

[A]ppraisal of a stressor involves several simultaneous processes in the child. At a cognitive level, the child must relate current stimuli to the memory of similar past stimulus encounters, define the parameters of the event (such as the potential intensity and duration of the stimuli), evaluate the likelihood of the event occurring, and orient the event in time (e.g., it will happen in 10 min versus in 10 days). (p. 380)

These processes, because they are dependent in part on memory, are contingent on developmental level and likely to be affected by emotional arousal (Peterson, 1989). Children's appraisals of the medical circumstances in which they find themselves thus presumably depend not only on their understanding of what those circumstances portend—to which their memories contribute—but also hinge on their awareness and understanding of their previous experiences and responses in similar contexts.

Research specifically addressing children's understanding of their medical experiences is relatively rare (see, e.g., Bachanas & Roberts, 1995; Bush & Holmbeck, 1987; Hackworth & McMahon, 1991; Steward & Steward, 1981). A foundation for examining this understanding is provided, however, by research on children's understanding of health and illness (e.g., Bibace & Walsh, 1981; Brewster, 1982; Whitt, Dykstra, & Taylor, 1979) and on their memories of specific episodes of medical care (e.g., Baker-Ward, Gordon, Ornstein, Larus, & Clubb, 1993; Steward et al., chapter 6, this volume).

Much of the research on children's understanding of wellness and illness has been conducted within a Piagetian framework, in which understanding of health and illness is believed to depend on the stage of cognitive development the child has attained. Recent "functionalist" reconceptualizations of children's understanding of health and illness place "greater emphasis . . . on children's experiences in their physical, social, and psychological worlds" (Rubovits & Siegel, 1994, p. 269) as contributing to and defining children's knowledge in specific domains:

> From the perspective of a functional model, children's knowledge of their chronic disease should be intimately related to what they need to know declaratively and procedurally to manage the disease successfully. . . . Thinking of disease knowledge in this way frames the child's understanding in a *need*-to-know rather than a *capacity*-to-know conception. In this way, disease understanding includes not only medical aspects of a disease but also social, emotional, and other behavioral issues associated with a particular child. (Rubovits & Siegel, 1994, p. 270).

The functionalist perspective suggests that children's understanding of their medical care experiences, and of strategies for coping with those medical care experiences they find distressing, threatening, or challenging, will be based on both the type and extent of their previous related experiences, and on individual differences in children's social and emotional characteristics and environments (see also Hackworth & McMahon, 1991). Rather than viewing the need-to-know and capacity-to-know perspectives as mutually exclusive, however, we suggest that level of cognitive development and experience in interaction with individual differences form the foundation for children's understanding of their medical care experiences. That is, children's memories of previous experiences with medical care—the content and qualitative aspects of which are shaped by level of cognitive development, affective experience, and other factors—contribute to, become integrated with, and are reflected in children's conceptions of medical care and their responses to the threats, challenges, and rewards offered by such care.

YOUNG CHILDREN'S UNDERSTANDING OF ROUTINE PEDIATRIC CARE

Faithful to this (modified) functionalist perspective, the framework within which we have conceptualized young children's understanding of routine medical care builds on Schank and Abelson's (1977) script theory, Nelson's (1986) event theory, and the work of Bowlby (1988) and others (e.g., Bretherton, 1985) on children's mental representations (or "working models") of themselves and their social and interactional worlds.

According to Nelson's (1986) developmental theory of event representation, the child's earliest mental representations are of routine everyday events; young children acquire event representations through direct experience with the world and through direct interactions with other individuals. Even children as young as about 2 years of age can use their experiences of routine events to begin to organize their real-world knowledge into event representations (e.g., Bauer & Hertsgaard, 1993; Bauer & Travis, 1993). These event representations then become the basic building blocks for the more sophisticated cognitive structures and processes that will follow, such as language acquisition, categorization, inference, logical reasoning, and interpersonal communication.

Event representations include goal-directed sets of actions that are hierarchically structured and consist of temporal-causal sequences of behavior beginning with an *opening act*, followed at some point by a central or *goal act*, and ending with a *closing act*. In addition, event representations include the agents or individuals involved in the actions and the variable resources ("slot fillers") to be acted on. Events are often conveniently packaged with a conventional label. For example, the event of "going shopping" opens with making a list of needed and usually variable items, includes the goal act of selecting items at the market, and closes with the placement of items in the kitchen pantry.

An event representation is, therefore, a complex mental unity in which the parts (acts, agents, and props or slot fillers) work together as one organized whole, such that invoking any one part or component of the representation will identify whether, and the range in which, the other parts will play out. Event representations are flexible and dynamic entities that enable individuals to predict how the sequences of actions comprising an event might change, to anticipate agents and outcomes, and to identify recurring events as well as events that are about to occur. This view suggests that event representations contribute uniquely to children's understanding of the predictability of their environment and interactions that may, in turn, form a foundation for children's coping.

The work of Nelson (1986) and other investigators (e.g., Bower, 1981; Bowlby, 1988; Bretherton, 1985; Schore, 1994) also indicates that the emotions associated with or evoked by specific constellations of actions and consequences comprise critical features of mental representations. Children's representations of their experiences, the specific features of which depend to some extent on various individual differences, become elaborated and modified through maturation, and through ongoing interactions with the world. Representations thus come to incorporate not only actions (of the child and important others involved in the experience), but also expectations of consequences and associated emotional responses. In this way, elaborated event representations also may come to serve as the foundation for children's appraisals of the threat and challenge in situations with which they are confronted, and for their responses in threatening, challenging, or otherwise emotionally arousing situations (see also Block, 1982; Schore, 1994).

Finally, mental representations act as lenses or filters through which experiences are interpreted and understood (e.g., Block, 1982), and thereby may serve to link children's early experiences (including nurturant and traumatic ones) and the ways in which children comprehend and attempt to cope with emotionally arousing events (Block, 1982; Schore, 1994; Thompson, 1994).

Routine well-child care and medical visits for acute illness and/or injury are common experiences in the lives of most preschool-age children in our society (e.g., Boyce, chapter 3, this volume; Parmelee, 1986). The episodic nature and emotionally salient character of such care suggest that young children would be likely to develop mental representations that reflect their general understanding of the event of going to the doctor. Furthermore, research on children's mental representations (e.g., Nelson, 1986; Schore, 1994) and on the acquisition of children's health attitudes and behaviors (e.g., Tinsley & Lees, 1995) suggests that children's representations of routine pediatric care would include not only the events experienced (e.g., getting a shot or being examined) but also their affective responses (e.g., being hurt or crying). Because children's visits to the doctor can be affectively laden for parents, too, especially parents with high levels of trait anxiety and medical fears (e.g., Bush et al., 1986), it seems probable that children's event representations would also reflect some aspects of their parents' health-related anxieties.

We thus hypothesized that children's mental representations of routine care would contain information about procedures and activities children experience as well as affective information, and would link children's own experiences with the health-related attitudes and behaviors of the parent typically involved in the event of going to the doctor. We predicted specifically that the affective and cognitive contents of children's mental representations of routine medical care would relate to their mothers' global concern about their children's health.

Data from the first phase of our research on children's representations of the event of going to the doctor were obtained from interviews conducted with 37 girls and 33 boys 4 years of age. These children were interviewed using a format based on Nelson (1986). The interviewer began by saying, "I know you know a lot about going to the doctor. Tell me what happens when you go to the doctor," and then proceeded with specific prompts based on the child's response.

The format of the Doctor Event Interview is as follows (I = Interviewer):

I: I know you know a lot about going to the doctor.
        Tell me what happens when you go to the doctor [waits for child's response].
I: You certainly know a lot about going to the doctor.
        Tell me something else about going to the doctor [waits for child's response].
I: [Repeats previous question until child says "I don't know" or "Nothing," then asks:]
        What's the first thing that happens when you go to the doctor? [waits for child's response].
I: What happens next? [waits for child's response].
I: What happens after that? [repeats until child says "I don't know" or "Nothing"]

Examples of children's responses include the following:

I: Tell me what happens when you go to the doctor.
C: *Well, they check you through a telescope. They check your ears and they check your body. And that's all I know.*
I: Tell me what happens when you go to the doctor.
C: *It hurts. You get a shot and then you get a sticker.*

I: Tell me something else about going to the doctor.

C: *You tick . . . You check your heart.*

I: What's the first thing that happens when you go to the doctor?

C: *You just wait in the waiting chair.*

I: And then what happens?

C: *You go to the doctor and then the nurse tells the doctor that somebody's here to go to the doctor.*

I: And then what happens?

C: *The doctor usually looks at the way you're growing.*

I: And then what?

C: *You do other things and then you're all done and you get a sticker.*

Children's responses were coded for representational complexity (Andreassen, Genevro, Baggeroer, & Bornstein, 1994; Nelson, 1986). Variables derived included the total number of acts (e.g., "You check your heart" is considered one act) and the ratio of acts to interviewer prompts. Because research indicates that specific elements of routine pediatric care, such as injections, can be particularly upsetting to young children (e.g., Peterson, 1989), children's responses were also coded for content related to specific aspects of routine medical care, including, for example, whether the child mentioned "getting a shot" or being "checked." To investigate affective components of children's representations of going to the doctor, responses were also coded for expressions of negative affect, defined for these purposes as statements including references to pain, distress, or disaffection, such as "it hurt," "I cried," or "I don't like to go to the doctor." Children also completed the *Wechsler Preschool and Primary Scale of Intelligence-Revised* (WPPSI–R; Wechsler, 1989).

Mothers of these children completed short forms of the *RAND Child Health Status Measures* and *Functional Status Questionnaire* (Lewis, Pantell, & Kieckhefer, 1989) and questions designed to assess mothers' treatment of their children's physical symptoms by medication (Maiman, Becker, & Katlic, 1985). The latter series of questions was expanded and modified to assess the degree of concern each mother expressed about her child's health relative to her perceptions of other mothers of children the same age. Mothers rated themselves on a 3-point scale, with scale points of 1 (*worry less than other mothers*), 2 (*worry about as much as other mothers*), and 3 (*worry more than other mothers*). Mothers' ratings of their child's general health status were also obtained using a 4-point scale, with a rating of 1 representing excellent health and a rating of 4 representing poor health.

The number of discrete acts in children's representations of the event of going to the doctor ranged from 0 to 15 (M = 3.8, SD = 3.4). The ratio of acts reported to the number of interviewer prompts ranged from 0 to 3 (M = 0.9, SD = 0.8). Almost one quarter (24%) of children's event representations included expressions of negative affect associated with routine pediatric care.

Girls' representations of going to the doctor were significantly more complex, as indexed by the ratio of the number of acts to interviewer prompts (see Table 4.1, β = .25, p < .05). Because research has indicated the existence of gender variation in the expression of emotion by young children (e.g., Fabes & Eisenberg, 1992), potential gender differences in representational content were evaluated. Evaluation of representations that included one or more acts indicated that girls' representations were not significantly more likely to include negative affect than were those of boys, $\chi^2(1)$ = 1.02.[1]

Boys were significantly more likely than girls, however, to produce responses (e.g., "I don't know" or "I don't want to talk about it") that included no acts, $\chi^2(1)$ = 7.0, p = .01. They were also less likely to mention being "checked" or "getting a check-up," $\chi^2(1)$ = 10.5, p = .001.

We found that mothers in this sample tended to view themselves as slightly less concerned about their children's health than they perceive other mothers of 4-year-old children to be, M = 1.8, SD = 0.5. Mothers, on average, also rated their children's general health as excellent, M = 1.3, SD = 0.5.

Hierarchical multiple regression analyses were conducted to test the hypothesis that mothers' level of concern about their children's health would relate to representational complexity and negative affective content in children's event representations of routine pediatric care. In these analyses, variance attributable to child gender, child IQ, and mothers' perceptions of their child's general health status was controlled. The results, presented in Table 4.1, indicated that higher levels of maternal concern were associated with the presence of negative affective content in children's event representations, β = .30, IR^2 = 8%, $F(1,65)$ = 6.17, p < .05. Maternal concern also was significantly positively associated with representational complexity, as measured using the ratio of acts to interviewer prompts, β = .29, IR^2 = 7%, $F(1,62)$ = 5.62, p < .05.

---

[1]Results of analyses examining all protocols also indicated that the representations of girls were not significantly more likely than those of boys to include negative affect, $\chi^2(1)$ = 3.26, p = .07.

TABLE 4.1
Affective and Cognitive Components of Preschoolers' Event Representations: Maternal Contributions

| | | Dependent Variables | | | | | |
| | | Negative Affective Content | | | Representational Complexity (Act to Interviewer Prompt Ratio) | | |
Step	Variable	β	IR^2	$F\Delta(df)$	β	IR^2	$F\Delta(df)$
1	Gender	.19	4.55	1.60 (2,67)	$.25^*$	10.16	3.62^* (2,64)
	WPPSI–R Full IQ	.07			.18		
2	Child's General Health (Maternal Rating)	-.04	.16	.11 (1,66)	-.03	.07	.05 (1,63)
3	Concern Re: Child's Health (Maternal Rating)	.30	8.26	6.17^* (1,65)	.29	7.46	5.62^* (1,62)
	Total Variance Explained		12.97	$2.42^\dagger$ (4,65)		17.69	3.33^* (4,62)

$^\dagger p = .06.$ $^* p < .05.$

69

Young children's representations of the event of going to the doctor thus frequently include information not only about various phenomena and procedures children typically experience in the process of receiving routine pediatric care, but incorporate their affective responses as well. Cognitive and affective features of these representations are predicted by mothers' concerns about their children's health. This suggests that children's representations are one means by which their own experiences are linked with the affective experiences and actions of others. We are in the process of investigating in more detail the roles played by children's event representations in the development of their understanding of medical care experiences. We also continue to explore the ways in which children's representations of medical care connect the affects and actions of significant others with children's own experiences and coping responses.

CHILDREN'S UNDERSTANDING OF STRATEGIES FOR COPING WITH STRESSFUL MEDICAL EXPERIENCES

Many children undergo medical treatments that are potentially more traumatic than those encountered in the course of routine pediatric care (Bush et al., 1986; Steward et al., chapter 6, this volume). How children respond to such treatments and to efforts to prepare them to cope effectively with aspects of medical care they find distressing or threatening, seems likely to depend to a great extent on children's understanding of that care—which in turn depends on factors such as age, developmental level, individual differences, and previous experiences. Thus, it is critical to ascertain how children appraise both the medical experiences they undergo and the internal and external resources available to them to respond to aspects of those experiences they perceive as threatening or distressing.

It has been proposed that, in addition to ascertaining whether demands constitute a threat, individuals also appraise whether and to what degree stressful situations (or elements of situations) are controllable (e.g., Folkman, 1984).[2] Uncontrollable stressors are characterized by circumstances that are not easily altered or that are not perceived as changeable. Being admitted to the hospital for surgery is an example of a situation in which many associated circumstances are beyond the control of the patient, especially when the patient is a young child.

---

[2]See Thoits (1991) for a discussion of how differences in perceptions of "controllability" and the use of a variety of coping strategies are related to differential coping outcomes in adults.

Evidence from studies with adults (e.g., Folkman, 1984) and some studies with children (e.g., Peterson & Toler, 1986) suggests that active, problem-focused, "approach" coping strategies (e.g., Altshuler & Ruble, 1989), such as seeking information about what is going to happen and implementing change strategies, can be effective in coping with controllable stressors. In contrast, the use of passive, emotion-focused, "avoidance" coping strategies (e.g., Altshuler & Ruble, 1989) appears to be most effective, at least initially, in response to stressful situations that are beyond the control of the individual (e.g., Compas, 1987; Lazarus & Folkman, 1984; Miller & Green, 1985). Some avoidance strategies, such as distraction, involve attempts to shift attention away from painful or distressing stimuli. Although researchers have indexed distraction-oriented strategies in a variety of ways, such strategies may be usefully categorized as either behavioral distraction or cognitive distraction (e.g., Altshuler & Ruble, 1989). *Behavioral distraction* involves physical activities such as drawing or playing board games that divert attention from distressing events or emotions. *Cognitive distraction* involves manipulating mental states to refocus attention. Thinking of a favorite activity or companion, or trying to mentally solve challenging mathematical problems, for example, are cognitive activities that are to some degree incompatible with the awareness of distressing stimuli.

Research on children's coping knowledge indicates that children of school age typically are aware of behavioral forms of distraction as ways of coping with distress or threat (e.g., Altshuler et al., 1995; Altshuler & Ruble, 1989; Yates, Yates, & Beasley, 1987). Age differences have been observed in children's awareness of cognitive distraction strategies, however: Children younger than 7 years rarely spontaneously mention cognitive distraction as a coping strategy (e.g., Altshuler & Ruble, 1989; Band & Weisz, 1988). Younger children also tend to think about managing distressing emotions in terms of changing situations, rather than using internal, cognitive strategies (such as distraction) to regulate emotional arousal (e.g., Carroll & Steward, 1984).

In addition, a dimension of cognitive abilities that seems likely to relate to children's coping in stressful medical situations is problem-solving skill (see also Compas et al., 1992). The process of problem solving includes appraisal (of the situation as well as available resources) and captures the potentially iterative nature of children's attempts to deal with difficult situations. Viewing problem solving, with the goal of managing distressing emotions, as integral to coping also suggests that cognitive problem-solving abilities, in combination with age, experience, and specific individual differences related to affective experience and expression (e.g., gender), would be particularly likely to affect children's coping capabilities in medical situations they find threatening or distressing.

We addressed issues of how children being hospitalized for elective surgery appraise and understand the coping options available for dealing with potentially stressful medical procedures in a sample of school-age children being admitted for relatively minor surgery (Altshuler et al., 1995; Genevro et al., 1995). Relations were examined among children's age, gender, problem-solving abilities, and knowledge of strategies for coping with potentially distressing medical experiences. Children's perceptions of the value and efficacy of specific coping strategies were also investigated.

In studying children's understanding of coping strategies, we were interested in (a) how age, as a proxy for maturation in general, relates to differences in children's coping knowledge; (b) how individual variation in problem-solving ability, adjusted for age, relates to children's coping capacities; (c) how problem-solving abilities affect relations between age and coping knowledge; and (d) how children perceive the value of specific strategies for coping in uncontrollable health care situations, and the efficacy of those strategies in changing feelings of fear.

Participants in the study were children between the ages of 5 and 13 years who were admitted to Bellevue Hospital in New York City for relatively minor surgery and who were scheduled to spend no more than 3 nights in the hospital. Children were interviewed prior to hospitalization about their coping knowledge and perceptions of coping strategy value and efficacy, and their problem-solving skills were assessed using two subscales of the *Kaufman Assessment Battery for Children* (Triangles and Matrix Analogies; Kaufman & Kaufman, 1983).

Knowledge of coping strategies was evaluated by children's verbal reports of the behavioral and cognitive options available to a child in a hypothetically stressful situation. Because knowledge of a coping strategy is not necessarily equivalent to a perception that the strategy would be a good thing to do (strategy value), or that it would be effective in changing feelings of fear (strategy efficacy), we also asked children to rate strategies in terms of value and efficacy both before and after hospitalization (Genevro et al., 1995). Value and efficacy were distinguished conceptually because children may think that using a particular strategy would change their feelings of fear (be efficacious), but would not be a good thing to do (be valuable) because it leads to other untoward consequences, such as the disapproval of parents or other involved adults.

Children were told a story about a child of their own gender who felt frightened about a visit to the dentist, and then were asked what the child could do to feel less scared (see Altshuler et al., 1995, for additional details).[3] Children subsequently responded to a series of open-ended questions about what the hypothetical child could do about feeling scared. In addition, children were presented with 11 cards depicting specific coping strategies. Their perceptions of the value of each strategy were obtained by asking them to indicate how bad or good each strategy would be for the hypothetical child to use; perceptions of strategy efficacy were obtained by asking children whether each of the strategies, if used, would change the hypothetical child's feelings of fear (see Genevro et al., 1995, for additional details).

Children's responses to the open-ended questions were coded into categories of coping strategies. The categories used in these analyses and the strategies comprising each category are presented in Table 4.2. Examples of children's responses to the open-ended questions about what hypothetical "Jill" or "John" could do about feeling scared in the hypothetical story are presented in Table 4.2 as well.

In response to the open-ended questions about what the hypothetical child could do about feeling scared, children most frequently suggested behavioral distraction strategies ($M = 1.0$, $SD = 1.1$) as coping options, followed by escape ($M = 0.7$, $SD = 1.0$), adaptive approach ($M = 0.4$, $SD = 0.8$), cognitive distraction ($M = 0.4$, $SD = 0.7$), and denial ($M = 0.3$, $SD = 0.8$). As predicted, and as has been found in other studies (e.g., Altshuler & Ruble, 1989), there was no relation between age in this range and knowledge of behavioral distraction strategies, $r = .08$. Age was positively and significantly related to knowledge of cognitive distraction strategies, $r = .30$, $p < .05$, and negatively related to suggestions of escape strategies, $r = -.38$, $p < .05$. Age also related positively to knowledge of denial strategies, $r = .33$, $p < .05$, and adaptive approach strategies, $r = .30$, $p < .05$.

Neither gender nor children's problem-solving scores related to any of the coping knowledge variables. Results of hierarchical multiple regression analyses of the effects of problem-solving scores on relations between age and knowledge of coping are presented in Table 4.3. Significant interactions between problem solving and age in several of these analyses indicated, however, that problem solving moderated relations between age and knowl-

---

[3]Stories about dental procedures were used because of ethical concerns regarding the use of hospitalization stories with children about to undergo surgery. Research on children's health attitudes (e.g., Bush & Holmbeck, 1987) indicates that children tend to have global attitudes toward health care providers and procedures rather than specific attitudes toward, for example, physicians or dentists (Bachanas & Roberts, 1995). The dental stories were used based on the premise that children's responses would accurately reflect their awareness of coping strategies while reducing their sense of personal involvement.

TABLE 4.2
Coping Strategies

Categories and Component Strategies	Examples of Children's Responses to Open-Ended Coping Question (Prehospitalization)
Avoidance Strategies	
Behavioral Distraction	
Do something fun.	"Play with someone."
Do something else.	"Go to a playroom and color."
Play.	"Read a book."
Read.	
Watch television.	
Cognitive Distraction	
Think about something fun.	"Think that she wants to play."
Think about something else.	"She'll think they'll give her a lollipop."
Fantasize.	"Think of something else."
Escape	
Leave the situation.	
Sleep/Close eyes/Nap.	"Not to look at what they're doing to him—close his eyes."
Try to get out of it.	"If the doctor isn't there yet, she could leave."
Argue.	
Go somewhere else/Go outside.	"Hit the doctor to make himself less scared; scream at the doctor and nurse."
Denial	
Deny that the situation exists.	"Not to think of the tooth coming out."
Don't think about it.	"Make believe it wasn't going to happen."
Approach Strategies	
Adaptive Approach	
Do what is asked.	
Seek information.	"Ask the doctor if [John] will be put to sleep or something else."
Social Support Strategies	
Social Support	
Talk with Mom (or Dad).	"His mother will tell him it's just nothing."
Talk with a friend.	"Sit down and talk with a friend."

74

TABLE 4.3
Knowledge of Coping Strategy Variables: Hierarchical Multiple Regression Results

Predictor Variables	df	Dependent Variables							
		Behavioral Distraction		*Cognitive Distraction*		*Adaptive Approach*		*Escape*	
		IR^2 (%)	$F\Delta$	IR^2 (%)	$F\Delta$	IR^2 (%)	$F\Delta$	IR^2 (%)	$F\Delta$
Gender	(1,34)	.66	.22	.84	.29	.76	.26	7.88	2.91
Problem-solving	(1,33)	.00	.00	8.46	3.08	3.13	1.07	2.02	.74
Age	(1,32)	3.31	1.10	10.39	4.14*	8.34	3.04	7.54	2.92
Age x Gender	(1,31)	.01	.00	.00	.00	6.59	2.52	21.87	11.17**
Gender x Problem solving	(1,30)	1.51	.48	1.60	.61	.85	.32	—	—
Age x Problem solving	(1,29)	19.24	7.41**	18.42	8.86**	11.47	4.81*	—	—
Total R^2 (%)		24.73		39.70		31.13		39.31	
F		1.59		3.18*		2.18		5.02**	

Note. n = 36. * *p* < .05. ** *p* < .01.

edge of specific types of coping strategies. That is, relations between age and knowledge of some strategies differed at different levels of problem-solving scores: As depicted in Figure 4.1, older children with higher problem-solving scores suggested both behavioral and cognitive distraction as possible coping options significantly more frequently than did younger children or older children with lower problem-solving scores. Knowledge of adaptive approach strategies was also predicted by the interaction of age with problem-solving scores; in this instance, however, older children with lower problem-solving scores were more likely to suggest adaptive ap-proach strategies.

Children's ratings of coping strategy value and efficacy, as presented in Table 4.4, indicated that they were fairly consistent in their estimates of good strategies and poor strategies. Adaptive approach strategies ("asking for information," "doing what is asked"), distraction strategies (both behav-ioral and cognitive), and social support strategies ("talk to mom," "talk to a friend") were characterized by children as valuable strategies that were also likely to change feelings of fear.

Escape and denial strategies, which included leaving the situation or pretending that it was not going to happen, and a maladaptive approach strategy, thinking about how the procedure would feel, were considered the worst coping options and least likely to change feelings of fear. These results provide some interesting contrasts to the results pertaining to coping knowledge. For example, although even 5-year-olds are quite aware that escape is a coping option available to them, they sensibly do not believe it is a good strategy to use in response to feeling afraid.

Children's perceptions and endorsements of the various strategies indi-cate that they are fairly knowledgeable about the coping options available and useful in a hypothetically stressful situation. These results also indicate to us that children were actively trying to understand how best to manage their feelings of distress in a situation in which it is unlikely that they would be able to exercise much control. For example, it is possible that children's high ratings of the value of the strategy of adaptive approach may be based on their perceptions of the importance of getting painful or stressful experiences "over and done with"—that by cooperating, they would be minimizing their exposure to distress-evoking experiences and interactions (which can include the disapproval and cajoling of adults engaged in providing treatment or care to the child, as well as the physical pain involved in undergoing medical procedures). Children as patients are confronted with the behavioral expectations, dictates, and interventions of a bewildering number and variety of adults—parents, nurses, physicians, Child Life workers, technicians, dietary workers, and volunteers—whose goals for

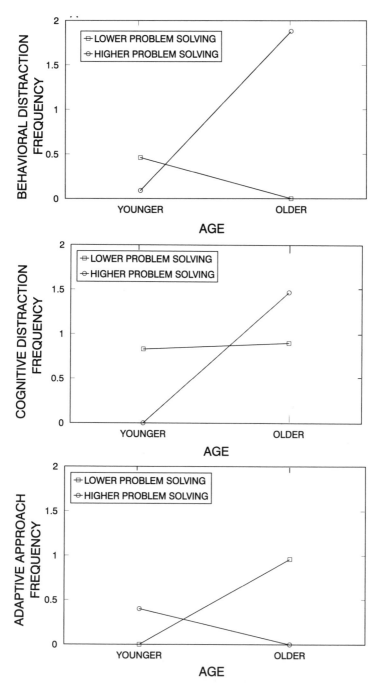

FIGURE 4.1. Significant interactions of age with problem-solving skills and gender in relation to knowledge of different coping strategies. Reprinted with permission from Ablex.

TABLE 4.4
A. Ratings of Value of Coping Strategies

Strategy Category	Prehospitalization		
	M	SD	Rank
Adaptive approach	5.28	1.08	1
Behavioral distraction	5.02	1.35	2
Cognitive distraction	4.79	1.55	4
Escape/Denial	3.15	1.60	6
Maladaptive approach	3.97	1.97	5
Social support	4.80	1.31	3

B. Ratings of Efficacy of Coping Strategies

Strategy Category	Prehospitalization		
	M	SD	Rank
Adaptive approach	.77	.37	1
Behavioral distraction	.75	.35	2
Cognitive distraction	.73	.34	4
Escape/Denial	.67	.40	5
Maladaptive approach	.53	.50	6
Social support	.73	.36	3

Note. All strategy categories are composed of two strategies except for maladaptive approach, which consists of one strategy.

intervention (e.g., maximization of long-term benefit or completing their work efficiently) may differ from children's own goals (e.g., avoidance or minimization of short-term distress and pain, or making sense of what is happening). "Asking what will happen" and "complying" thus may reflect children's attempts to understand the parameters of the situation and to bring their behaviors into accord with adults' expectations.

CONCLUSIONS

Our research on young children's mental representations of going to the doctor indicates that these representations constitute a strong foundation for further investigation of the growth of children's understanding of medical care. In addition to providing information about specific elements of their health care experiences, these representations evidence links among children's experiences, their affective responses, and the affects and behaviors of their parents and care providers. This research also indicates that specific individual differences in children (in this instance, gender) relate to systematic differences in the content and complexity of representations of routine care reported by same-age peers.

In addition, our investigations of school-age children's knowledge of coping strategies and their estimations of the value and efficacy of those strategies indicate that, generally, they are aware of strategies that may be useful in coping with a potentially distressing medical experience. We also found, however, that factors such as age, in combination with level of cognitive problem-solving abilities, predicted children's knowledge of strategies—such as behavioral and cognitive distraction—thought to be particularly useful in the initial stages of uncontrollable stressful experiences. This, in combination with evidence of children's perceptions that some strategies are more effective and valuable in managing emotions in a potentially distressing medical encounter than others, indicates that children are not simply passive recipients of care, but rather that they actively seek to cope with health care experiences and operate on those cognitions in ways that make sense to them.

Our research thus suggests that information about children's understanding of their medical experiences and of the coping options and resources available to them may prove valuable to pediatricians, psychologists, and other health care providers in their efforts to promote the coping and adaptation of individual children in diverse medical situations. Because in our society children's contacts with routine medical care typically begin early, are frequent in the preschool years, and have the potential to be very distressing, such experiences are likely to be both salient to children and play an integral role in their physical and psychological development (Parmelee, 1986, chapter 8, this volume). Children's early medical experiences (and related affects) may influence their later health attitudes and behaviors (e.g., Steward & Steward, 1981).

Helping children cope with aversive medical situations while supporting their development and long-term adaptation may depend on the ways in which we assist children in appraising and making sense of their current experiences in light of their previous experiences and developmental level, and also the ways we help them to identify, use, and benefit from the resources they themselves bring to such situations. In particular, children may benefit if time is taken to help them understand what behaviors are expected of them in medical treatment situations and how they can meet those expectations; the adults in the situation also need to understand and communicate their awareness of the specific types of help children may need to do what is asked of them.

Our research further suggests that as we seek to refine interventions designed to prepare children for potentially distressing medical experiences, it is important to recognize that coping is a complex, multidimensional regulatory process that integrates affect, cognition, interpersonal resources, and behaviors (e.g., Greenberg, Kusche, & Speltz, 1991). Coping depends to some degree on problem-solving abilities and it develops over time and with experience. These investigations lead us to speculate that children's efforts to cope with aversive medical treatments originate in part from their prior experiences in similar situations and in part from what is possible—and expected—in a specific medical situation. Children's coping in specific situations and the development of children's coping capabilities over time and through experience thus can be facilitated or impeded by both individual and environmental factors. In determining how best to intervene (or not intervene if help is not necessary) to prepare children and families for potentially challenging or distressing medical experiences, we also urge the careful assessment of children's and (their families') understanding of the present situation, past experiences (medical and nonmedical) that were distressing to them; their past efforts to cope, and their own internal and external resources.

ACKNOWLEDGMENTS

The study of children's understanding of routine medical care was supported by the Division of Intramural Research of the National Institute of Child Health and Human Development and by National Research Council Research Associate Awards to the first and second authors. We are grateful to Alisa Ainbinder, Cheryl Baggeroer, Abigail Herron, and Allison Wiles, who also contributed to this work. The research reported here on children's coping with hospitalization for elective surgery was supported by three grants from the National Institute of Mental Health—a predoctoral National Research Service Award (MH09288) to J. L. Altshuler, and Grant 37215 and a Research Scientist Development Award (00484) to D. N. Ruble—and by a National Research Council Research Associate Award to the first author. We thank Dr. B. Dreyer, E. Dickey, and the Child Life Staff at Bellevue Hospital for their support of this research.

REFERENCES

Altshuler, J. L., Genevro, J. L., Ruble, D. N., & Bornstein, M. H. (1995). Children's knowledge and use of coping strategies during hospitalization for elective surgery. *Journal of Applied Developmental Psychology, 16*, 53–76.

Altshuler, J. L., & Ruble, D. N. (1989). Developmental changes in children's awareness of strategies for coping with uncontrollable stress. *Child Development, 60*, 1337–1349.

Andreassen, C. J., Genevro, J. L., Baggeroer, C. E., & Bornstein, M. H. (1994, March). *Contributions of toddler play to temporal and causal ordering in preschoolers' event representations.* Paper presented at the Conference on Human Development, Pittsburgh, PA.

Bachanas, P. J., & Roberts, M. C. (1995). Factors affecting children's attitudes toward health care and responses to stressful medical procedures. *Journal of Pediatric Psychology, 20,* 261–275.

Baker-Ward, L., Gordon, B. N., Ornstein, P. A., Larus, D. M., & Clubb, P. A. (1993). Young children's long-term retention of a pediatric examination. *Child Development, 64,* 1519–1533.

Band, E. B., & Weisz, J. R. (1988). How to feel better when it feels bad: Children's perspectives on coping with everyday stress. *Developmental Psychology, 24,* 247–253.

Bauer, P. J., & Hertsgaard, L. A. (1993). Increasing steps in recall of events: Factors facilitating immediate and long-term memory in 13.5–16.5-month-old children. *Child Development, 64,* 1204–1223.

Bauer, P. J., & Travis, L. L. (1993). The fabric of an event: Different sources of temporal invariance differentially affect 24-month-olds' recall. *Cognitive Development, 8,* 319–341.

Bibace, R., & Walsh, M. (1981). *New directions in child development: Children's conceptions of health, illness, and bodily functions.* San Francisco: Jossey-Bass.

Block, J. (1982). Assimilation, accommodation, and the dynamics of personality development. *Child Development, 53,* 281–295.

Bower, G. (1981). Mood and memory. *American Psychologist, 36,* 129–148.

Bowlby, J. (1988). Developmental psychiatry comes of age. *American Journal of Psychiatry, 145,* 1–10.

Bretherton, I. (1985). Attachment theory: Retrospect and prospect. In I. Bretherton & E. Waters (Eds.), Growing points of attachment theory and research (pp. 3–35). *Monographs of the Society for Research in Child Development, 50*(1–2, Serial No. 209).

Brewster, A. B. (1982). Chronically ill hospitalized children's concepts of their illness. *Pediatrics, 69,* 355–362.

Bush, J. P., & Holmbeck, G. N. (1987). Children's attitudes about health care: Initial development of a questionnaire. *Journal of Pediatric Psychology, 12,* 429–443.

Bush, J. P., Melamed, B. G., Sheras, P. L., & Greenbaum, P. E. (1986). Mother–child patterns of coping with anticipatory medical stress. *Health Psychology, 5,* 137–157.

Carroll, J., & Steward, M. S. (1984). The role of cognitive development in children's understanding of their own feelings. *Child Development, 55,* 1486–1492.

Compas, B. (1987). Coping with stress during childhood and adolescence. *Psychological Bulletin, 101,* 393–403.

Compas, B. E., Worsham, N. L., & Ey, S. (1992). Conceptual and developmental issues in children's coping with stress. In A. M. LaGreca, L. J. Siegel, J. L. Wallander, & C. E. Walker (Eds.), *Stress and coping in health* (pp. 7–24). New York: Guilford.

Fabes, R. A., & Eisenberg, N. (1992). Young children's coping with interpersonal anger. *Child Development, 63,* 116–128.

Folkman, S. (1984). Personal control and stress and coping processes: A theoretical analysis. *Journal of Personality and Social Psychology, 46,* 839–852.

Gaynard, L., Wolfer, J., Goldberger, J., Thompson, R. H., Redburn, L., & Laidley, L. (1990). *Psychosocial care of children in hospitals: A clinical practice manual from the ACCH Child Life Research Project.* Bethesda, MD: Association for the Care of Children's Health.

Genevro, J. L., Bornstein, M. H., Ruble, D. N., & Altshuler, J. L. (1995). *Children's perceptions of the value and efficacy of strategies for coping with hospitalization for elective surgery.* Unpublished manuscript, NICHD.

Greenberg, M. T., Kusche, C. A., & Speltz, M. (1991). Emotion regulation, self-control, and psychopathology: The role of relationships in early childhood. In D. Cicchetti & S. L. Toth (Eds.), *Internalizing and externalizing expression of dysfunction: Rochester Symposium on Developmental Psychopathology, Vol. 2* (pp. 21–55). Hillsdale, NJ: Lawrence Erlbaum Associates.

Hackworth, S. R., & McMahon, R. J. (1991). Factors mediating children's health care attitudes. *Journal of Pediatric Psychology, 16*, 69–85.

Kaufman, A. S., & Kaufman, N. L. (1983). *KABC: Kaufman Assessment Battery for Children.* Circle Pines, MN: American Guidance Service.

Lazarus, R., & Folkman, S. (1984). *Stress, appraisal, and coping.* New York: Springer.

Lewis, C. C., Pantell, R. H., & Kieckhefer, G. M. (1989). Assessment of children's health status: field test of new approaches. *Medical Care, 27*, S54–S65.

Maiman, L. A., Becker, M. H., & Katlic, A. W. (1985). How mothers treat their children's physical symptoms. *Journal of Community Health, 10*, 136–155.

Melamed, B. G., & Bush, J. P. (1985). Family factors in children with acute illness. In D. C. Turk & R. D. Kerns (Eds.), *Health, illness, and families* (pp. 183–209). New York: Wiley.

Miller, S. M., & Green, M. L. (1985). Coping with stress and frustration: origins, nature, and development. In M. Lewis & C. Saarni (Eds.), *The Socialization of emotions* (pp. 263–314). New York: Plenum.

Nelson, K. (1986). *Event knowledge: Structure and function in development.* Hillsdale,NJ: Lawrence Erlbaum Associates.

Parmelee, A. H., Jr. (1986). Children's illnesses: Their beneficial effects on behavioral development. *Child Development, 57*, 1–10.

Parmelee, A. H. (1992). Wellness, illness, health, disease concepts. In E. J. Susman, L. V. Feagans, & W. J. Ray (Eds.), *Emotion, cognition, health, and development* (pp. 165–187). New York: Basic Books.

Peterson, L. (1989). Coping by children undergoing stressful medical procedures: Some conceptual, methodological, and therapeutic issues. *Journal of Consulting and Clinical Psychology, 57*, 380–387.

Peterson, L., Mori, L., & Carter, P. (1985). The role of the family in children's responses to stressful medical procedures. *Journal of Clinical Child Psychology, 14*, 98–104.

Peterson, L., & Toler, S. M. (1986). An information disposition in child surgery patients. *Health Psychology, 5*, 343–358.

Rubovits, D. S., & Siegel, A. W. (1994). Developing conceptions of chronic disease: A comparison of disease experience. *Children's Health Care, 23*, 267–285.

Rudolph, K. D., Dennig, M. D., & Weisz, J. R. (1995). Determinants and consequences of children's coping in the medical setting: Conceptualization, review, and critique. *Psychological Bulletin, 118*, 328–357.

Schank, R. C., & Abelson, R. P. (1977). *Scripts, plans, goals, and understanding.* Hillsdale, NJ: Lawrence Erlbaum Associates.

Schore, A. N. (1994). *Affect regulation and the origin of the self: The neurobiology of emotional development.* Hillsdale, NJ: Lawrence Erlbaum Associates.

Steward, M. S. (1988). Illness: a crisis for children. In J. Sandoval (Ed.), *Crisis counseling, intervention, and prevention in the schools: School psychology* (pp. 109–129). Hillsdale, NJ: Lawrence Erlbaum Associates.

Steward, M. S., & Steward, D. (1981). Children's conceptions of medical procedures. In R. Bibace & M. Walsh (Eds.), *New Directions for child development: Children's conceptions of health, illness, and bodily functions* (No. 14). San Francisco: Jossey-Bass.

Thoits, P. A. (1991). Patterns in coping with controllable and uncontrollable events. In E. M. Cummings, A. L. Greene, & K. H. Karraker (Eds.), *Life-span developmental psychology: Perspectives on stress and coping* (pp. 235–258). Hillsdale, NJ: Lawrence Erlbaum Associates.

Thompson, R. A. (1994). Emotion regulation: A theme in search of definition. In N. A. Fox (Ed.), The development of emotion regulation. *Monographs of the Society for Research in Child Development, 59* (2-3, Serial No. 240), pp. 25–52.

Tinsley, B. J., & Lees, N. B. (1995). Health promotion for parents. In M. H. Bornstein (Ed.), *Handbook of parenting: Vol. 4. Applied and practical parenting,* (pp. 187–204). Mahwah, NJ: Lawrence Erlbaum Associates.

Wechsler, D. (1989). *Wechsler Preschool and Primary Scale of Intelligence–Revised, Manual.* San Antonio, TX: The Psychological Corporation/Harcourt Brace Jovanovich.

Whitt, J. K., Dykstra, W., & Taylor, C. A. (1979). Children's conceptions of illness and cognitive development. *Clinical Pediatrics, 18,* 327–339.

Yates, G. C. R., Yates, S. M., & Beasley, C. J. (1987). Young children's knowledge of strategies in delay of gratification. *Merrill-Palmer Quarterly, 33,* 159–169.

5

Anxiety in Children During the Perioperative Period

Zeev N. Kain
Yale University School of Medicine

Linda C. Mayes
Yale Child Study Center

More than half a million children undergo elective surgical procedures annually in the United States (Graves, 1993). Surgical procedures with and without subsequent hospitalization represent potential stressors for children and contribute to significant anticipatory anxiety and fear. Children may be threatened by anticipated parental separation, pain or discomfort, loss of control, uncertainty about "going to sleep," and by masked strangers working in an often highly technical, sterile, non-child-friendly setting. These factors contribute to children's experiencing anxious reactions prior to anesthesia and surgery. Preoperative anxiety may be operationally defined as a subjective feeling of tension, apprehension, nervousness, worry, and vigilance associated with increased autonomic nervous system activity. Although the exact prevalence of preoperative anxiety in children is difficult to estimate because of difficulties in measurement as well as developmental variations in what is fear provoking and upsetting, from 40% to 60% of children are reported to exhibit psychological and/or physiological manifestations of anxiety in the presurgical period (Beeby & Morgan-Hughes, 1980; Corman, Hornick, Kritchman, & Terestman, 1958; Melamed & Siegel, 1975; Vernon, Foley, Sipowicz, & Shulman, 1965)

Appropriate identification and treatment of this clinical phenomenon is important because it may lead to both psychological and physiological adverse outcomes (Boeke, Duivenvoorden, Verhage, & Zwaveling, 1991; Haavik, Soreide, Hofstad, & Steen, 1992; Vernon et al., 1965). Preoperative anxiety may prolong the induction of anesthesia and the immediate postoperative recovery period. In addition, increased preoperative anxiety among adults has been shown to correlate with increased postoperative pain, increased postoperative analgesic requirements, and prolonged recovery and hospital stay (Badner, Nielson, Munk, Kwiatkowska & Gelb, 1990; Boeke et al., 1991). Short-term (2 to 4 weeks) postsurgical behavioral problems such as sleep and eating disturbances and enuresis (Schulman, Foley, Vernon, & Allan, 1967; Vernon et al., 1965) have been reported in varying numbers of children (Brophy & Erikson, 1990). Long-lasting negative psychological effects (6 to 12 months postsurgery), including persistent sleep disturbances and separation anxiety, may impact children's responses to subsequent medical care and interfere with normal development, socialization, and adjustment to school (Vernon et al., 1965).

Concern over such physiologic and short- or long-term behavioral reactions has prompted the development and evaluation of a number of different intervention strategies designed to reduce children's preoperative anxiety (Melamed & Ridley-Johnson, 1988; Melamed & Siegel, 1980; Schulman et al., 1967). These strategies include premedication and behavioral interventions such as parental presence during the anesthesia induction process and preoperative preparation programs. Premedication, although effective in most cases, may increase anesthesia risk and prolong postoperative recovery (Kain, 1995). Additionally, routine preoperative use of sedatives may result in increased pharmacy costs, additional nursing staff, and increased need for appropriately equipped bed space in the holding area (Kain, 1995). Behavioral interventions offer theoretical advantages in that they may provide the child with coping strategies that will be effective in subsequent medical encounters, and through the involvement of parents, more members of the family are cognizant of the potential stressors presented to the child by anesthesia and surgery (Rasnake & Linscheid, 1989). Behavioral interventions such as presurgical preparation programs (play therapy, orientation tours, books, modeling, joint parent–child preparation, and teaching children coping skills) are modeled on learning theory (Melamed & Ridley-Johnson, 1988; Melamed & Siegel, 1980; Schulman et al., 1967).

There is a widely held belief that all children will benefit from behavioral preparation for surgery, and an estimated 70% of hospitals routinely offer such programs to all children and parents (Melamed & Ridley-Johnson, 1988; Peterson & Ridley-Johnson, 1980). Also, routine preoperative modeling for all children undergoing surgery has been advocated recently in the anesthesia literature, and commercial videotapes demonstrating modeling are now available (Hain, 1983; Karl, Pauza, Heyneman, & Tinker, 1990). Although most studies suggest that preoperative preparation of the child may reduce stress and enhance coping (Edwinson, Arnbjornsson, & Ekman, 1988; Elkins & Roberts, 1983; McGill & Hannallah, 1992; Melamed & Ridley-Johnson, 1988; Melamed & Siegel, 1980; Schwartz, Albino, & Tedesco, 1983; Vernon & Bailey, 1974), other reports indicate that such programs have no effect on some children and may potentially increase anxiety in younger children who are not cognitively able to integrate the different aspects of the preparation program (Ferguson, 1979; Field, 1992; Melamed, Meyer, Gee, & Soule, 1976; Melamed & Ridley-Johnson, 1988; Robinson & Kobayashi, 1991). Moreover, some work documents that a significant number of children (61%) develop postsurgical behavioral problems that may or may not be linked to children's anxiety in response to a hospital stressor (Brophy & Erikson, 1990; Lumley, Melamed, & Abeles, 1993). As these programs are often expensive in terms of personnel time and resources, the more efficient, as well as informed, use of preoperative behavioral interventions may be achieved by targeting children most at risk for immediate and longer term reactions related to the stress of anesthesia and surgery. Similarly, recommendations for parental presence during anesthesia induction for every child do not take into account individual factors in both child and parent that may serve to diminish how effective parents may be, or perceive themselves to be, in reducing their child's anxiety.

Systematic study of both preoperative preparation programs and the effectiveness of parental presence during anesthesia may highlight aspects of both interventions that are clinically useful in reducing anxiety and indicate for which groups of children (and parents) these interventions are more likely to be effective. In this chapter, we present data on (a) the factors that appear predictive of individual variation in 4- to 10-year-old children's anxiety reactions prior to elective minor surgery without subsequent hospitalizations, (b) children's and families' responses to a preoperative preparation program, (c) children's responses to parental presence during anesthesia induction, and (d) the prevalence of behavioral changes 2 weeks postsurgery.

ANESTHESIA INDUCTION

Based on both behavioral (Manifest Upset Scale) and physiological (heart rate) responses, the induction of anesthesia appears to be the most stressful procedure a child experiences during the preoperative period (Schwartz et al., 1983). Anesthesia induction exposes children to situations that potentially elicit some of their most basic fears in medical situations: choking or suffocation (particularly with the application of the anesthesia mask) and injections (Cuthbert & Melamed, 1982). Individual variation in children's responses to stressors such as anesthesia induction and surgery has its origin in at least four general areas: (a) age and developmental competency of the child; (b) previous experience with medical procedures, illnesses, or hospitalizations; (c) individual capacities for affect regulation and the child's anxiety at baseline; and (d) parental state and trait anxiety. Attention has been paid in varying degrees to each of these variables in studies of children's anxiety reactions to anesthesia induction.

Children's age and developmental capacity to understand the various stressors in anesthesia induction play crucial roles in their reactions. For younger children, it is likely that the greater stress is imposed (a) by being separated from their parents despite their feeling afraid and distressed, and (b) by that separation being achieved by strangers whose faces are often concealed by masks. The younger child (ages 1–6 years) does not necessarily have the cognitive capacity to anticipate potential dangers or painful situations during the induction, whereas the older child may anticipate pain and the fear of "going to sleep." Conversely, older children (over the age of 6 years) may rely on a number of coping strategies, including verbal questioning and cognitive mastery (e.g., learning about heart monitors or about what surgeons do) to mediate their anxiety, whereas younger children are generally more dependent during times of extreme distress on adults' comforting interventions (Cuthbert & Melamed, 1982; Hyson, 1983; Lumley et al., 1993).

Several studies have examined the effects of previous hospitalization and previously complicated medical encounters on children's anxiety responses. Based on a conditioned learning model, the preoperative situation may be viewed as presenting many unconditioned fear stimuli occurring repeatedly over short intervals. This research indicates that children's previous surgical and medical histories may either exacerbate or attenuate fear conditioning and that the quality of the previous experience (e.g., how distressing it was) is as crucial as its occurrence (Dahlquist et al., 1986; Melamed & Siegel, 1985).

Children's own capacities for affect regulation have been considered less often in studies of reactions to medical procedures. Domains included in a number of temperament measures are, for example, approach-withdrawal, emotional lability, or activity level. *Approach-withdrawal* describes some aspect of children's typical behavioral response to novel situations or individuals; *emotional lability* or affect regulation describes children's responses to unexpected situations and/or the predictability of their usual emotional state and range of state. Relations among these domains and dimensions such as "shyness" or "inhibition/disinhibition" have been studied extensively. Although beyond the scope of this chapter, it is important to note that aspects of these different dimensions appear to measure the child's tendency to become anxious in novel settings and that there are some biological correlates of behavioral responses in terms of adrenocortical response and elevated heart rate (Kagan, Reznick, & Snidman, 1987). Moreover, although there are few data examining the link between these aspects of temperament and anxiety-based disorders in children, it may be that children who are more anxious, shy, or inhibited appear more vulnerable to the disruptive effects of stressful events.

Finally, parental anxiety may increase children's anxious responses to fearful or stressful situations through at least two pathways. First, in the framework of social learning theory, parents act as stress reducers for their children. Parents who are themselves more anxious in a given situation are less available to respond to their child's needs and their child's signals of increasing distress. Indeed, in these instances, children's distress may further compound parental anxiety, thus rendering the parent increasingly less able to respond effectively. Several investigators have found that mothers who were more anxious in the surgical setting had children who were also more anxious and that mothers were less able to respond in these situations (Bevan et al., 1990). The second pathway of the effect of parental anxiety on children's responses reflects the genetic contribution of a parental disposition to being overanxious. An increased risk of anxiety disorders is found among children of women with panic disorders and depression (Turner, Beidel, & Costello, 1987; Weissman, Leckman, Merikangas, Gammon, & Prusoff, 1984). Conversely, among children with overanxious disorders, more parents report similar histories in their own childhood (Last, Hersen, Kazdin, Francis, & Grubb, 1987; Last, Phillips, & Statfeld, 1987). Fewer data are available to permit examination of the association between maternal anxiety traits and similar traits in children, the relation between which may be accounted for by both genetic and environmental factors.

GENERAL METHODS IN THE STUDY
OF CHILD ANESTHESIA INDUCTION

In the studies described here, children and their families were assessed at several different points during the perioperative period starting with their arrival at the preoperative holding area until 2 weeks after surgery. A repeated-measures design was utilized in which the child or parent was evaluated by both observational and self-report measures of anxiety at three stress points, including (a) the holding area, (b) separation to the operating room, and (c) during anesthesia induction. Previous research indicates that entry to the operating room (OR) is more stressful for children than waiting in the holding area, and introduction of the anesthesia mask is more stressful than either previous period. The study cohorts were drawn from children between the ages of 3 and 10 years undergoing minor outpatient surgery and general anesthesia at the Children's Hospital at Yale-New Haven. Children with a history of prematurity, chronic illness, or repeated hospitalizations were excluded, as were children or parents who were developmentally delayed or did not speak English. All subjects underwent a nitrous-oxide/oxygen/halothane mask induction followed by a balanced general anesthetic in a pediatric operating suite. Duration of anesthesia induction ranged from 3 to 12 minutes, and the standard of care was not affected by the presence of either a video camera or an observer.

For each child and family participating in the study, we collected the following measures:

1. *Baseline measures of child.* Mothers described their child's temperament using the EASI (Buss, Plomin, & Willerman, 1973), which includes 20 items in four main behavioral domains: emotionality, activity, sociability, and impulsivity. Additionally, baseline demographic measures included age of child and parent, ethnicity, parental education, marital and employment status, number of siblings, birth order, day-care experience, previous history of surgery or hospitalization, and previous history of child's being distressed during a medical or surgical visit.

2a. *Observational assessment of parent's anxiety.* Clinicians working with the families completed an observational measure of the parent's anxiety in the holding area and at the moment of entry into the OR using a continuous *visual analog scale* (VAS) scoring system for anxiety. The VAS rating system consists of a 100-mm line that pictorially represents two behavioral or perceptual extremes at either end of a continuum, "not anxious" and "extremely anxious" (Huskisson, 1983). The VAS has been used in a number of studies of preoperative anxiety in children and adults.

2b. *Self-report of parental anxiety.* Parents were asked to complete the *State-Trait Anxiety Inventory* (STAI; Spielberger, 1983) while they waited with their child in the holding area. This inventory includes 40 statements, that describe how they feel now (state) or usually (trait), which parents rate on a 4-point scale. Additionally, parents rated their own state of anxiety using the VAS at two time points: first in the holding area, and then at the point of the child's entry into the OR.

3a. *Observational assessment of child's anxiety.* In the holding area and at the moment of separation to enter the OR, children's anxiety was assessed using the VAS completed by both an observer and the parent. Additionally, observers completed the *Clinical Anxiety Rating Scale* (CARS; Vernon, Foley, & Shulman, 1967). The scale utilizes a 6-point Likert scale ranging from 0 (*relaxed, smiling, willing and able to converse*) to 5 (*general loud crying . . . makes no effort to cope*). Good to excellent observer reliability has been documented for the CARS.

3b. *Self-report measure of anxiety for children prior to entry into the OR.* Self-reported anxiety was measured for children older than 3 years by the *Venham Picture Scale* (VPS; Venham, Bengston, & Cipes, 1977). The VPS consists of six pairs of pictures, each depicting a distressed and a nondistressed child. Children were asked to choose the child who looked most like they felt. Test–retest agreement of the revised instrument was 97% on a sample of 38 subjects. For children between 2 and 3 years of age, a second self-report measure of anxiety was developed for the study consisting of three pictures: a frightened, sad, or happy bear. Children were asked to choose the picture most reflecting themselves, or by implication, their feelings at the time. When applied to a subject population of 53 children, this self-report measure for younger children showed a test–retest agreement of 95.3%.

3c. *Observation of children's behavior during anesthesia induction.* Instruments for assessing children's response to the operating room and to anesthesia induction generally rate behaviors that reflect the consequences of anxiety, such as diminished cooperativeness, rather than the direct behavioral markers of an anxious state such as motor activity, irritability, crying, or active withdrawal (Bevan et al., 1990; Hannallah & Rosales, 1983; Mikawa et al., 1993). For these studies, we created and validated an observational rating scale to assess children's responses to anesthesia induction, the *Yale Preoperative Anxiety Scale* (YPAS). Five domains of behavior indicating anxiety were operationally defined as indicators of an anxious state. These five domains were activity, emotional expressivity, state of arousal, vocalization, and use of adults. Twenty-one behavioral categories within the five major domains were specified, and nonoverlapping, clinically meaningful descriptive anchors for each rating point were defined, covering a range from minimal to maximal expression of behaviors in a domain (Table 5.1).

The child's response was rated during two "stress periods": from entering the OR until the introduction of the anesthesia mask, and from introduction of the mask until anesthesia was achieved. The highest behavioral category that occurred in each of the five domains during each stress period was rated.

TABLE 5.1
The Yale Preoperative Anxiety Scale (YPAS)

Category	Score	Operational Definition of Score
Activity	1	Looking around, curious, may move toward equipment, or mainly still
	2	Not exploring, may look down, may fidget with hands or suck thumb
	3	Squirming, moving on table, may push mask away
	4	Activity trying to get away, pushes with feet and arms, may move whole body
Vocalizations	1	Asking questions, making comments, babbling
	2	Responding to adults but uses whispers, "baby talk," or only head nodding
	3	Quiet, no sound or responses to adults
	4	Whimpering, moaning, groaning
	5	Crying, may be screaming "no", sustained through mask
	6	Crying and/or screming loudly, sustained through mask
Emotional expressivity	1	Manifestly happy, smiling
	2	Neutral, no visible expression on face
	3	Worried, sad, frightened, may have tears in eyes
	4	Distressed, crying, extreme upset, may have wide eyes
State of apparent arousal	1	Alert, looks around occasionally, watches anesthesiologist, could be relaxed
	2	Withdrawn, sitting still and quiet, may suck thumb, turn face to adult
	3	Vigilant, looking quickly around, may startle to sound, eyes wide, body tense
	4	Panicked, whimpering, may be crying or pushing others away
Use of parent	1	Reaches out to parent, seeks and accepts comfort
	2	Looks to parent quietly, doesn't seek contact or comfort, accepts if offered
	3	Keeps parent at a distance, actively withdraws from parent, pushes parent away

Note. Within each category, a score of 0 was given if the child was not visible to the rater and a score of 9 was given if the rater was uncertain as to how a behavior should be scored.

The timing of when the mask was introduced was ascertained by the attending anesthesiologist and thus varied among children. However, the usual standard of practice in our hospital is for the anesthesiologist to spend a brief time period, usually 2 to 4 minutes, interacting with the child before introducing the mask. The YPAS showed excellent interobserver reliability across the five domains (Table 5.2) and high correlation with more global measures of anxiety including the VAS, $r = .59$, and the CARS, $r = .64$.

4. *Follow-up at 2 weeks following surgery.* Families were mailed the *Post-Hospitalization Behavior Questionnaire* (PHBQ; Vernon et al., 1967) to assess children's behavior changes. This questionnaire lists 27 specific problems that potentially occur after a medical procedure or hospitalization (e.g., problems with aggression, withdrawal, separation, and sleep). This instrument has acceptable test–retest reliability over a 1-month interval.

PREDICTORS OF ANXIETY
DURING ANESTHESIA INDUCTION

One hundred and forty-two consecutive patients were enrolled. The mean age of the children was 61 months ($SD = 32$) with 92 boys (65%) and 50 girls (35%). One hundred and ten (80%) were White and 15 (11%) were African American. Sixty-one (43%) of the mothers completed college or had an advanced degree, and 68 (48%) completed high school. Seventy

TABLE 5.2
Interobserver Reliability of the YPAS

YPAS Domain	Observed Agreement (PO)	Chance Agreement (PC)	Weighted kappa (KW)	Clinical Significance
	Subject Enters the OR			
Use of parent	0.96	0.79	0.84	Excellent
Activity	0.96	0.79	0.81	Excellent
State arousal	0.89	0.59	0.30	Good
Vocalization	0.90	0.69	0.69	Good
Emotional expressivity	0.90	0.68	0.68	Good
	Anesthesia Mask Applied			
Use of parent	0.88	0.66	0.66	Good
Activity	0.97	0.52	0.94	Excellent
State arousal	0.91	0.50	0.81	Excellent
Vocalization	0.95	0.65	0.85	Excellent
Emotional expressivity	0.94	0.67	0.83	Excellent

TABLE 5.3
Demographic Characteristics of 142 Subjects and Their Parents

	M(SD)
Child's age in months	61(32)
Gender (percent)	
Female	31
Male	69
Anxiety Score of Previous Medical Encounters (VAS)	21(21)
EASI	
Emotionality	50(16)
Activity	66(18)
Sociability	70(12)
Impulsivity	56(16)
STAI-Mother	36(8)
Premedication (percent)	
No	79
Yes	21
Preparation Program (percent)	
No	35
Yes	65
Parental Presence (percent)	
No	78
Yes	22

children (49%) had a previous hospitalization. Mean parental trait anxiety rating using the STAI was 36 ($SD = 8$; see Table 5.3)

In the holding area, 40 (32.3%) of the children had a VAS score above 50. The mean VAS score in the holding area was 37 ($SD = 27$). Maternal anxiety was significantly correlated with child's anxiety, $r = .43$, $p = .02$. Additionally, older children (> 7 years) were more anxious than younger children (VAS $M = 49$, $SD = 31$ vs. $M = 31$, $SD = 25$, $p = .02$). Children of separated or divorced mothers were significantly more anxious than children of either married or single mothers (ANOVA, 55 ± 24 vs. 54 ± 27 vs. 10 ± 14, $p = .02$). Also, children (under 4 years) who were enrolled in day care were rated as significantly less anxious (51 ± 27 vs. 18 ± 31, $p = .02$). The most anxious group of children (upper quartile) was characterized by high self-reported maternal anxiety in holding, VAS mean of 46 ($SD = 31$) versus mean of 61 ($SD = 31$), $p = .04$; higher paternal anxiety in holding, VAS $M = 52$ ($SD = 22$) versus $M = 26$ ($SD = 16$) $p = .02$; previous history of extreme upset with medical visits, VAS $M = 17$ ($SD = 16$) versus $M = 31$ ($SD = 21$), $p < .05$; being older than 4 years, VAS $M = 44$ ($SD = 34$) versus

$M = 65$ ($SD = 38$), $p = .02$. Presurgical tour, gender, trait anxiety of mother, birth order, and number of siblings did not affect the child's anxiety in the holding area. On entry to the OR, children's anxiety increased, and the mean VAS score of the child was 62 ± 41, $p = .001$. Children's anxiety related to maternal anxiety in the holding area, $r = .42$, $p = .01$, and at separation, $r = .43$, $p = .04$, and to their own anxiety in the holding area, $r = .38$, $p = .01$.

HOSPITAL PREPARATION PROGRAMS

Our first approach to evaluating the preoperative preparation program has been to study a consecutive sample of children coming for elective surgery, some of whom had received preoperative preparation and some of whom had not. The preoperative preparation program offered by the Child Life department of our hospital consists of the provision of information and modeling (sensory expectations, role identifications, rehearsals, and support) that is related to the specific surgery the child will undergo. These interventions are based in large part on learning theory, which suggests that exposing children to certain aspects of fear-inducing situation conditions, in effect, desensitizes them to stress. Families of all children scheduled for elective surgery are contacted by the Surgery Center and participation in the presurgical program is strongly recommended. The program lasts about 45 minutes and is offered 4 days a week. In addition, during the visit, evaluation and informative preoperative teaching are performed by an anesthesiologist and a nurse. If the parents choose not to participate in the extended preoperative program, they are instructed to arrive 1 hour before the planned surgery to receive anesthesia and nursing evaluations along with a short (5–10 minute) preparation by the nurses aimed primarily toward parents. About 60% to 75% of families participate in the preoperative program. Based on a survey of 106 parents' responses to the program, most (98%) felt that it helped them and their child to be better prepared for surgery. Almost all reported that they would choose to participate in the program again if their child ever needed surgery, and 95% stated that other parents should be encouraged to participate in such a program.

Of the 143 subjects, 93 children (65%) received the preoperative preparation program and 49 (34%) did not receive the program. We first examined differences between children who did and did not receive the preoperative preparation program on baseline demographic, socioeconomic, and clinical variables. The two groups of children and parents did not differ significantly with regard to gender, age of child, ethnicity, type of surgery, or parental education. Previous surgery, administration of premedication, and parental presence during induction of anesthesia were also similar. Baseline temperament of the child in all EASI categories (emotionality, activity, sociability, and impulsivity) did not differ between the children who received the preparation and those who did not. Similarly, trait anxiety of the parents as measured by the STAI was similar between the two groups.

Next, we examined differences between the two groups on measures of preoperative anxiety in the holding area using the VAS and STAI. There were no differences between those children who did receive and those who did not receive the preoperative preparation in the observational measures of children's anxiety in either the holding area (VAS $M = 43$, $SD = 26$ and $M = 38$, $SD = 30$) or at entry to the OR (CARS $M = 3.1$, $SD = 1.4$ and $M = 2.9$, $SD = 1.5$). Maternal self-reported state anxiety was higher in the group that received the program (Spielberger state for preparation program $M = 46$, $SD = 9.8$ vs. $M = 40$, $SD = 9.6$ with no preparation program). Similarly, on entry to the OR, mothers who received the preparation program were rated by the observers as more anxious (VAS $M = 56$, $SD = 26$ vs. $M = 41$, $SD = 27$ for no program, $t = 3.2$, $p = .002$).

When we examined the relation between the four independent variables (age of child, previous hospitalization, baseline temperament, and maternal anxiety) combined with the occurrence and timing of the preparation program, we found the following interactions between preoperative preparation and child and family characteristics:

1. Younger children (< 48 months) receiving the preoperative preparation were rated as more anxious by observation in the holding area than those older than 48 months (VAS $M = 46$, $SD = 37$ vs. $M = 25$, $SD = 24$, $p = .01$).
2. Children with a history of previous medical encounters were significantly more anxious at separation to the OR if they received the preoperative preparation (VAS $M = 36$; $SD = 28$ vs. $M = 23$, $SD = 13$, $p = .04$).
3. Children rated higher on emotionality on the EASI by their parents were more anxious if they had received preoperative preparation (VAS $M = 41$, $SD = 34$ vs. $M = 13$, $SD = 20$, $p = .01$).
4. Preoperative preparation programs scheduled 1 day before the surgery appeared to increase the anxiety of the oldest age group (> 72 months), whereas programs scheduled at least a week in advance appeared to diminish children's anxiety in this older group (VAS $M = 63$, $SD = 22$ vs. $M = 47$, $SD = 23$, $p = .05$).

TABLE 5.4
Behavioral and Physiological Anxiety Scores

Measure	Group	Holding Area		Induction 1		Induction 2	
		M	SD	M	SD	M	SD
VAS	Control	32.0	25.0	36.0	30.0	50.0	41.0
	Intervention	33.0	26.0	34.0	29.0	57.0	42.0
YPAS	Control			39.0	21.0	46.0	23.0
	Intervention			36.0	13.0	54.0	28.0
CARS	Control			0.9	1.3	2.1	2.1
	Intervention			0.6	0.9	2.6	2.1
Cortisol	Control					95.0	54.0
(mµ/ml)	Intervention					84.0	31.0

Note. Induction 1 = Subjects entering the induction room; Induction 2 = Anesthesia mask is introduced; VAS = Visual Analog Scale; YPAS = Yale Postoperative Anxiety Scale; CARS = Clinical Anxiety Rating Scale.

Thus, preoperative preparation programs appear not to have a uniformly anxiety-reducing effect for children or their families. The beneficial aspects are moderated by the age and temperament of the child, by the timing of the intervention, and by previous experience with hospitalizations and medical encounters. Further, parents who have received the intervention report feeling increased anxiety at the time of separation, a factor that may interfere with their being able to comfort the child at the time of separation to the OR.

PARENTAL PRESENCE DURING INDUCTION

We used a similar design to study the effectiveness of parental presence during anesthesia induction. In addition to the two assessment periods described earlier, we also measured children's anxiety during the induction process using the YPAS for the two stress points: entry into the OR and introduction of the anesthesia mask. For this ongoing study, the sample to date includes 48 children whose parents were present (intervention group) and 42 whose parents were not (control group). Once again, there were no differences between those children whose parents were present and those whose parents were not for child's age, gender, EASI ratings, maternal age, level of education, and self-reported trait anxiety. When the control group was compared to the intervention group, there were no significant differences in any of the behavioral or physiological measures tested in the holding area and during induction of anesthesia (Table 5.4). A detailed analysis for each one of the five YPAS anxiety domains failed to demonstrate any difference between the two groups. Also, cooperation of both groups as measured by a VAS was similar (37 ± 42 vs. $47 \pm 43, p = ns$). The length of induction did not differ between the two groups (2.6 ± 1.2 minutes vs. $2.8 \pm 0.9, p = ns$).

Application of the Pearsonian correlation coefficient between child's age and induction anxiety scores revealed that younger children appeared more anxious during induction as measured by both serum cortisol, $r = -.45$, and the YPAS, $r = -.54$. Also, a significant correlation was noted between the anxiety of the parent (VAS) immediately after induction and the anxiety of the child during induction, $r = .57, p = .01$.

Next, we developed several linear regression models with parental presence as an interactive variable to predict which subgroup of children would benefit most from this intervention. The predictors in these models included variables suggested in the literature, in our clinical practice, and in our data as likely to affect the response of the child to parental presence during induction of anesthesia. In an overall model, using serum cortisol as the outcome and parental presence as an interactive variable, child age and baseline temperament (EASI activity) and baseline anxiety of the parent were identified as independent predictors of the child's anxiety during induction, $R^2 = 0.41, F = 3.7, p = 0.04$). As shown in Figure 5.1, univariate analysis demonstrated that serum cortisol for children who had a parent with

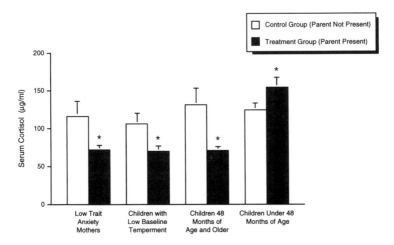

FIGURE 5.1.   Variables predicting the child's response to parental presence during induction are shown.

a low trait anxiety (lower 25% of the STAI), $p = .04$, or children who had a low baseline level of activity (lower 25% of the EASI activity), $p = .03$, was significantly less in the presence of their parents. Similarly, children over 4 years of age had lower serum cortisol levels in the presence of their parents during induction, $p = .02$. In contrast, children under 4 years of age had higher serum cortisol levels if their parent was present, p = .04 (Figure 5.1).

In both examples, introduction of the anesthesia mask may represent the most stressful moment for the child and a moment for which the parent cannot offer protection, thus potentially increasing both the child's and the parent's anxiety and concern. Other studies have shown that parental presence during procedures such as venipuncture is often associated with more crying and distress in children under 5 years of age (Shaw & Routh, 1982). Similar to the results we obtained regarding the differential effects of the preoperative preparation program, these findings suggest that clinical modifications in helping parents and children be together during the induction process are needed. Such modifications might take into account the age of the child, their typical response to novelty or stressful times, and how parents might be most helpful during the induction process.

FOLLOW-UP 2 WEEKS AFTER SURGERY

The PHBQ was mailed to the families of 143 children (93 boys and 50 girls) with a mean age of 61 months ($SD = 30$). All of these children had been observed in the earlier study of predictors of anxiety. At 2 weeks, 68 children (48%) did not change on any of the 27 behaviors of the PHBQ. Fifty-nine (41%) developed some problematic behaviors, and within that group, behavior problems were of small magnitude for most children: 30% of the children had a change in only one to three behaviors and only 8% of the children had more than 7 behavioral changes. The most common changes among the children were eating disturbances (23%) and separation anxiety (40%). The prevalence of reported behavioral *improvements* ranged from 0% to 9% (better appetite) with most (73%) behavioral *improvements* occurring in subjects who underwent either myringotomy or a tonsillectomy and adenoidectomy.

Spearman correlation coefficients demonstrated that age of the child, $r = -.36$, $p = .01$, number of siblings, $r = -.35$, $p = .04$, observed child's, $r = .32$, $p = .01$, and maternal, $r = .38$, $p = .05$, anxiety in the preoperative holding area and on entry to the OR, $r = .31$, $p = .03$, were associated with a high problematic behavior summary score. In a stepwise logistic regression model for the presence of any problematic behavior 2 weeks after surgery, two independent risk factors were identified. A child with no siblings had 2.7 times the risk for behavioral problems than a child with siblings, 95% confidence interval, 1.4 to 5.4, and a child who was very anxious (defined as the upper quartile of the CARS score) on entry to the OR had 1.4 times the risk for later behavioral problems than a calm child (lower CARS quartile score), 95% confidence interval, 1.1 to 3.4. These findings are consistent with other reports (Lumley et al., 1992) and suggest that for younger children who have more difficulties preoperatively, more intensive follow-up and intervention with parents may be warranted.

CONCLUSIONS

These studies demonstrate the complexities in assuming that a modeling and information-based preoperative preparation program or parental presence during anesthesia induction prior to surgery are equally effective for all children. Similar to previous studies, we found that not all children exhibit anxiety in response to anesthesia and surgery, and that few show severe behavioral changes following surgery. Also, our findings indicate the individual factors (e.g., child's age, previous hospital experience, individual reactivity to novel or stressful situations, timing of the intervention, and parental anxiety) contribute to individual variation in a child's response to a medical procedure. These factors, along with children's cognitive level of functioning, are likely determinants of how any intervention designed to help the child during the procedure is actually experienced as beneficial by both child and parent.

The findings from this work suggest several potential areas for development and refinement of interventions to help children faced with medical procedures. Assessing children's past history of response to medical procedures, how they and their parents respond in general to novelty or stress, and tailoring interventions according to the developmental age of the child will provide clinical indicators for those children and families most likely to need and benefit from preoperative preparation. More studies are needed linking detailed assessment of these factors with children's anxiety responses over the course of the procedure and their behavioral symptoms afterward.

The timing of the intervention and its goals also merit consideration. For example, for older children having more time between the preoperative preparation and the surgery was beneficial. However, for younger children, it may be more efficacious to meet families an hour before the surgery and provide intensive preoperative preparation at that point. In regard to parental presence in the OR, more careful studies are needed as it appears that parental presence is not manifestly beneficial for all children. It may be that for children sensitive to stress or for younger children, having a parent present but unable to intervene and protect them is, in and of itself, too novel and stressful and thus not beneficial. It also may be that the goal of any preoperative behavioral intervention is not to reduce children's anxiety response but rather to provide them with more effective strategies for dealing with stress and novelty. It may be essential and unavoidable that children are frightened and anxious, but if they are able to use external as well as internal strategies to master that anxiety, there will be fewer immediate and postoperative sequelae. This suggestion underscores that future studies of children's anxiety in preoperative situations may also need to focus on measures of children's efforts toward coping and mastery as well as their anxiety and also that interventions might focus on enhancing coping strategies. Finally, settings such as the OR permit studies that focus on normal or expected anxiety and fear in response to naturally occurring stressors such as illness and medical intervention.

REFERENCES

Badner, N., Nielson, W., Munk, S., Kwiatkowska, C., & Gelb, A. (1990). Preoperative anxiety: Detection and contributing factors. *Canadian Journal of Anaesthsiology, 37*, 444–447.

Beeby, D. G., & Morgan-Hughes, J. O. (1980). Behavior of nonsedated children in the anesthetic room. *British Journal of Anaesthesia, 52*, 279–281.

Bevan, J. C., Johnston, C., Haig, M. J., Tousignant, G., Lucy, S., Kirnon, V., Assimes, I., & Carranza, R. (1990). Preoperative parental anxiety predicts behavioral and emotional responses to induction of anesthesia in children. *Canadian Journal of Anaesthsiology, 37*, 177–82.

Boeke, S., Duivenvoorden, H., Verhage, F., & Zwaveling, A. (1991). Prediction of postoperative pain and duration of hospitalization using two anxiety measures. *Pain, 45*, 293–297.

Brophy, C., & Erikson, M. (1990). Children's self-statements and adjustment to elective outpatient surgery. *Journal of Developmental and Behavioral Pediatrics, 11*, 13–16.

Buss, A., Plomin, R., & Willerman, L. (1973). The inheritance of temperament. *Journal of Personality, 41*, 513–524.

Corman, H., Hornick, E., Kritchman, M., & Terestman, N. (1958). Emotional reactions of surgical patients to hospitalization, anesthesia and surgery. *American Journal of Surgery, 96*, 646–653.

Cuthbert, M. I., & Melamed, B. G. (1982). A screening device: Children at risk for dental fears and management problems. *Journal of Dentistry for Children, 49*, 432–436.

Dahlquist, L. M., Gil, K. M., Armstrong, F. D., DeLawyer, D. D., Greene, P., & Wuori, D. (1986). Preparing children for medical examinations: The importance of previous medical experience. *Health Psychology,* 249–259.

Edwinson, M., Arnbjornsson, E., & Ekman, R. (1988). Psychologic preparation program for children undergoing acute appendectomy. *Pediatrics 82,* 30–36.

Elkins, P. D., & Roberts, M. C. (1983). Psychological preparation for pediatric hospitalization. *Clinical Psychology Review, 3,* 275–295.

Ferguson, B. (1979). Preparing young children for hospitalization: A comparison of two methods. *Pediatrics, 64,* 656–664.

Field, T. (1992). Infants' and children's responses to invasive procedures. In A. La Greca (Ed.), *Stress and coping in child health* (pp. –). New York: Guilford.

Graves, E. (1993). National hospital discharge survey: Annual summary, 1991. *Vital and Health Statistics, 114,* 1–62.

Haavik, P. E., Soreide, E., Hofstad, B., & Steen, P. A. (1992). Does preoperative anxiety influence gastric fluid volume and acidity? *Anesthesia and Analgesia, 75,* 91–94.

Hain, W. R. (1983). Peer modeling and paediatric anaesthesia. *Anaesthesia, 38,* 158–161.

Hannallah, R. S., & Rosales, J. K. (1983). Experience with parent's presence during anesthesia induction in children. *Canadian Journal of Anaesthesiology, 30,* 236–239.

Huskisson, E. C. (1983). Visual Analogue Scales. In R. Melzack (Ed.), *Pain measurement and assessment* (pp. 33–37). New York: Raven Press.

Hyson, M. C. (1983). Going to the doctor: A developmental study of stress and coping. *Journal of Child Psychology and Psychiatry, 24,* 247–259.

Kagan, J., Reznick, S. J., & Snidman, N. (1987). The physiology and psychology of behavioral inhibition in children. *Child Development, 58,* 1459–1473.

Kain, Z. N. (1995). Parental presence during induction of anesthesia [Editorial]. *Paediatric Anaesthesiology, 5,* 209–212.

Karl, H. W., Pauza, K. J., Heyneman, N., & Tinker, D. E. (1990). Preanesthetic preparation of pediatric outpatients: The role of a videotape for parents. *Journal of Clinical Anesthesia, 2,* 172–177.

Last, C. G., Hersen, M., Kazdin, A. E., Francis, G., & Grubb, H. (1987). Psychiatric illness in the mothers of anxious children. *American Journal of Psychiatry, 144,* 1580–1583.

Last, C. G., Phillips, J. E., & Statfeld. A. (1987). Childhood anxiety disorders in mothers and their children. *Child Psychiatry and Human Development, 18,* 103–112.

Lumley, M. A., Melamed, B. G., & Abeles, L. A. (1993). Predicting children's presurgical anxiety and subsequent behavior changes. *Journal of Pediatric Psychology, 1,* 481–497.

McGill, W. A., & Hannallah, R. S. (1992). Parental presence during induction of anesthesia in children. *Seminars in Anesthesia, 11,* 259–264.

Melamed, B. G., Meyer, R., Gee, C., & Soule, L. (1976). The influence of time and type of preparation on children's adjustment to hospitalization. *Journal of Pediatric Psychology, 1,* 31–37.

Melamed, B. G., & Ridley-Johnson, R. (1988). Psychological preparation of families for hospitalization. *Developmental and Behavioral Pediatrics, 9,* 96–102.

Melamed, B. G., & Siegel, L. J. (1975). Reduction of anxiety in children facing hospitalization and surgery by use of filmed modeling. *Journal of Consulting and Clinical Psychology, 43,* 511–521.

Melamed, B. G., & Siegel, L. J. (1980). Psychological preparation for hospitalization. In C. M. Franks & F. J. Evans (Eds.), *Behavioral medicine: Practical applications in health care* (pp. 307–355). New York: Springer.

Melamed, B. G., & Siegel, L. J. (1985). Children's reactions to medical stressors: An ecological approach to the study of anxiety. In A. H. Tuma & J. D. Maser (Eds.), *Anxiety and its disorders* (pp. 369–386). Hillsdale, NJ: Lawrence Erlbaum Associates.

Mikawa, K., Maekawa, N., Nishina, K., Takao, Y., Yaku, H., & Obara, H. (1993). Efficacy of oral clonidine premedication in children. *Anesthesiology, 79*, 926–931.

Peterson, L., & Ridley-Johnson, R. (1980). Pediatric hospital responses to survey on prehospital preparation for children. *Journal of Pediatric Psychology, 5*, 1–7.

Rasnake, L. K., & Linscheid, T. R. (1989). Anxiety reduction in children receiving medical care: Developmental considerations. *Developmental and Behavioral Pediatrics, 10*, 169–175.

Robinson, P. J., & Kobayashi, K. (1991). Development and evaluation of a presurgical preparation program. *Journal of Pediatric Psychology, 16*, 193–212.

Schulman, J. L., Foley, J. M., Vernon, D. T. A., & Allan, D. (1967). A study of the effect of the mother's presence during anesthesia induction. *Pediatrics, 39*, 111–114.

Schwartz, B. H., Albino, J. E., & Tedesco, L. A. (1983). Effects of psychological preparation on children hospitalized for dental operations. *Journal of Pediatrics, 102* 634–638.

Shaw, E. G., & Routh, D. K. (1982). Effects of mothers' presence on children's reactions to aversive procedures. *Journal of Pediatric Psychology, 7*, 33–42.

Spielberger, C. D. (1983). *Manual for the State-Trait Anxiety Inventory (STAI: Form Y)*. Palo Alto, CA: Consulting Psychologists Press.

Turner, S. M., Beidel, D. S., & Costello, A. (1987). Psychopathology in the offspring of children with anxiety disorders patients. *Journal of Consulting and Clinical Psychology, 55*, 229–235.

Venham, L., Bengston, D., & Cipes, M. (1977). Children's response to sequential dental visits. *Journal of Dental Research, 56*, 454–459.

Vernon, D. T. A., & Bailey, W. C. (1974). The use of motion pictures in the psychological preparation of children for induction of anesthesia. *Anesthesiology, 40*, 68–72.

Vernon, D. T. A., Foley, J. M., & Shulman, J. L. (1967). Effect of mother–child separation and birth order on young children's responses to two potentially stressful experiences. *Journal of Personality and Social Psychology, 5*, 162–74.

Vernon, D., Foley, J., Sipowicz, R., & Shulman, J. (1965). *The psychological responses of children to hospitalization and illness*. Springfield, IL: Thomas.

Weissman, M. M., Leckman, J. F., Merikangas, K. R., Gammon, G., & Prusoff, B. (1984). Depression and anxiety disorders in parents and children: Results from the Yale Family Study. *Archives of General Psychiatry, 41*, 845–852.

6

The Trauma and Memory of Cancer Treatment in Children

Margaret S. Steward
Jacqueline O'Connor
Curt Acredolo
University of California, Davis

David S. Steward
Graduate Theological Union, Berkeley

On October 26th, 1994, 2 months into twice-monthly chemotherapy and 2 days before his next treatment, Bill Best, a 16-year-old boy diagnosed with Hodgkin's disease, ran away from home. His experience was reported in the popular press by Ritter (1994). The note he left his parents said, "I feel like the medicine is killing me instead of helping me." Billy was receiving standard treatment for Hodgkin's disease, chemotherapy and radiation. The side effects were reported to be comparatively mild: no vomiting, no infections, no hospitalizations. Evidently he was offered medication for nausea. Yet his mother, Susan Best, reported that he refused. He had "toughed it out" accepting antinausea pills for the first time only on the last visit. Although his treating physician, Dr. Cliff Takemoto, was "baffled" by his running away, Billy's mother reported that Billy could not cope with the hair loss, the nausea, and weakness that followed chemotherapy. In addition to the pain of the treatments and distressing side effects, Billy was isolated. His mother noted that "few of Billy's friends knew that he had cancer." He had access to social workers and psychologists, but his mother said, "I'm sure he said no. He's not the type of kid who'd have wanted that." Dr. Takemoto reported that Billy "seemed to be tolerating treatment extremely well, better than most. There must've been something more, issues of control, loss of freedom. It's all speculation. *It's not clear what's going on in Billy's mind*" (italics added).

Beyond the individual case report, compelling though it is, what is the evidence of child trauma in oncology treatment settings today? We believe that longitudinal research with children who have experienced extensive physical and psychosocial trauma is needed to inform theories of development and to influence clinical practice with child patients. We have studied the experiences of 3- to 6-year-old children, videotaped and interviewed during a pediatric visit, as well as their memory of the visit across a period of 6 months (Steward et al., in press). Forty-six of the 130 children in that study, drawn from the Pediatric Hematology/Oncology Clinic at the University of California Davis Medical Center, experienced the same kinds of medical procedures as did the long-term cancer survivors we wished to study longitudinally (e.g., bone marrow, spinal tap, venipuncture, etc.).

There are options available to make many medical procedures less traumatic (such as Zofran for control of nausea and vomiting, behavioral strategies to increase a sense of control, and EMLA cream for venipunctures), but the diagnosis and treatment of childhood cancer still present children with experiences falling well outside the normal range, and well beyond the parameters of most children's coping repertoires. We found that interventions to lessen the pain of the physical trauma of necessary procedures are not always offered, and even if offered—as in the case of Billy Best—they are not always accepted by children or their families. Furthermore, our recent review of research conducted with children across a broad range of troubled and traumatic family and community settings revealed that many adults (parents and professionals) have difficulty relating to traumatized children, and often employ denial or inattention to shield themselves from what such children are thinking and feeling (Steward & O'Connor, 1994).

In this chapter, we first review the theoretical, empirical, and clinical literatures that link childhood cancer with trauma. Next, we present a developmental model for investigating the effects of traumatic cancer experiences on personality and behavior across the transition from middle childhood to adolescence. Finally, we discuss issues related to cross-disciplinary research on children's health and illness.

Several factors make the longitudinal study of survivors of childhood cancer both unique and timely in the field of trauma research. They include

(a) the unprecedented number of long-term survivors of childhood cancer, (b) theoretical and empirical advances in the study of childhood trauma and the presence of trauma-related disorder in pediatric cancer patients, and (c) the methodological possibility of assessing both the relative impact of well-documented traumatic events, and also survivors' memories and *reappraisals* of those events, on the development of health behavior patterns and personality characteristics most closely associated with them.

CHILDHOOD CANCER PATIENTS: SURVIVORS OF TRAUMA

Recent advances in pediatric oncology are creating a new population of individuals who have shared the traumatic experiences of childhood cancer. Prior to 1960, few children with cancer survived, but since the early 1960s, highly effective diagnostic and therapeutic regimens have been introduced. Over the past 30 years, survival rates of children with acute lymphocytic leukemia (ALL), the most prevalent of the child childhood cancers, have jumped from less than 1% to nearly 70% (Bearison & Mulhern, 1994). Today, most children diagnosed with cancer share the characteristic of early diagnosis, a regular regimen of treatments, and a return to health within 2 to 5 years.

Concomitant with advances in treatment and increased rates of long-term survival, research concerns and research strategies with survivors of childhood cancer have shifted across the decades. Studies conducted in the 1960s and 1970s focused on how to help parents prepare for and cope with death. Researchers relied on retrospective accounts, anecdotal information, or observation of single events (Kupst, 1992). In the 1980s, the focus of research shifted to the psychosocial processes that children employed to cope with the diagnosis and treatment of cancer, and data collection strategies broadened to include direct observation, self-report instruments, and structured interviews with children and parents (Cairns, Klopovich, Hearne, & Lansky, 1982; Jay, Ozolins, Elliott, & Caldwell, 1983; Kellerman, 1980; Ross & Ross, 1988; Spinetta & Deasey-Spinetta, 1981; Zeltzer, Jay, & Fisher, 1989).

Koocher and O'Malley (1981) conducted the first comprehensive follow-up study of childhood cancer survivors and their families. They identified coping with the chronicity of cancer, coping with the aftermath of treatment, and coping with life as a long-term survivor as the next issues to be studied. Kupst (1992) asserted that research on the survival of the childhood cancer patient continues to be necessary, as little is known about what happens to patients physically or psychologically as the survival period lengthens. Cella and Tulsky (1990) noted that there is increased interest, beyond survival, in the quality of life following childhood cancer.

Although improvements in rates of long-term survivorship constitute good news for patients, families, and health care professionals, it is important to recognize that, although highly effective, the medical procedures required for the diagnosis and treatment of pediatric cancer are profoundly traumatic. They are likely to impact behavior and personality in diverse ways throughout life. As Bush (1987) succinctly noted, "One byproduct of advancing medical technology is increasing numbers of children in pain—children who previously would have survived for much shorter periods of time" (p. 215). Parents and children alike rate the experience of medical procedures as extremely distressing (Dolgin, Katz, Zeltzer, & Landsverk, 1989; Jay & Elliott, 1990; McGrath, 1987; Steward, Steward, Joye, & Reinhart, 1991; Watt-Watson, Everden, & Lawson, 1991). Cancer treatments are physically invasive and extremely painful, and for many children—like Billy Best—the side effects of treatment such as nausea, vomiting, weight fluctuations, and hair loss compound the physical and psychological stress (Claflin & Barbarin, 1991). For children, loss of control is frightening as well:

> Several hours after experiencing a spinal tap, 6-year-old Sandra spoke to me in a hushed voice, extremely fearful that a doctor would overhear her: "When they do one I feel too much. I get mad. I say, 'don't do no more!' They say they're do one more. . . . They do one more, and they do one more again, and then they do three times that." When she had finished dictating, she insisted that I conceal her words and drawing in my bag, and not reveal it to any doctor who had been involved in her medical procedures. (Lewis, 1978, p. 18)

The trauma of childhood cancer is not limited to the bodily assaults suffered by children in the course of diagnosis and treatment. According to Nir (1985):

> The diagnosis of cancer plunges a child into this new medical reality, creating a series of overwhelming problems for young patients and their families. *The issues are both physical and emotional in nature.* Although initially distinct, in the course of the child's illness, the physical and emotional components tend to interdigitate, often becoming almost indistinguishable from one another. (p. 124, italics added)

The psychological dynamics of children's cancer treatments are an integral aspect of the trauma they experience. A defining feature of childhood trauma, according to Terr (1991), is that the event renders the child temporarily helpless and breaks past normal coping and defensive responses. Children with cancer undergo necessary, painful procedures while they are awake, and often they must be held down physically by medical staff to ensure that they will not be injured when they struggle to free themselves. These children are rendered helpless, and young children especially cannot employ the favored coping strategy of their age or stage—escape (Altshuler & Ruble, 1989; Band & Weisz, 1988). Indeed, children reported to Steward and her colleagues (1991) that during a spinal tap the nurse's arms across their shoulders—the physical restraint—was more stressful than the needle inserted in their backs.

Traumatic conditions include not only those in which a child is unprepared for an event, but also conditions that are "marked by prolonged and sickening anticipation" (Terr, 1991, p. 11). Many cancer treatment regimens involve repetitive procedures (e.g., chemotherapy and spinal taps) endured over an extended time. As the quote by 6-year-old Sandra powerfully illustrates and observational research documents, both the unexpected and the anticipated events that mark the experience of cancer for most children are sources of extreme distress (Jay et al., 1983).

For many victims of childhood cancer, the trauma is compounded by their parents' distress responses. The process of cancer diagnosis and treatment has long been understood as a very intense and stressful experience for parents (Jay et al., 1983; Kellerman, 1980; Koocher & O'Malley, 1981; Nir, 1985). Although some parents are intuitively able to facilitate their child's coping, many are unprepared and confused about how to help their child. Among parental reactions that may be detrimental to the child's ability to cope or derive comfort from the parents are denial (Byrne, Lewis, Halamek, Connelly, & Mulvihill, 1989; Koocher & O'Malley, 1981; Nir, 1985; Watt-Watson et al., 1991), embarrassment (Blount et al., 1989; Bush, Melamed, & Cockrell, 1989; Steward, 1993), and overt manifestations of distress or anger that tend to magnify the child's behavioral protests and increase the child's attention to the physical pain (Blount et al., 1989). Watt-Watson et al. (1991) found that 9% of parents whose children experienced painful, invasive medical procedures claimed that their children did not experience any pain, a defensive response that may seriously diminish the parents' ability to empathize, offer comfort, and validate their distressed children's thoughts and feelings. Many children display intense behavioral distress during painful procedures, and parents sometimes are embarrassed by and threaten to punish these behavioral responses. The trauma is again compounded—and attachment bonds challenged—when the parent threatens to punish the child's attempts at coping, or "joins the opposition" and helps restrain the child (Blount et al., 1989; Steward, 1993).

Anna Freud (1952) asserted that it is not only the severity of the injury or illness that is important in determining the relative stressfulness of that experience for a child, but also the meaning of the illness to the child. When children cannot make sense of what is happening to them—for example, when there is incongruity of a medical procedure with the child's sense of his or her needs—the stress is compounded (Steward, 1988). Billy Best told his parents that the "medicine was killing" him. Furthermore, because children rarely understand the etiology and treatment rationales (Steward & Steward, 1981), they may be vulnerable to distorted attributions regarding their illness and treatment experiences. For example, children may misidentify repeatedly painful medical procedures as deserved punishment for their own real or imagined misbehavior (Brewster, 1982), thus heightening their distress. The withholding of information and mislabeling of events by parents or medical staff to "protect the child" compound the misinformation (Bearison, 1990; Byrne et al., 1989; Claflin & Barbarin, 1991; Everhart, 1991) and increase the child's susceptibility to distorted appraisals.

Thus, victims of childhood cancer experience significant physical and psychological trauma during their diagnosis and treatment. The physical aspects of their trauma may be described in terms of painfulness, invasiveness, and the physical restraint of movement. Psychologically traumatic factors may include anticipatory distress, maladaptive parental coping, and developmental and situationally imposed constraints of the child's attempts at cognitive mastery of experiences. Because survivors of childhood cancer are, in virtually every sense, survivors of childhood trauma, they constitute a unique and rapidly growing population for the study of trauma and its long-term effects on behavior, personality, and development.

POSTTRAUMATIC STRESS DISORDER AND SYMPTOMATOLOGY IN SURVIVORS OF CHILDHOOD CANCER

Ever since Freud (1924/1953), childhood trauma has been assumed to have a lifelong influence on personality and behavior. However, the nature and magnitude of its effects, and their moderators—the factors that may accentuate or diminish the influence of childhood trauma—are relatively unknown. Recent advances in the definition of childhood trauma (Terr, 1991), the criteria for the diagnosis of Posttraumatic Stress Disorder (PTSD; *Diagnostic and Statistical Manual of Mental Disorders* (4th ed.), 1994), and the study of posttraumatic stress and related disorders (Fletcher, 1991) have begun to organize our understanding of the short- and long-term effects of childhood trauma. There is growing evidence of trauma-induced symptomatology in children suffering from cancer, both during the course of the illness and treatment, and even after a return to health. Having defined trauma as "the mental result of one sudden, external blow or series of blows, rendering the young person temporarily helpless and breaking past ordinary coping and defensive operations," Terr (1991, p. 10) reported that the characteristic sequelae of childhood trauma—strongly visualized or otherwise repeatedly perceived memories, repetitive behaviors, trauma-specific fears, and a sense of severely limited future—are found regardless of the source of the traumatic event or the age of the child. Terr (1991) differentiated among three categories of trauma: (a) A one-time occurrence, that is, an unanticipated "single blow" (Type I); (b) repeated exposure to extreme external events (Type II); and (c) crossover stressors, which are one-time events that have long-term catastrophic consequences (Type III). The trauma of childhood cancer may be conceptualized and studied in terms of Terr's model: Leukemia patients, for example, experience a lengthy course of intense, repetitive treatments and fit Terr's definition of Type II repeated trauma, whereas children who have other forms of cancer, such as solid tumors (Crist & Kun, 1991), may have a significantly shorter course of treatment (e.g., surgery) and may best be understood as instances of Type III crossover trauma. These classifications are important because in Terr's model each category of trauma is associated with distinct coping mechanisms, differential influences on memory, and potentially different developmental trajectories.

All children who experience trauma do not necessarily develop PTSD. Initially the diagnosis was applied to adults, particularly combat veterans, although there is a growing recognition that it may be applicable to children as well (Lyons, 1987). Clinicians have shown great interest in childhood trauma, but opportunities to study the long-term effects of childhood trauma systematically have been rare (Eth & Pynoos, 1985; Johnson, 1989; Terr, 1991). Although many individuals have experienced some form of trauma during childhood, it is difficult to find large, heterogeneous populations of individuals who have shared traumatic experiences, where it is also possible to measure individual differences in the degree and duration of trauma on precise scales and according to several distinct indices of trauma. Moreover, research on the effects of early trauma has usually focused on survivors of natural disasters such as hurricanes (Saylor, Swenson, & Powell, 1992), wars (Realmuto et al., 1992), and interpersonal violence (Pynoos & Eth, 1984; Pynoos & Nader, 1989; Terr, 1981) including child abuse (Briere, 1992; Goodwin, 1985; Green, 1985; Herman, 1992). As a group, these studies share many or all of the following limitations: (a) Samples may be small and homogeneous, as well as unusual in their demographic makeup; (b) there are no systematic observations or detailed records of the traumatic event(s) available for quantification, analyses, or comparison with victims' self-reports; and (c) outcome variables are studied almost exclusively in terms of their relation to the original event; in other words, developmental and personal *transformations* of these early traumatic experiences are not treated as potential mediating variables in the study of trauma survivorship.

Nir (1985), reflecting on 5 years of providing psychiatric liaison services to families and children in treatment for cancer, observed that "post-traumatic stress disorders accompanied, almost without exception, the diagnosis of childhood cancer" (p. 131). There are virtually no longitudinal follow-up studies indicating whether or when cancer-induced PTSD is resolved. However, preliminary results from a prospective longitudinal study of children undergoing bone marrow transplantation revealed the persistence of PTSD symptoms 12 months following the transplant procedure (Stuber, Nader, Yasuda, Pynoos, & Cohen, 1991), and support the use of a PTSD diagnostic model in investigating the long-term psychosocial development of childhood cancer survivors.

Koocher and O'Malley (1981) did not consider the formal diagnosis of PTSD in their report of 117 survivors of childhood cancer; however, they documented that there are potential long-range emotional and medical risks for survivors of childhood cancer. In their sample, which included children ages 0 to 18 years at diagnosis, and 5.6 to 37 years at follow-up, 53% were well adjusted, 26% evidenced mild problems, 10% had moderate problems, and 11% had marked to incapacitating problems. Greenberg, Kazak, and Meadows (1989) found that 8- to 16-year-old survivors who had to cope with severe physical late effects (e.g., relapses and secondary malignancies) demonstrated poorer self-concept, a more external locus of control, and more depressive symptoms than those with no or moderate to mild late effects. Kazak and Meadows (1989) called for closer attention to how survivors change over time, and these changes might be either adaptive or stressful. We believe that attention to the potential for both negative and positive changes during the transition to adolescence is particularly important, as developmental transitions may involve reorganizations on many physical and emotional levels, and therefore represent periods of heightened vulnerability.

In general, the methods for assessment of children's trauma and responses to trauma have been borrowed from adult concepts and instruments. However, Fletcher (1991) created a set of interview and self-report instruments that parallel the *DSM* format, with versions for parent and child. He also created an instrument that allows one to formally review and rate 26 dimensions of stressful events. Cancer may not have been the only stressful event in the lives of children diagnosed with childhood cancer. Employing Fletcher's instruments, it is possible to assess both the intensity and complexity of traumatic events in children's lives, and to match more adequately survivors of childhood cancer with control children.

MEMORY AND APPRAISALS OF EARLY CHILDHOOD EVENTS AND THE LONG-TERM IMPACT OF CHILDHOOD TRAUMA

Since Freud's (1924/1953) initial description of infantile amnesia, "which veils our earliest childhood from us and estranges us from it" (p. 335), memory researchers have believed that the timing of traumatic events in an individual's life cycle is critical to memory. Although the repression mechanism used by Freud to explain his adult patients' retrieval problems has been challenged as far too simple (e.g., Loftus, 1993), current researchers continue to characterize most of the content of young children's memory as being inaccessible to retrieval later in life (Fivush & Hammond, 1990; Nelson, 1989; Wetzler & Sweeney, 1986), and therefore not available as a basis for self-understanding or future decision making.

Pillemer and White (1989) proposed a dual memory system that controls both the way in which experiences are stored and the type of cueing needed to access memory. The first memory system is present at birth and continues to predominate into early childhood. It contains memories that are organized and evoked by context and emotion, and that are manifested in images, behaviors, or emotional responses. Children develop the second language-based memory system during the preschool years. Event representations may then be encoded in narrative form, and can be elicited and shared verbally.

The development of autobiographical memory parallels the development of a young child's sense of self and coincides with the emergence of the second memory system (Fivush, 1993). It overlays the first memory system suggested by Pillemer and White, but does not replace it. This may mean that memories of experiences that are powerful enough (regardless of the positive or negative valence of the experience) to leave a person speechless are stored in the first memory system and cannot be retrieved easily by a simple verbal request by the self or another. This theoretical perspective provides a framework within which to conceptualize memory—including its accuracy and affective qualities—not only as a function of the age at which trauma occurs, but also as a mediator of the impact of early trauma on later psychological development.

An important focus of our research and clinical interests is the memories that childhood cancer survivors have of their early medical experiences. Byrne and colleagues (1989) found that 20% of a sample of 1,928 adults diagnosed with cancer before the age of 5 years, and 21.6% of those diagnosed between 5 and 10 years of age, claimed that they had never been told of their diagnosis. These former patients may have forgotten, or they may never actually have been told of their cancer diagnosis. Although physicians are more likely to discuss cancer with their young patients and their parents today than they were 30 years ago, even today some children undergoing cancer treatment have striking gaps in what they remember about their own diagnosis and the rationale for their treatment (Claflin & Barbarin, 1991). This lack of information can result in gross distortions of their diagnostic and treatment experiences. For example, a 12-year-old girl reported to Everhart (1991) that, following her nephrectomy for Wilm's tumor at age 2, she was given another stomach and cannot eat a lot. Although this child's misinformation may not directly threaten her health, she uses it to make appraisals regarding her food intake that may ultimately have consequences for her health. In the case of other survivors of childhood cancer, a memory lapse may compromise current health decisions or even threaten future health. Byrne and her colleagues reported that 80% of those who did know their cancer diagnosis also knew the modes of treatment. The authors failed to report, and may not have pursued, the question of memory of treatment procedures with those persons who did not know or remember their cancer diagnosis. An important question is whether "fragments" of the cancer experiences have been retained, as Terr described, or are accessible to memory but have been mislabeled or misinterpreted.

Taylor (1991) developed a mobilization/minimization model that suggests that, although negative experiences initially elicit more physiological, cognitive, and affective responses than do positive experiences, with time the memory of negative experiences fades; but Terr (1991) and Loftus (1993) both asserted that it is naive to assume that children forget negative experiences. We know that adults who observe or are responsible for administration of pain often underestimate children's pain (Schechter, 1989), use different criteria than the child victim for assessing the child's distress (Manne, Jacobsen, & Redd, 1992), or attempt to elicit the memories of distressing events only with verbal inquiry (Pipe, Gee, & Wilson, 1993).

McGrath (1987) termed self-report data as the gold standard for assessing the intensity of pain. She found strong correlations between actual tissue damage caused by medical procedures and children's self-reports of pain.

A significant link among children's judgment of painful medical procedures, interview strategies, and children's subsequent memory of the event has been documented (Steward, 1993; Steward et al., in press; Steward et al., 1991). Children's reports of body touch and handling (elicited with anatomical drawings or dolls) and judgments of the relative stressfulness of medical procedures (elicited with the Faces Scale; Bieri, Reeve, Champion, Addicoat, & Ziegler, 1990) significantly predicted completeness of their memory at 1-month follow-up and both accuracy and completeness of their report at 6-month follow-up. It should be noted that judgments of the children's distress by physicians and nurses who administered the procedures were not correlated with either measure of children's memory.

The children in Steward's research were 3 to 6 years old, and were followed for only 6 months. What happens to children's pain judgments and memories of the experiences that evoked the pain as children develop? Everhart (1991) believed that children's concepts of cancer and its treatment may be arrested at the cognitive level they had achieved at the time of diagnosis and treatment. Adolescents diagnosed and treated as children may have more cognitive limitations, especially with regard to understanding the possible long-term sequelae of the disease. Their focus is likely to fall on the mechanics of, and distress caused by, the medical procedures per se, rather than the reason for the procedure (diagnosis vs. treatment) or the results of the procedures (Steward & Steward, 1981).

There is considerable controversy about whether it is the actual event(s) one experienced early in childhood, or one's current memories and evaluation—and the consequent stress that accompanies these reevaluations—that actually influence personality and behavioral development. Rutter (1989) argued that polarization of this issue is inappropriate, because the past and the present are inextricably linked in the role they play as shapers of development. With this premise in mind, we anticipate that both the accuracy and the affective quality of memories and reappraisals vary as a function of age at diagnosis and treatment, and also differentially mediate the effects of the cancer experiences on subsequent psychological functioning, including perceptions of personal vulnerability and vitally important health-related judgment and behavior. Understanding this issue clearly carries more than academic interest, for survivors of childhood cancer may be especially vulnerable later in life if they cannot accurately inform their physicians of their medical history. Also, there is increasing documentation that survivors of childhood cancer face clinically significant late effects ranging from relapses and second malignancies to problems with dentition, growth, and reproduction (Byrne et al., 1989).

THE EFFECTS OF CHILDHOOD TRAUMA
ON HEALTH BEHAVIOR AND PERSONALITY
DEVELOPMENT IN ADOLESCENCE

Health-related behavior in cancer survivors is an area particularly in need of comprehensive study, because increasing numbers of pediatric cancer survivors are living into adolescence. Adolescence is the period of development in which the issues of independence and autonomy, ranging from the intrapersonal to the interpersonal, are experienced through the lens of risk-taking behaviors (Baumrind, 1987; Dryfoos, 1990; Leffert & Petersen, chapter 7, this volume). It is during adolescence that parents (usually mothers) initiate the transfer of health "surveillance," turning over many health-related decisions to their children (Freud, 1952; Millstein & Litt, 1990). This transfer process, although developmentally significant, does not always go smoothly. Although most adolescents perceive themselves to be invulnerable, the leading causes of morbidity and mortality in adolescence are in fact related to risky decisions made by adolescents themselves (Irwin & Millstein, 1987). Indeed, Gochman and Saucier (1982) found perceived vulnerability to be negatively related to preventive health behaviors and self-concept and positively related to anxiety and health risk behaviors such as smoking.

Tinsley (1992) called for longitudinal studies and attention to individual differences to increase our understanding of the acquisition and socialization of children's health attitudes and behavior, as current models are limited by self-report and cross-sectional data. In a recent review of adolescent health, Millstein and Litt (1990) noted that relatively little work has been done to improve our understanding of the natural history from childhood of health behaviors and their meaning to adolescents. They note that even survey data are rarely collected on adolescents younger than 15 years of age. Although high school freshmen are included in the 10 annual surveys of adolescent health behaviors being conducted nation-wide from 1990 through 2000 by the Centers for Disease Control and Prevention, those data will not yield information on the processes by which young adolescents move into health risk or health-enhancing behaviors because, unfortunately, a cross-sectional design has been selected. Millstein and Litt (1990) called for the study of factors that affect adolescents' perceptions of their vulnerability to harm, their current beliefs about health-promoting behaviors, conceptual schemata used in interpreting body sensation and symptomatology, decision making in relationships, health and beliefs about the health care system, treatment seeking behavior, and sick role behavior. Rutter (1989) made the methodological point that, although longitudinal studies document that the outcome of transitions is partially determined by an individual's past experience, it is too simple to ask what behavior is a function of past versus present experience: "Life transitions have to be considered both as end products of past processes and as instigators of future ones . . . as both independent and dependent variables" (p. 46).

Adolescent survivors of childhood cancer, having faced a life-threatening illness, may provide unique evaluations and choices of both health-enhancing and health risk behaviors. We perceive an urgent need to begin studying systematically the ways, both positive and negative, in which childhood cancer experiences influence the development of adolescent health-related judgment and behavior. Nir (1985), for example, observed adolescent cancer patients' "acting out" and risk-taking behaviors. He wrote about an "adolescent girl (who) coped with loss of control by becoming sexually active. This resulted in a pregnancy between two courses of chemotherapy. 'I don't have time to wait,' was her explanation" (p. 131). Thus, health-related appraisals and behavior in adolescent survivors of childhood cancer may be influenced significantly by the foreshortened view of the future that is not only a symptom of PTSD across all types of trauma (Terr, 1991), but in this case is based on the objective reality of a possible relapse or recurrence of the life-threatening illness.

Individuals who have an internal locus of control are generally reported to adjust better to illness than those with an external locus of control. Yet Bearison (1994) observed that the construct of locus of control is particularly problematic as it pertains to children with cancer. Children cannot be expected to assume responsibility for the cause of their cancer, nor is there much they can initiate or refuse in the treatment of their cancer. In fact, Bearison and his colleagues (Bearison, Sadow, Granowetter, & Winkel, 1993) found better coping and adjustment in families in which both parents and children expressed an external locus of control and were able to state an identifiable external "cause" of the child's cancer. At the same time they acknowledged that their physicians had told them that the etiology of childhood cancer is unknown. Others have reported, but played down, slight differences in locus of control that demonstrate cancer children to report more external locus of control than healthy peers (Greenberg et al., 1989).

A critical set of questions can be raised as survivors of childhood cancer return to health and continue to develop into adolescence. What proportion of these children maintain that external locus of control? Does the external locus of control that served children well during treatment make them vulnerable to outside pressures that lead to risky health behaviors in adolescence, and make it less likely that they will initiate or maintain health-enhancing behaviors? Our pilot study data suggest that, as survivors of early childhood cancer make the transition into early adolescence, their own estimates of risk behavior begin to diverge from that of their parents. Responses to a series of open-ended questions and to the "Risk Wall" (Bush & Ianotti, 1991) reveal that parent and child estimates of peer influence on risky behavior also differ. It is important to include parental judgments in the study of health-enhancing and health risk behaviors reported by adolescent and adult survivors of childhood cancer. Dyadic parent–child information from normal samples would be useful as well.

MODELING THE LINK BETWEEN CHILDHOOD TRAUMA AND ADOLESCENT EXPERIENCE

We have developed a theoretical model, as shown in Figure 6.1, to enable longitudinal investigation of the link between childhood trauma and adolescent experiences based on a review of the literature, our own research and clinical experience with traumatized children, and pilot work with adolescent survivors of childhood cancer. The model can be applied to children identified initially during middle to late childhood who are followed into adolescence. In this model we identify both "stable" and "moving" predictors (one of which is influenced by the subjects' repeated participation in a longitudinal study).

The pivotal independent variable is the presence and relative severity of traumatic episodes, here operationalized as diagnosis and treatment for childhood cancer. The treatment group is expected to differ from a control

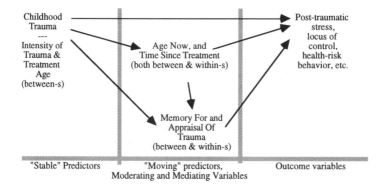

FIG. 6.1.   A model of "stable" and moving variables that link childhood trauma and adolescent experience.

group on a variety of indices of posttraumatic stress and on a variety of personality and behavioral measures, including perception of vulnerability, locus of control, and health risk behavior.

Among survivors of childhood cancer, however, several additional variables are of interest, two of which remain constant over the arbitrary time span of a longitudinal study, and four of which "move" (change, or at least have the potential for change). These additional stable and moving variables are expected to influence whether or not those who have experienced a severe traumatic episode in childhood actually demonstrate evidence of posttraumatic stress, manifest dysfunctional personalities, and/or manifest dysfunctional behaviors. It is also possible with this data set to document children's strategies for successful coping.

The two stable variables are the objective measure of the degree of trauma experienced and the age at which treatment is completed (with one analysis testing whether treatment completion and the traumatic episode pre- or postdates the onset of autobiographical memory; Fivush, 1993; Fivush & Hammond, 1990) and, concordantly, the onset of Pillemer and White's (1989) notion of the second stage of memory. The "moving" variables, which are expected to moderate and/or mediate the effect of the intensity of traumatic experience, include age, time since treatment, the memory for the traumatic episodes, and the current appraisal of the traumatic episodes. It is hypothesized that, at any point in time, the effects of childhood trauma differ in kind and intensity depending on whether the events are easily recalled and whether they are appraised as having engendered great stress. Moreover, recall and appraisal can be expected to change with time, particularly in a context in which one is being questioned about a prior traumatic episode (Janoff-Bulman, 1992). As documented by Acredolo and O'Connor (1991), questioning brings to light one's uncertainty, promoting curiosity and reflection, and ultimately a change in one's understanding. Thus, through repeated assessments, it would be important to monitor changes in cancer survivors' memories for and appraisals of their traumatic episodes as well as concomitant changes demonstrated in their personalities and behaviors (i.e., in the indices of posttraumatic stress, locus of control, health risk behavior, etc.). The impact on the children's memory for pediatric events as a consequence of participating in research about their own medical history would constitute a worthwhile research topic.

A matter of central interest in this model is how trauma interacts with the cognitive, physical, and psychosocial developments that accompany the transition into adolescence—for example, the emergence of a capacity for abstract self-reflection, physical growth and development, and the transfer of health care responsibility from parent to child.

We believe that degree of trauma should be assessed both in terms of an objective score and a subjective score. That is, given children's medical records, one could document all procedures each child endured and use previously reported behavioral data to code and weigh the stressfulness of those procedures (Jay & Elliott, 1990; Steward et al., 1991). Individuals will also vary in the degree to which they recall the event surrounding their illness and treatment, and subjective ratings of the trauma they endured may vary considerably from the objective level of trauma deduced from knowing their medical histories. Some children in our pilot study carried powerful memories of their own "bad feelings like scariness and sadness and fears," and others vividly described "people who were sicker than me, who were dying." Subjective ratings may be more or less severe than objectively derived scores. Both measures of trauma may independently "explain" a reliable portion of the variance in personality and behavior.

It is not clear at this time how childhood trauma affects adolescent personality and health-enhancing or health risk behavior. Specific hypotheses can be proposed on the basis of existing theory and empirical data. Given Taylor's (1991) work on diminished memory for negative events over time, one could test the strength of the relation between subjective and objective trauma with the prediction that this relation will grow weaker with age and years since treatment as children forget the trauma of their experiences with medical procedures. However, Steward (1993) documented that most children possess accurate, although incomplete recall about specific medical procedures and our adolescent pilot data suggest that memory of subjective trauma will have a very shallow slope, declining little if at all with age. Brainerd and Reyna's (1990) work on fuzzy trace theory would predict an increase in amount of recall as a function of being questioned by researchers over the course of a longitudinal study. Along similar lines, Acredolo and O'Connor's (1991) theory on the motivational role of uncertainty on the acquisition of knowledge would predict that adolescents will become increasingly inquisitive regarding their medical histories and gain increasing certainty as to the events surrounding their illness and treatment. Adolescents may initiate discussions with parents, grandparents, siblings, and family physicians or even recontact hospitals where they received treatment to clarify or augment their memories.

We anticipate that, as the parameters of objective and/or subjective trauma increases, risk-taking behavior will become increasingly bimodal. That is, having survived a life-threatening event, some individuals will respond by becoming compulsively life protecting and conservative in regard to risky behaviors. Other individuals will respond with either an increased attitude of invulnerability or an increased sense of external control (or both) leading to a liberal attitude toward risky behavior.

In general, we anticipate that the severity of trauma will predict an external locus of control, a pessimistic attributional style, and an identity that includes explicit mention of sufferer or survivor status. That is, with increased levels of trauma, the helplessness one experienced pervades more and more of the individual's personality and behavior even to the point of dominating the individual's sense of self and hope for the future. Evidence for this prediction can be seen in Wallerstein and Blakeslee's (1989) study of adolescents and adults whose parents divorced when they were children. Many years later, that complex set of events continued to dominate their sense of who they were and influenced their interactions with their parents and peers.

CROSS-DISCIPLINARY COMMUNICATION AND COLLABORATION BETWEEN DEVELOPMENTAL PSYCHOLOGISTS AND PEDIATRICIANS

When developmental psychologists and pediatricians work together it is possible to sharpen theories about children and their families, and at the same time to improve the delivery of clinical care. These two groups share an advocacy and a special affection for children and their families. Many developmental psychologists and pediatricians also share a focus on process, contexts, and change. They are interested in perturbations in the lives of children and their families that offer opportunities for coping and competence, and they are alert to early signs of maladaption or dysfunction (Parmelee, 1986, 1989). Cross-disciplinary research is one natural outcome of these common interests and concerns.

In collaborative research, when the same child is seen as both a patient and a research subject, there are a number of issues that must be addressed before the beginning or the different assignments of the cross-disciplinary colleagues may interrupt the best work of both. Three issues come to mind that merit collegial discussion. First, we believe that ground rules need to be established in collaborative research about the conditions under which patient care takes precedence over research access or vice versa. For example, in a recent study we conducted, the clinic director asked us not to contact the family of potential research subjects at home prior to their appointment because he believed that the parents' commitment to the child's treatment regime was fragile, and our request for participation might be sufficient to induce a "no show" to the detriment of the child. However, once the family arrived in the clinic, the director was happy to add his endorsement to our invitation to the child and family to participate in the study.

A second issue involves the problem of gaining informed consent from pediatric patients. It is already pro forma that when children are included as research subjects, Human Subjects Review Committees require consent from parents as well as children. However, in medical settings, consent from both parents and children may be unduly influenced by the pressure to respond quickly to a child's injury or illness. Parental permission is nearly isomorphic with bringing the child to a medical facility, and children are expected to comply with little consultation with necessary and sometimes painful diagnostic and treatment procedures for their own good. Therefore, research team members should exert extra caution when approaching pediatric patients and their families about participation in a research study (Fisher, 1993). Automatic, perfunctory compliance should not be expected or tolerated from children or their parents.

A third issue, related closely to the second, is that researchers must be cautious that the child's involvement in the research project does not add to the child's burden of stress or pain. We all must be sensitive to children who are especially vulnerable physically and/or psychosocially, because they may be ill, injured, tired, frightened, angry, or lonely. Thorough research team discussion parameters can be established so that the unique medical circumstances and personality of each child patient can be respected. Practically, this means that each child who is a research subject is given a real choice, not only of participating in a study, but of calling for a break, or even terminating participation in a research study without penalty.

Because research and clinical care have different purposes, different access to patients, and different pacing, cross-disciplinary research is time consuming and often frustrating. There is also the potential for miscommunication among colleagues. But we believe that cross-disciplinary teams can ask more interesting and sometimes even more important questions. We also know that the answers can make a positive difference in the lives of children and their families. Finally, we note a benefit not often acknowledged. The professional respect necessary to plan and conduct such research and the hard work necessary to complete it successfully often result in deep, lifelong professional friendships among cross-disciplinary colleagues.

ACKNOWLEDGMENT

We appreciate the support of the Gertrude Carter Cancer Research Fund, awarded to M. Steward, C. Acredolo, and C. Abildgaard.

REFERENCES

Acredolo, C., & O'Connor, J. (1991). On the difficulty of detecting cognitive uncertainty. *Human Development, 34*, 204–223.

Altshuler, J. L., & Ruble, D. N. (1989). Developmental changes in children's awareness of strategies for coping with uncontrollable stress. *Child Development, 60*, 1337–1349.

Band, E. B., & Weisz, J. R. (1988). How to feel better when it feels bad: Children's perspective on coping with everyday stress. *Developmental Psychology, 24*, 247–253.

Baumrind, D. (1987). A developmental perspective on adolescent risk-taking in contemporary America. In C. E. Irwin (Ed.), *Adolescent social behavior and health* (pp. 93–125). San Francisco: Jossey-Bass.

Bearison, D. J. (1990). *They never want to tell you*. Cambridge, MA: Harvard University Press.

Bearison, D. J. (1994). Medication compliance in pediatric oncology. In D. J. Bearison & R. K. Mulhern (Eds.), *Pediatric psycho-oncology: Psychological perspectives on children with cancer* (pp. 84–98). New York: Oxford University Press.

Bearison, D. J., & Mulhern, R. K. (Eds.) (1994). *Pediatric psycho-oncology: Psychological perspectives on children with cancer*. New York: Oxford University Press.

Bearison, D. J., Sadow, A. J., Granowetter, L., & Winkel, G. (1993). Patient's and their parent's causal attributions of childhood cancer. *Journal of Psychosocial Oncology, 11*, 47–61.

Bieri, D., Reeve, R. A., Champion, G. D., Addicoat, L., & Ziegler, J. B. (1990). The faces pain scale for the self-assessment of the severity of pain experienced by children: Development, initial validation, and preliminary investigation for ratio scales properties. *Pain, 41*, 139–150.

Blount, R. L., Corbin, S. M., Sturges, J. W., Wolfe, V. V., Prater, J. M., & James, L. D. (1989). The relationship between adults' behavior and child coping and distress during BMA:LP procedures: A sequential analysis. *Behavior Therapy, 20*, 585–601.

Brainerd, C. J., & Reyna, V. F. (1990). Gist is the grist:Fuzzy-trace theory and the new intuitionism. *Developmental Review, 10*, 3–47.

Brewster, A. B. (1982). Chronically ill hospitalized children's conceptions of their illness. *Pediatrics, 69*, 355–362.

Briere, J. (1992). *Child abuse trauma: Theory and treatment of the last effects*. Newbury Park, CA: Sage.

Bush, J. P. (1987). Pain in children: A review of the literature from a developmental perspective. *Psychology and Health, 1*, 215–236.

Bush, J. P., & Ianotti, R. J. (1991). A children's health belief model. *Medical Care, 28*, 69–80.

Bush, J. P., Melamed, B. G., & Cockrell, C. S. (1989). Parenting children in a stressful medical situation. In T. W. Miller (Ed.), *Stressful life events* (pp. 643–658). Madison, WI: International Universities Press.

Byrne, J., Lewis, S., Halamek, L., Connelly, R. R., & Mulvihill, J. J. (1989). Childhood cancer survivors' knowledge of their diagnosis and treatment. *Annals of Internal Medicine, 110*, 400–403.

Cairns, N. U., Klopovich, P., Hearne, E., & Lansky, S. B. (1982). School attendance of children with cancer. *Journal of School Health, 3*, 152–155.

Cella, D., & Tulsky, D. S. (1990). Measuring quality of life today: Methodological aspects. *Oncology, 4*, 29–37.

Claflin, C. J., & Barbarin, O. A. (1991). Does "telling" less protect more? Relationships among age, information disclosure, and what children with cancer see and feel. *Journal of Pediatric Psychology, 16*, 169–191.

Crist, W. M., & Kun, L. E. (1991). Common solid tumors of childhood. *The New England Journal of Medicine, 324*, 461–471.

Diagnostic and Statistical Manual of Mental Disorders (4th ed.). (1994). Washington, DC: American Psychiatric Association.

Dolgin, M. J., Katz, E. R., Zeltzer, L. K., & Landsverk, J. (1989). Behavioral distress in pediatric patients with cancer receiving chemotherapy. *Pediatrics, 84*, 103–110.

Dryfoos, J. G. (1990). *Adolescents at risk.* New York: Oxford University Press.

Eth, S., & Pynoos, R. S. (Eds.). (1985). *Post-traumatic stress disorder in children.* Washington, DC: American Psychiatric Press.

Everhart, J. A. (1991). Overcoming childhood cancer misconceptions among survivors. *Journal of Pediatric Oncology Nursing, 8*, 46–48.

Fisher, C. B. (1993). Integrating science and ethics in research with high-risk children and youth, Social Policy Report. *Society for Research in Child Development, VII*, 1–27.

Fivush, R. (1993). Developmental perspective on autobiographical recall. In G. S. Goodman & B. L. Bottoms (Eds.), *Child victims, child witnesses: Understanding and improving testimony* (pp. 1–24). New York: Guilford.

Fivush, R., & Hammond, N. R. (1990). Autobiographical memory across the preschool years: Towards reconceptualizing childhood amnesia. In R. Fivush & J. A. Hudson (Eds.), *Knowing and remembering in young children* (pp. 223–248). New York: Cambridge University Press.

Fletcher, K. E. (1991). *Childhood PTSD Interview, Childhood PTSD Interview—Parent Form, When Bad Things Happen, Parent Report of the Child's Reaction to Stress,* and *Dimensions of Stressful Events Rating Scale.* Worcester: University of Massachusetts.

Freud, A. (1952). The role of bodily illness in the mental life of children. *Psychoanalytic Study of the Child, 7*, 69–80.

Freud, S. (1953). *A general introduction to psychoanalysis.* New York: Pocket Books. (Original work published 1924)

Gochman, D. S., & Saucier, J. F. (1982). Perceived vulnerability in children and adolescents. *Health Education Quarterly, 9*, 46–59.

Goodwin, J. (1985). Post-traumatic symptoms in incest victims. In S. Eth & R. Pynoos (Eds.), *Post-traumatic stress disorder in children* (pp. 155–168). Washington, DC: American Psychiatric Press.

Green, A. H. (1985). Children traumatized by physical abuse. In S. Eth & R. Pynoos (Eds.), *Post-traumatic stress disorder in children* (pp. 133–154). Washington, DC: American Psychiatric Press.

Greenberg, H. S., Kazak, A. E., & Meadows, A. T. (1989). Psychologic functioning in 8–16 year old cancer survivors and their parents. *Journal of Pediatrics, 114*, 488–493.

Herman, J. L. (1992). *Trauma and recovery.* New York: Basic Books.

Irwin, C. E., & Millstein, S. G. (1987). Biopsychosocial correlates of risk-taking behaviors during adolescence. *Journal of Adolescent Health Care, 7*, 825–835.

Janoff-Bulman, R. (1992). *Shattered assumptions: Towards a new psychology of trauma.* New York: The Free Press.

Jay, S. M., & Elliott, C. H. (1990). A stress inoculation program for parents whose children are undergoing painful medical procedures. *Journal of Consulting and Clinical Psychology, 58,* 799–804.

Jay, S. M., Ozolins, M., Elliott, C. H., & Caldwell, S. (1983). Assessment of children's distress during painful medical procedures. *Health Psychology, 2,* 133–147.

Johnson, K. (1989). *Trauma in the lives of children.* Claremont, CA: Hunter House.

Kazak, A. E., & Meadows, A. T. (1989). Families of young adolescents who have survived cancer: Social-emotional adjustment, adaptability, and social support. *Journal of Pediatric Psychology, 14,* 175–191.

Kellerman, J. (Ed.). (1980). *Psychological aspects of childhood cancer.* Springfield, IL: Thomas.

Koocher, G. P., & O'Malley, J. E. (1981). *The Damocles syndrome: Psychosocial consequences of surviving childhood cancer.* New York: McGraw-Hill.

Kupst, M. J. (1992). Long-term family coping with acute lymphoblastic leukemia in childhood. In A. M. LaGreca, L. J. Siegel, J. L. Wallander, & C. E. Walker (Eds.), *Stress and coping in child health* (pp. 242–261). New York: Guilford.

Lewis, N. (1978, January–February). The needle is like an animal. *Children Today,* 18–21.

Loftus, E. F. (1993). The reality of repressed memories. *American Psychologist, 48,* 518–537.

Lyons, J. A. (1987). Post-traumatic stress disorder in children and adolescents: A review of the literature. *Developmental and Behavioral Pediatrics, 8,* 349–356.

Manne, S. L., Jacobsen, P. B., & Redd, W. H. (1992). Assessment of acute pediatric pain: Do child self-report, parent ratings, and nurse ratings measure the same phenomenon? *Pain, 48,* 45–52.

McGrath, P. A. (1987). An assessment of children's pain: A review of behavioral, physiological, and direct scaling techniques. *Pain, 31,* 147–176.

Millstein, S. G., & Litt, I. F. (1990). Adolescent health. In S. S. Feldman & G. R. Eliott (Eds.), *At the threshold: The developing adolescent* (pp. 431–456). Cambridge, MA: Harvard University Press.

Nelson, K. (1989). Remembering: A functional developmental perspective. In P. R. Solomon, G. R. Goethals, C. M. Kelley, & B. R. Stephens (Eds.), *Memory: Interdisciplinary approaches* (pp. 127–150). New York: Springer-Verlag.

Nir, Y. (1985). Post-traumatic stress disorder in children with cancer. In S. Eth & R. S. Pynoos (Eds.), *Post-traumatic stress disorder in children* (pp. 123–132). Washington, DC: American Psychiatric Press.

Parmelee, A. H. (1986). Children's illnesses: Their beneficial effects on behavioral development. *Child Development, 57,* 1–10.

Parmelee, A. H. (1989). The child's physical health and the development of relationships. In A. J. Sameroff & R. N. Emde (Eds.), *Relationship disturbance in early childhood* (pp. 145–162). New York: Basic Books.

Pillemer, D. B., & White, S. H. (1989). Childhood events recalled by children and adults. In H. W. Reese (Ed.), *Advances in child development and behavior* (pp. 297–340). New York: Academic Press.

Pipe, M. E., Gee, S., & Wilson, C. (1993). Cues, props and context: Do they facilitate children's event reports? In G. S. Goodman & B. L. Bottoms (Eds.), *Child victim, child witness: Understanding and improving testimony* (pp. 25–46). New York: Guilford.

Pynoos, R. S., & Eth, S. (1984). The child as witness to homicide. *Journal of Social Issues*, *40*, 87–108.

Pynoos, R. S., & Nader, K. (1989). Children's memory and proximity to violence. *Journal of the American Academy of Child and Adolescent Psychiatry*, *28*, 236–241.

Realmuto, G. M., Masten, A., Carole, L. F., Hubbard, J., Groteluschen, A., & Chhun, B. (1992). Adolescent survivors of massive childhood trauma in Cambodia: Life events and current symptoms. *Journal of Traumatic Stress*, *5*, 589–599.

Ritter, J. (1994, November 11). Mass. teen on the run—from chemotherapy. *USA Today*, p. 1.

Ross, D. M., & Ross, S. A. (1988). *Childhood pain: Current issues, research and management*. Baltimore: Urban & Schwarzberg.

Rutter, M. (1989). Pathways from childhood to adult life. *Journal of Child Psychiatry and Psychology*, *30*, 23–51.

Saylor, C. F., Swenson, C. C., & Powell, P. (1992). Hurricane Hugo blows down the broccoli: Preschoolers' post-disaster play and adjustment. *Child Psychiatry and Human Development*, *22*, 139–149.

Schechter, N. L. (1989). The undertreatment of pain in children: An overview. *Pediatric Clinics of North America*, *36*, 781–794.

Spinetta, J. J., & Deasey-Spinetta, P. (Eds.). (1981). *Living with childhood cancer*. St. Louis, MO: Mosby.

Steward, M. S. (1988). Illness: A crisis for children. In J. Sandoval (Ed.), *Crisis counseling, intervention and prevention in the schools* (pp. 109–129). Hillsdale, NJ: Lawrence Erlbaum Associates.

Steward, M. S. (1993). Children's memory of medical procedures: "He didn't touch me and it didn't hurt!" In C. A. Nelson (Ed.), *Minnesota symposium on child psychology: Memory and affect in development* (pp. 171–225). Hillsdale, NJ: Lawrence Erlbaum Associates.

Steward, M. S., & O'Connor, J. (1994). Pediatric pain, trauma, and memory. *Current Opinion in Pediatrics*, *6*, 411–417.

Steward, M. S., & Steward, D. S. (1981). Children's concepts of medical procedures. In R. Bibace & M. Walsh (Eds.), *The development of children's conceptions of health and related phenomena* (pp. 67–83). San Francisco: Jossey-Bass.

Steward, M. S., Steward, D. S., Farquhar, L., Reinhart, M., Myers, J. E. B., Walker, J., & Joye, N. (in press). Interviewing children about body touch and handling. *Monographs of the Society for Research in Child Development*.

Steward, M. S., Steward, D. S., Joye, N., & Reinhart, M. (1991). Pain judgments by young children and medical staff. *Journal of Pain and Symptom Management*, *6*, 202.

Stuber, M. L., Nader, K., Yasuda, P., Pynoos, R. S., & Cohen, S. (1991). Stress responses after pediatric bone marrow transplantation: Preliminary results of a prospective longitudinal study. *Journal of the American Academy of Child and Adolescent Psychiatry*, *30*, 952–957.

Taylor, S. E. (1991). Asymmetrical effects of positive and negative events: The mobilization-minimization hypothesis. *Psychological Bulletin*, *110*, 67–85.

Terr, L. (1981). Psychic trauma in children: Observations following the Chowchilla school-bus kidnapping. *American Journal of Psychiatry, 138,* 14–19.

Terr, L. (1991). Childhood traumas: An outline and overview. *American Journal of Psychiatry, 148,* 10–20.

Tinsley, B. J. (1992). Multiple influences on the acquisition and socialization of children's health attitudes and behavior: An integrative review. *Child Development, 63,* 1043–1069.

Wallerstein, J. S., & Blakeslee, S. (1989). *Men, women and children a decade after divorce.* New York: Tichnor & Fields.

Watt-Watson, J., Everden, C., & Lawson, C. (1991). Parents' perceptions of children's acute pain experience. *Journal of Pain and Symptom Management, 6,* 149.

Wetzler, S. E., & Sweeney, J. A. (1986). Childhood amnesia: An emprical demonstration. In D. Rubin (Ed.), *Autobiographical memory* (pp. 191–202). New York: Cambridge University Press.

Zeltzer, L. K., Jay, S. M., & Fisher, D. M. (1989). The management of pain associated with pediatric procedures. *Pediatric Clinics of North America, 36,* 941–964.

7

Biology, Challenge, and Coping in Adolescence: Effects on Physical and Mental Health

Nancy Leffert
Search Institute
Minneapolis, Minnesota

Anne C. Petersen
University of Minnesota

Adolescence is a time in the life course that is filled with potential opportunity, challenge, and risk. It is a time of opportunity because the child enters the period generally still possessing the child's body and the child's ways of thinking and emerges with a new body, many new skills, and the thinking and reasoning ability to use those new skills in sophisticated ways (Petersen & Leffert, 1995b). Along the way, the adolescent is confronted with many challenges. We deliberately use the word *challenge* instead of stress because a challenge may lead to positive outcomes. However, challenges may become stressful for many young people. As adolescents begin to experience adultlike stresses and challenges, there is some risk that they may also experience pressures to engage in health-compromising behavior. Many of the challenges they experience, such as sexual behavior and substance use, are related to their impending adult status. These challenges or stresses require the adolescent to learn ways of coping. Some coping methods, such as problem solving, are effective; others, such as substance use, are not effective. The methods of coping that adolescents learn will ultimately shape their development and the trajectory of health into, and perhaps through, adulthood. Because of the mutual influence of challenge and opportunities, and the potential risk of health-compromising behaviors, adolescence is an excellent period in which to examine the links between developmental psychology and behavioral pediatrics.

The scientific study of adolescence has emerged over the past 20 years as a significant field, with an especially large amount of research appearing just during the last 10 years (e.g., Dornbusch, Petersen, & Hetherington, 1991; Feldman & Elliott, 1990; Petersen, 1988, 1993). There have been many effective collaborations between pediatrics and developmental psychology as part of this emerging body of research. These types of collaborations are especially important because many lifelong patterns of health and behavior are laid down during adolescence. Adolescence is a time in which we can intervene into these behaviors, influencing more positive outcomes. The linkages between pediatrics and developmental psychology particularly inform the field in the area of developmentally appropriate interventions.

This chapter examines adolescence as a time of change and challenge. We review the concept of adolescence as a developmental transition and key aspects of adolescent development such as biological, cognitive, and social change. We also examine models for understanding the relations of hormones to behavior, and the physiological, behavioral, and health factors associated with stress and coping as they relate to physical and mental health during adolescence. We draw some examples from our research and that of others to illuminate these inferences.

ADOLESCENCE: A DEVELOPMENTAL TRANSITION

The adolescent decade begins with biological change and ends with entrance into the adult social roles of work and family. The developing person shapes and is shaped by the experiences of the period. Scholars describe adolescence as the second decade of life, with three subphases: early adolescence (ages 10–14 years), middle adolescence (15–17 years), and late adolescence (18–20 years; e.g., Elliott & Feldman, 1990). Each of these subphases has distinct features. Early adolescence is dominated by puberty, which is also thought to be the time when the actual transition from childhood to adolescence is made. Middle adolescence is generally what is called to mind when we think of adolescence, in that it involves an intense preoccupation with peers and the music and attire so often associated with young people. Late adolescence is yet another time of transition; as the young person begins to take on the roles and responsibilities of adulthood (Crockett & Petersen, 1993).

The traditional view of adolescence is that it is a time of "storm and stress" (Hall, 1904), a time in which it is considered normative to experience conflicts in all areas (e.g., Blos, 1970; Freud, 1958). Research has clearly demonstrated that a "stormy" or "stressful" decade is not the case for all adolescents, but instead the experience of a minority of young people (e.g., Douvan & Adelson, 1966; Offer, Ostrov, & Howard, 1981; Rutter, 1980). Adolescence is indeed characterized by change and transition, and it is challenging, but it is not inevitably problematic (Petersen & Leffert, 1995b).

A developmental transition is characterized by significant change in the biological or social domains of life, or both (e.g., Emde & Harmon, 1984). Adolescence is considered a time of transition because major changes take place in all domains of development (e.g., physical, cognitive) and in all social contexts (Petersen, 1988). Experiencing so much change across domains within a brief period, such as during early adolescence, may exacerbate typical responses. For example, research has demonstrated that negative outcomes are linked to the experience of too many simultaneous changes during this period (Petersen, Sarigiani, & Kennedy, 1991; Simmons, Burgeson, Carlton-Ford, & Blyth, 1987). The concept that many changes within a short period may be stressful to young people supports Coleman's (1978) focal theory that developmental tasks can be managed more effectively if they occur sequentially, or at least without too many changes occurring at once. The experience of many changes occurring simultaneously is especially likely during early adolescence, and therefore early adolescence may be a time of particular risk (Petersen & Spiga, 1982). In addition to the normative challenges of adolescence, some young people come into the period "weakened" by chronic disease or sociobiological deficits, such as nutritional deficiencies (e.g., Petersen, Susman, & Beard, 1989). These factors combined with the changes of normal adolescent development may be especially challenging and stressful.

A model for factors influencing mental health during early adolescence is shown in Figure 7.1. The nature, number, and timing of changes are all important. The nature of some changes, such as the death of a parent, may have many direct (e.g., loss) and indirect (e.g., changes in income or living arrangements) effects, whereas other changes, such as the death of a pet, may have less extensive effects. As noted earlier, the sheer number of changes can also be overwhelming and lead to negative outcomes (e.g., Simmons & Blyth, 1987). If changes are sequential, the adolescent is more able to cope. If changes are simultaneous, the "pile up" can lead to ineffective coping. Peer and parent support during this period can buffer

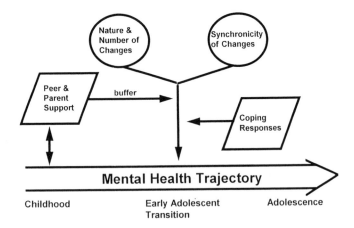

FIGURE 7.1.   A model of developmental transitions.   (Adapted with permission from Petersen & Ebata, 1987).

responses to external or internal changes and challenges. Coping responses can also be more or less effective. We argue that health-related behaviors, such as emerging sexuality or experimentation with alcohol or tobacco, may be conceptualized in the same way.

Biological Change

The physical changes of puberty are dramatic and take place relatively rapidly but with a great deal of individual variation in terms of their timing and tempo (Eichorn, 1975; Petersen & Taylor, 1980; Tanner, 1972). Pubertal change takes place within an already existing endocrine system that was established prenatally but then suppressed until the beginning of puberty (Petersen & Taylor, 1980). Many of the hormones involved in puberty show fivefold increases over their prepubertal levels. Although prepubertal boys and girls are similar in their levels of circulating gonadal hormones, mature boys have much higher levels of testosterone, and mature girls have markedly elevated levels of estradiol (Petersen & Taylor, 1980).

The internal endocrine changes associated with puberty begin a few years prior to their external manifestations. For girls, most of the observable changes take place between 10 and 15 years of age, whereas for boys the span is typically from 11 to 16 years of age (Marshall & Tanner, 1969, 1970). During puberty, the adolescent experiences genital development, breast development (in girls), pubic and axillary hair development, development of facial hair and voice deepening (in boys), changes in the oily secretions of the skin, and rapid gains in both height and weight (Tanner, 1962).

All adolescents experience puberty (except those individuals with endocrine disorders that may prevent or interfere with normal puberty), although there are gender differences in the timing of pubertal development (see Figure 7.2). Girls may begin puberty as early as 8 years of age and as late as 13 ½. Boys may begin puberty approximately 1 ½ to 2 years later than girls; beginning as early as 9 ½ and as late as 13 years of age. The duration of puberty averages 4 years, although it ranges from 1 ½ to 6 years. These variations may add to the adolescent's feelings of uncertainty during this period of time (Petersen et al., 1989). Young adolescents may feel somewhat anxious about when and what they will experience (Petersen et al., 1989).

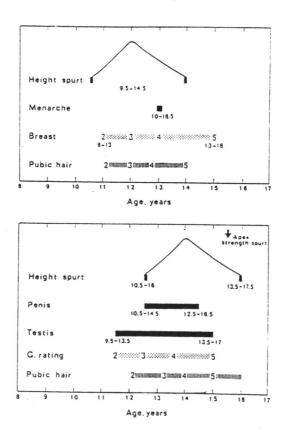

FIGURE 7.2.   Schematic sequence of events at puberty. An average girl (upper) and boy (lower) are represented. The range of ages within which each event charted may begin and end is given by the figures placed directly below its start and finish. (Reproduced by permission from Tanner, 1974)

Direct Effects Model

Mediated Effects Model

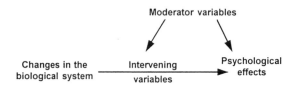

FIGURE 7.3.   The direct effects and mediated effects models. In *Handbook of Adolescent Psychology,* edited by J. Adelson. Copyright 1980, by Petersen and Taylor. Reprinted with permission of John Wiley & Sons, Inc.

It is not yet known whether the gonadal hormone system has different effects on behavior at the beginning of puberty compared to the effects on mature adults. However, there is some reason to believe that the effects are different. The question here is whether the same amount of hormone has different effects at different developmental stages (Petersen et al., 1989). For example, Brooks-Gunn and Warren (1987) reported that midpubertal estrogen levels were related to depressed mood in girls at menarche. This suggests that the brain may be differentially responsive to hormone levels earlier in the pubertal process compared to later (Petersen et al., 1989). Hormone-behavior studies have not been feasible until recently, and much more research is needed in this area.

A great deal of research has accumulated regarding the interrelation of the hormonal changes of puberty and adolescent behavior. Two models have been used to investigate these relations, as can be seen in Figure 7.3 (Petersen & Taylor, 1980). The *direct-effects model* specifies that the hormonal changes associated with puberty directly influence psychological development. The organizing and activating influence of hormones related to puberty on behavior is consistent with a direct-effects model. The *mediated-* or *indirect-effects model* is inclusive and suggests that the psychological effects of puberty are mediated by complex relations among intervening variables, or moderated by contextual or situational aspects of the adolescent's life (Petersen & Taylor, 1980; Richards, Abell, & Petersen, 1993) These can be variables that are psychological or endogenous to the individual, or factors that are exogenous to the personality. For example, in this model, the hormone-induced physical maturational changes of puberty serve as a social stimulus to peers, parents, and other adults, requiring that adolescents begin to behave like adults. Adolescents then may change their behaviors to fit the demands of their social contexts, which they may view as requiring "adultlike" behaviors, such as smoking and use of alcohol.

The direct-effects model suggests that pubertal hormones cause normative adolescent turmoil (e.g., Kestenberg, 1968). Several lines of research have now demonstrated that this hypothesis is inadequate, at least in its simplistic form. First, not all adolescents manifest significant turmoil (e.g., Bandura, 1964; Offer & Offer, 1975). Therefore, universal change, such as puberty, is unlikely to be the cause of specific psychological difficulties. Second, except for one study (Rutter, 1980), most research finds no link between becoming pubertal and manifesting turmoil or psychological problems (e.g., Crockett & Petersen, 1987). Specific pubertal changes, however, may play a causal role with some individuals. Third, difficulties in adolescence are not transient but rather typically foretell diagnosable problems in adolescence or young adulthood (Rutter, Graham, Chadwick, & Yule, 1976; Weiner & DelGaudio, 1976). Therefore, the onset of puberty is unlikely to lead inevitably to psychological problems. However, as described earlier, puberty does involve major and significant changes in the lives of young adolescents.

The mediated-effects model suggests the way in which puberty may serve as a stressor for young people. It does not specify the domains in which puberty may interact with mediating and/or moderating variables to produce stress for the adolescent. There are individual differences in what these stressors may be. Changes in hormones and somatic characteristics and their relations to psychological functioning depend on such factors as age, gender, and contextual components (e.g., number of other changes experienced by a young person at any one given time; Simmons & Blyth, 1987). For example, we have found that both boys and girls who were pubertal before or during the move to a middle or junior high school had more difficulties than those who became pubertal after changing schools (Petersen, Kennedy, & Sullivan, 1991).

In general, there are few effects of actually becoming pubertal, although the timing of puberty has consequences (e.g., Magnusson, 1987). For

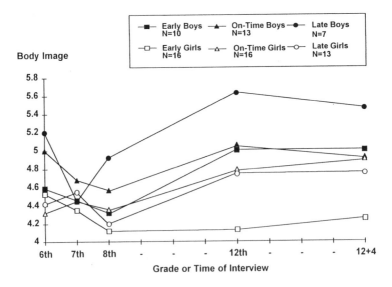

FIGURE 7.4.   Pubertal timing by gender on Body Image. (Reprinted by permission of the Jacobs Institute of Women's Health. From "Depression and Body Image Disorders in Adolescence" by Petersen, Leffert, Graham, Ding, & Overbey. In *Women's Health Issues,* 4(2), pp. 98–108. Copyright 1994)

example, Magnusson (1987) and colleagues reported that early-maturing girls have lower educational attainment in adulthood. Pubertal timing also affects body image. In an example from our own research, we examined body image relative to pubertal timing (Petersen, Kennedy, et al., 1991; Petersen, Leffert, Graham, Ding, & Overbey, 1994). As can be seen in Figure 7.4, early-maturing girls have declining body image that remains lower over the course of adolescence into early adulthood (Petersen et al., 1994). Later-maturing boys show an initial decline in body image at seventh grade, but they then "recover" and become the highest group by 12th grade and into young adulthood.

Cognitive Change

During adolescence the capacity to use formal logic (Inhelder & Piaget, 1958), think hypothetically, and use abstract reasoning all increase (Keating & Clark, 1980). In addition, adolescents become more capable of making decisions (e.g., Weithorn & Campbell, 1982), although the ability to make decisions is not always consistent and is affected by novel and stressful contexts. Because adolescents are more likely than older age groups to find themselves in situations that are new to them, they are particularly vulnerable to thinking that is considerably less sophisticated than what they are capable of in situations that are more familiar or comfortable (Crockett & Petersen, 1993; Hamburg, 1986). Like adults, adolescents are susceptible to "hot cognitions" (Hamburg, 1986), thoughts that are emotionally laden and that may interfere with decision-making processes (e.g., Gilligan & Belenky, 1980). These hot cognitions may lead to impulsive behavior that may contribute to the special risks of adolescence. In novel situations adolescents may respond impulsively without giving consideration to either the consequences of their actions or possible alternative decision options (Furby & Beyth-Marom, 1990). For example, adolescents may have difficulty negotiating the complexity of social relationships as they pertain to sexuality. They may be overcome by their "feelings." The adult, on the other hand, is better able to make decisions because the novelty of the situation has "worn off" (Petersen & Leffert, 1995a).

Researchers report that by age 14 (midadolescence) decision-making ability and reasoning is as good as that of adulthood and certainly involves the same flaws (Lewis, 1981; Weithorn & Campbell, 1982). Despite research evidence that the reasoning of adolescents is as good as the reasoning of adults, policies exist today (e.g., states' decisions regarding abortion and contraceptive services) that limit adolescents' ability to make decisions and/or choices that are independent of parental involvement (Adler, 1994; Petersen & Leffert, 1995a; Quadrel, Fischhoff, & Davis, 1993).

Social Change

In the same way that the hormonal changes of puberty and their manifestations are not inherently stressful to the young adolescent, the social challenges and uncertainties experienced by young adolescents are also not inherently stressful. However, social changes in the domains of family relationships, school transitions, and peer relationships may be stressful, particularly if they take place simultaneously with several other changes (e.g., Simmons & Blyth, 1987).

Parent–Child Relationships.   Traditionally, parent–child relationships during adolescence have been characterized as stormy at best. Psychoanalytic models have characterized parent–child conflict during adolescence as being a necessary part of autonomy development and the process of individuation (Blos, 1970; Freud, 1958). In most cases, research has shown that individuation does not lead to detachment from parents (e.g.,

Crockett & Petersen, 1993). In fact, closeness to parents continues into adulthood (Youniss & Smollar, 1985). However, adolescents report decreased closeness to parents over the adolescent decade (e.g., Petersen, Leffert, Miller, & Ding, 1993).

The view that parent–child relationships over the course of adolescence are basically positive does not mean that these relationships during adolescence are conflict-free. In fact, research has shown that conflict increases during early adolescence, an increase that has been demonstrated to relate to pubertal development (Hill, Holmbeck, Marlow, Green, & Lynch, 1985; Steinberg, 1981). Conflict reaches a plateau during midadolescence and then declines (Montemayor, 1983). Conflicts that occur between most parents and their adolescent children center on mundane issues (e.g., clothing, hairstyles; Laursen & Collins, 1994); only approximately 15% of families report severe conflicts that are thought to be related to psychopathology (Montemayor, 1983; Rutter et al., 1976). Generally, these are families in which childhood psychopathology was evident as well.

School Transitions.   A great deal of research evidence has accumulated demonstrating that the transition from elementary school to middle school or junior high can have negative effects on certain groups of young people (Eccles & Midgley, 1989; Simmons & Blyth, 1987). In the United States, this transition generally involves a change to a much larger and more anonymous school that is farther from home than the neighborhood elementary school. The adolescent must interact with many more peers and teachers, most of whom are not previously known to the adolescent (Epstein & Karweit, 1983). This transition has the potential to be challenging or stressful. Eccles and Midgley (1989) have further demonstrated that middle school and junior high school teachers are less supportive of autonomy and more demanding of compliant behavior than are elementary school teachers, despite the increased capacities of adolescents relative to children.

Research also has demonstrated that academic performance drops with every school transition (Blyth, Simmons, & Carlton-Ford, 1983) when compared to the achievement of same-aged peers who are not making a school transition. The effects are stronger with more transitions or with other changes occurring at the same time or closely spaced temporally (Crockett, Petersen, Graber, Schulenberg, & Ebata, 1989). There are also negative effects on self-esteem, although only for girls (Simmons & Blyth, 1987) and not in all populations (Crockett et al., 1989; Fenzel & Blyth, 1986).

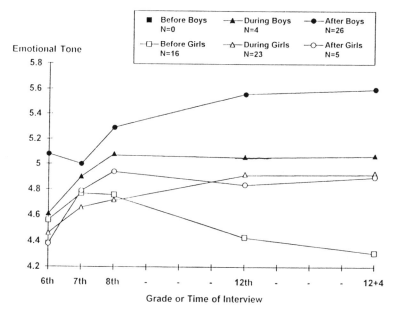

FIGURE 7.5.   Synchronicity by gender on Emotional Tone.

Very few boys transit puberty before school change, whereas girls often experience puberty during this transition (Petersen, Kennedy, et al., 1991; Simmons & Blyth, 1987). We examined the effects of the synchrony of pubertal timing and school transitions on psychosocial variables (Leffert, Graham, & Petersen, 1994; Petersen, Kennedy, et al., 1991). We analyzed our data controlling for the synchronicity of puberty and school changes on Emotional Tone, a measure of negative as well as positive feelings of well-being (Petersen, Schulenberg, Abramowitz, Offer, & Jarcho, 1984). Boys and girls are very similar when the data are analyzed in this way. As can be seen in Figure 7.5, boys who experience puberty after the school transition have more positive Emotional Tone. Synchronicity explains the emergence of depression in adolescence in both boys and girls, and entirely explains the gender difference in depression that emerges during adolescence (Petersen et al., 1994; Petersen, Sarigiani, et al., 1991). We also found that parent support (Petersen, Sarigiani, et al., 1991), but not peer support (Petersen, Sarigiani, Camarena, & Leffert, in press), makes a difference or moderates this effect during early adolescence.

Peer Relationships.   Peer relationships also change during adolescence. The change from the smaller elementary school generally increases the size of the peer group, and because adolescents have increased mobility, they move from small neighborhood groups of friends to large school-based groups (see Brown, 1990). The peer group not only becomes larger, but peer relationships also change in complexity compared to those of younger children (e.g., Berndt, 1982; Crockett, Losoff, & Petersen, 1984). Adolescents also spend more time engaged in peer relationships.

Although it is popularly thought that peers hold a large degree of influence over adolescent opinions and behaviors, research suggests that peer groups do not dramatically influence values that are considered family based (e.g., religious, educational; Brown, Clasen, & Eicher, 1986). Peers do hold more influence over aspects of adolescent appearance and preferences associated with the teen culture (e.g., music). However, peer pressure to participate in problem behaviors often increases over adolescence, although not as much as pressure in other areas (Brown, 1982; Brown, Lohr, & McClenahan, 1986). Some young people are more at risk for the influence of negative peer pressure, particularly early-maturing girls and young people who come from disrupted families (Magnusson, 1987).

Secondary Change

A number of secondary changes also occur during the adolescent decade. They are related to changes in biological and cognitive development and the effects of the major contextual change, school transition.

Psychological Change.   Self-image and self-esteem are constructs of adolescent psychological development that have been researched a great deal (see Harter, 1990). Overall self-esteem increases over the adolescent period (McCarthy & Hoge, 1982; O'Malley & Bachman, 1983). Certain aspects of self-image evidence different patterns of change (Abramowitz, Petersen, & Schulenberg, 1984). In addition to the global assessments of self-esteem, researchers have often assessed self-esteem in specific domains, such as physical attractiveness, peer relationships or acceptance, academic competence, athletic competence, and behavior (e.g., Harter, 1990). Although global assessments of self-esteem are typically highly correlated with self-esteem in specific domains, developmental trends may vary for an individual across domains (e.g., Fend & Schrörer, 1985). This general positive trend contrasts sharply with the popular or media impression that adolescents are falling apart psychologically and with data that evidence increased rates of problem behaviors (e.g., Elliott, 1993). The fact that not all adolescents engage or participate in problem behaviors such as delinquency, drug and alcohol use, and precocious sexuality gives at least a partial explanation for the different trends seen in self-esteem (see Petersen & Leffert, 1995, for more discussion of this issue).

In addition, and consistent with the overall increases in self-esteem, longitudinal studies have shown increasing capacity for autonomy during the course of adolescence (e.g., Steinberg & Silverberg, 1986). Conformity to parental opinion decreases steadily over the course of adolescence. Conformity to peers, however, peaks during early adolescence, at about age 13 or 14, and then declines during mid- and late adolescence (Berndt, 1979).

Experience.   Experience also plays a role in influencing the reasoning capacity and resulting behavior of adolescents. Emotion may interfere with clear thinking among adults as well as adolescents, but a lack of experience with a particular situation may increase anxiety and emotionality among adolescents. As mentioned earlier, adolescents may be especially suscepti- ble to hot cognitions, situations that are emotionally laden and that may lead them to respond impulsively. For example, initial experiences with sexually charged situations, such as being touched in erogenous areas, may befuddle adolescents, whereas the same touches may not be confusing or anxiety producing in a more experienced adult (e.g., Petersen & Leffert, 1995a). As adolescents begin to understand their own feelings elicited in particular situations, they become more able to use their reasoning abilities and behave in ways consistent with their values and expectations.

Summary of Adolescent Development

Adolescence may be characterized as a developmental period involving change in every domain of development and all major contexts (Petersen, 1988). Puberty and the transition to middle or junior high school have particular importance because of their direct impact on the developing adolescent and because of their effects on other aspects of change. For example, puberty results in adult-sized individuals with mature reproduc- tive capacity, both factors that have major social significance. School transitions involve change from the neighborhood-based peer group to a larger network of peers; this also is associated with changes in friendship patterns.

Adolescence brings an atmosphere of uncertainty for the individual. In addition to the normative developmental changes in adolescence, non-nor- mative changes may occur as well. For example, death or illness of family members, parental divorce, or changes in the economic position of the family all occur at predictable frequencies for adolescents.

PHYSICAL AND MENTAL HEALTH
IN ADOLESCENCE

The amount of change experienced by young people during adolescence may be stressful and exceed their capacity to cope. Some adolescents will meet the challenge and develop more effective coping styles. Others, unfortunately, are likely to develop ineffective coping styles that can become lifelong patterns. The following section examines examples of the physiological, behavioral, and health factors associated with stress and coping during adolescence.

Stress in Adolescence

Some research suggests that the extent of challenge in early adolescence produces a divergence in developmental patterns of psychological functioning (e.g., Petersen, Ebata, & Graber, 1987). In brief, the individual's ability to adjust or use coping responses during early adolescence may be altered by two related processes. First, because the brain is a target tissue for some puberty-related hormones (e.g., estrogen) that alter the biochemical milieu of the brain, adolescent behavior may be altered by direct hormone effects on the central nervous system (Petersen et al., 1989). Second, hormones may alter behavior indirectly by the physical maturational changes that occur as a result of puberty. Changes in height, weight, and body proportions are a stimulus to adolescents themselves and to others. Because of their more mature status, adolescents are exposed to increasing demands for more independent and responsible behavior (Petersen et al., 1989). In addition, these hormonal factors may interact with aspects of the social context in such a way as to affect health, and, in turn, further affect development.

Hormones have long been thought to account for behavior changes during adolescence (Petersen et al., 1989). However, hormones as influences on adolescent behavior were not the focus of empirical study until recently (see Susman, Nottelmann, Inoff-Germain, Dorn, & Chrousos, 1987, for a review of hormones and behavior in adolescence). Pituitary-gonadal axis hormones (e.g., luteinizing hormone and follicle stimulating hormone) and their manifestations, physical maturation and reproductive function, are the presumed causal influences that potentially affect behavior in adolescence (Petersen et al., 1989). For example, gonadal steroids (e.g., testosterone) have been linked to changes in aggression at puberty (Olweus, Mattsson, Schalling, & Low, 1980).

As we have discussed previously (Petersen et al., 1989), the hypotheses linking the increase in androgens at puberty and the increase in aggression during human adolescence grew out of studies showing consistent associations between androgen levels and aggressive behavior in male animals, with somewhat less consistent links in female animals (Bouissou, 1983; Eleftherious & Sprott, 1975). In human adolescents, published reports link levels of puberty-related hormones and aggressive behavior. For example, Olweus et al. (1980) reported that higher levels of testosterone in male adolescents related to higher levels of aggressive behavior. Olweus (1986) also reported that testosterone levels exert an indirect causal influence on provoked aggression with low frustration tolerance as a mediating variable; high levels of testosterone may result in impatience and/or irritability, which may then lead to unprovoked and destructive aggression. Similarly, Susman, Inoff-Germain, et al. (1987) hypothesized that higher testosterone levels as well as androgens of adrenal origin, such as androstenedione, were related to mother-reported levels of aggressive attributes in male and female adolescents. Further, they posited that irritability, anxiety, and sadness were involved in the pathways between hormone levels and aggression. The general findings suggested that a profile of lower gonadal steroid levels and higher adrenal androgen levels was related to acting out and rebellious behavior in boys. Finally, Nottelmann et al. (1987) reported that the profile of lower levels of gonadal steroids and higher levels of adrenal androgens also was associated with indices of other aspects of psychosocial adjustment as well as aggressive behavior. Specifically, the adjustment problems of boys were higher in those with lower pubertal stage for chronological age (later maturers) and lower gonadal steroid levels for chronological age. For girls the findings were fewer and less consistent. Adjustment problems for girls were associated with higher levels of gonadotropins, lower levels of the adrenal androgen dehydroepiandrosterone sulfate, and higher levels of androstenedione, sometimes in combination with lower pubertal stage (Nottelmann et al., 1987). Thus, the asynchrony of hormone levels and age may be related to adjustment in both boys and girls.

The profile of an interaction of lower gonadal steroid levels and higher levels of androstenedione together with aggressive behavior, negative emotions, and adjustment problems identified in young adolescents is consistent with a similar profile that has been reported in studies of animals and human adults encountering endogenous and exogenous stressors (see Petersen et al., 1989). The profile of lower levels of hormones of gonadal origin and higher levels of hormones of adrenal origin is illustrative of the interaction between the endocrinology of reproduction and the endocrinology of stress response (see Collu, Gibb, & Ducharme, 1984).

The causal influences of hormones on behavior changes and behavior on hormone changes are undoubtedly part of ongoing developmental processes rather than simply bidirectional causal influences unique to adolescence (Petersen et al., 1989). However, the rapid nature of change in the puberty-related hormones is unique to adolescence. Longitudinal studies of adolescents across the period during which they are experiencing rapid puberty-related hormone changes provide the ideal design for testing hypotheses regarding the causal links between the neuroendocrine changes of puberty and behavioral development (Petersen et al., 1989).

Health Factors

One example of the interaction of contextual "stressors" and development is adolescent iron deficiency. Among adolescent boys between 11 and 14 years of age, approximately 11% have very low levels of serum ferritin, a biochemical indicator of iron status (Petersen et al., 1989). The absence of iron stored in the body results most often in anemia, but other organ systems are affected as well (Beard & Finch, 1985).

The causes of this deficiency are not entirely clear, although they are most likely related to the increase in demand from the adolescent growth spurt and inadequate diet during this period of time. The literature suggests that iron deficiency may result in behavioral and cognitive changes in infancy, childhood, and adolescence (e.g., Pollitt, 1986). The cognitive changes reported are related to deficits in attention and concentration (e.g., Groner, Holtzman, Charney, & Mellits, 1986; Pollitt, Loibel, & Greenfield, 1983). Iron deficiency alters the individual's capacity to respond to stimuli by affecting central nervous system neurotransmission (e.g., Beard & Tobin, 1987; Oski, Honig, Helu, & Howanitz, 1983). Oral iron therapy of 2 to 3 months in duration has been shown to normalize cognitive measures, although not necessarily achievement. We would expect that correcting achievement would take longer given the prolonged period in which nutritional deficits might affect learning capacity (Petersen et al., 1989).

A poor socioeconomic setting correlates positively with iron deficiency in the United States. Adolescents in this situation often have limited nutritional intake. A long-term marginal intake of iron and short-term acute deficit prior to and during the adolescent growth spurt can potentially result in an adolescent who is tissue deficient in iron. It is highly probable that, given this situation, the result will be difficulties in cognition, achievement, task-oriented tests, and attentional skills (Petersen et al., 1989). In addition, iron deficiency may affect the development of normal coping strategies in adolescence and perhaps throughout the life span.

Coping in Adolescence

The changes in all domains during adolescence create a great deal of uncertainty, especially in early adolescence. In addition, normal adolescent development may be exacerbated by stressful life events or chronic illness or disability. How do adolescents cope with the degree of change and challenge and the uncertainty that may result? Although little research exists on this question, we address the conceptual issues in terms of coping styles, effects on physical health, and effects on mental health (see also Genevro, Andreassen, & Bornstein, chapter 4, this volume; Steward, O'Connor, Acredolo, & Steward, chapter 6, this volume).

Coping Styles. A widely used classification of coping styles distinguishes between problem-focused and affect or emotion-focused coping strategies (e.g., Compas, 1987; Hauser & Bowlds, 1990). Problem-focused coping styles refer to the use of problem-solving strategies such as addressing aspects of the social context that pose a threat or reframing the problem. In contrast, emotion-focused strategies relate to the distress caused by the problem. The affect-focused styles are sometimes thought to be less effective forms of coping because they do not directly address the problem, but instead deal with feelings about the problem (Hauser & Bowlds, 1990).

Both strategies are influenced by the circumstances involved. For example, reframing the problem may be most effective in a situation in which the young person has some control. School concerns are often dealt with by problem solving, and health concerns may be more often dealt with through affect-focused coping (Compas, 1987).

Effects on Physical Health. Cognitive, emotional, and behavioral aspects of individual development during adolescence may affect physical health and the course of a chronic illness. For example, in addition to the normative areas of transition during adolescence, the adolescent with Type I or Insulin Dependent Diabetes Mellitus (IDDM) must adhere to a treatment regimen. This includes the maintenance of insulin levels, proper diet, regular mealtimes, and adequate exercise (Hanson, Harris, et al., 1989; White, 1991). However, the adolescent's day-to-day life includes changes in routines that were established during childhood in both school and home contexts, and the inclusion of longer school days because of involvement in sports or other extracurricular activities. These changes do not necessarily favor glycemic control (Leffert, Susman, & Collins, 1993).

In addition, responsibility for maintaining healthy behaviors (e.g., diet, exercise, insulin administration) is one part of the responsibilities transferred to children during the transition to adolescence (Leffert et al., 1993). There is evidence that difficulties in managing diabetes may intensify for some children during this period. There are several possible reasons for these difficulties in management: (a) pubertal changes affect metabolic processes, (b) routines are affected by time spent away from home and parents, (c) stress itself may affect metabolic control, (d) the treatment regimen may be neglected because the child does not want to appear "different" from peers (Leffert et al., 1993), and (e) adolescents with IDDM may be noncompliant with their treatment and dietary regimens as a way of asserting autonomous decision making (Hamp, 1984). Treatment noncompliance affects the maintenance of diabetic control (White, 1991) and also increases the likelihood of diabetic complications earlier in life because of additional stress put on the circulatory and endocrine systems (Leffert et al., 1993).

Studies comparing children with diabetes and those without have revealed few psychological differences (Simonds, 1977). However, within-group differences have shown more psychological symptoms (e.g., anxiety, depression, behavioral problems) in diabetic children with poor metabolic control compared to those children with good metabolic control. One source of these differences may be the compilation or "pile up" of life stresses as the child moves into adolescence. For example, Hanson, Henggeler, Harris, Burghen, and Moore (1989) reported that stress and adherence to the therapeutic regimen are directly associated with metabolic control. Barglow et al. (1983) reported that metabolic control as measured by hemoglobin A_1 (HbA_1) was significantly related to age, duration of illness, life event changes, and ego development. Thus, adolescence may be a time of particular risk to metabolic control because of the major changes occurring in all developmental domains.

Individual development and physical health during the course of adolescence may also be affected by the presence of a disability. For example, pubertal maturation may be delayed or precocious in children and youth with disabilities and may increase the isolation of the young adolescent already set apart because of a disability (Blum, 1988).

Psychosocial development may be affected as well. For example, Blum, Resnick, Nelson, and St. Germaine (1991) reported that adolescents with spina bifida and cerebral palsy had restricted social lives in terms of best friends or dating. In addition these young people reported close relationships with their parents with an absence of parent–adolescent conflict. Blum et al. (1991) suggested that, in actuality, this perceived harmony may reflect parental overprotectiveness and infantilization, which may ultimately delay normal adolescent development.

Chronic illness such as IDDM or a disability such as spina bifida serve only as examples of the interaction of physical health and adolescent development. Other health issues such as experimentation with tobacco, alcohol, and use of other substances; violence; vehicular accidents; and early or unprotected sexuality are equally important factors (see Millstein, Petersen, & Nightingale, 1993, for a review of these topics).

Effects on Mental Health.   Although the media may still stereotype adolescents as moody and preoccupied, research suggests that the majority of adolescents experience no significant psychological difficulties, continue to have close relationships with their families and peers, and develop a healthy sense of themselves by the time they reach adulthood (Petersen, Compas, et al., 1993). These data (e.g., Rutter et al., 1976; Weiner & DelGaudio, 1976) indicate that depression is not a normal state of adolescence (Petersen, Compas, et al., 1993) and that adolescents do not "grow out of" psychological disturbances (Petersen, 1993). In fact, studies have shown that the young people who experience psychological disturbance during adolescence go on, if left untreated, to have serious psychiatric difficulties in adulthood (Rutter et al., 1976; Weiner & DelGaudio, 1976).

Adolescents may be sufficiently stressed or challenged so that their coping resources are overwhelmed, resulting in expressions of various mental health problems. There is indeed an increase in the incidence of psychological disorders during adolescence (Rutter et al., 1976). For example, rates of clinical depression or depressive affect increase during adolescence, especially among girls (Achenbach, Howell, Quay, & Conners, 1991; Petersen, Compas, et al., 1993). Studies of nonclinical samples report averages of 7% depressed adolescents, with a median of 4% (see Petersen, Compas, et al., 1993, for a review), whereas community samples evidence base rates of depressive disorders ranging from 3% (Rohde, Lewinsohn, & Seeley, 1991) to 8% (Kashani et al., 1987). Although young people can be taught coping strategies with short-term improvement in depressed affect, we find no consistent long-term effects (e.g., Petersen, Ding, Leffert, Graham, & Alwin, 1995).

CONCLUSIONS

Developmental changes tend to be generally positive over the adolescent decade in biological, cognitive, and psychosocial domains. However, rates of problem behaviors also increase during this time. Adolescents begin to experience challenges that may be quite like the challenges that adults face, and they may consequently experience pressures to engage in behaviors that may ultimately compromise their health over the course of adolescence and into adulthood. The normative challenges of adolescence may also be exacerbated by stressful life events, poor life conditions (e.g., nutritional insufficiency), or chronic disease or disability. Effective coping skills may permit successful passage through the adolescent decade into adulthood. In addition to effective coping skills, adolescents need parental support to meet these challenges, especially during early adolescence. We believe that the skills learned in adolescence are skills necessary throughout life.

It is essential to understand the nexus of interaction between physiology and behavior in both naturally occurring and stressful situations during this age period in order to effectively help adolescents meet the challenges of this time. For most adolescents, biological changes can be accommodated into healthy developmental patterns. However, without intervention, those young people who experience difficult social circumstances or particularly stressful lives may initiate unhealthy biological and behavioral responses. As mentioned earlier, adolescents with a chronic illness such as IDDM may develop poor metabolic control as a result of changes in routine, the stress accompanying the changes in early adolescence, or treatment noncompliance. Adolescents with difficult or stressful life situations may cope with their situation by using alcohol or other substances instead of using effective problem-solving strategies. Alternatively, adolescents may participate in other risky behaviors, such as precocious or unprotected sexual activity. Future research into the complex interactions of change occurring during adolescence and behavioral outcomes may inform the field in terms of interventions that help adolescents cope most effectively with the challenges they face.

REFERENCES

Abramowitz, R. H., Petersen, A. C., & Schulenberg, J. E. (1984). Changes in self-image during early adolescence. In D. Offer, E. Ostrov, & K. Howard (Eds.), *Patterns of adolescent self-image* (pp. 19–28). San Francisco: Jossey-Bass.

Achenbach, T. M., Howell, C. T., Quay, H. C., & Conners, C. K. (1991). National survey of problems and competencies among four-to-sixteen-year-olds. *Monographs of the Society for Research in Child Development, 56.*

Adler, N. (1994). *Adolescent sexual behavior looks irrational—but looks are deceiving.* Washington, DC: Federation of Behavioral, Psychological, and Cognitive Sciences.

Bandura, A. (1964). The stormy decade: Fact or fiction? *Psychology in Schools, 1,* 224–231.

Barglow, P., Edidin, D. V., Budlong-Springer, A. S., Berndt, D., Phillips, R., & Dubow, E. (1983). Diabetic control in children and adolescents: Psychosocial factors and therapeutic efficacy. *Journal of Youth and Adolescence, 12*(2), 77–94.

Beard, J. L., & Finch, C. A. (1985). Iron deficiency. In K. Weiner & F. Clyesdale (Eds.), *Iron fortification of foods* (pp. 3–16). New York: Academic Press.

Beard, J. L., & Tobin, B. (1987). Feed efficiency and norepinephrine turnover in iron deficiency. *Proceedings Society for Experimental Biology and Medicine*, 337–344.

Berndt, T. J. (1979). Developmental changes in conformity to peers and parents. *Developmental Psychology, 15*, 608–616.

Berndt, T. J. (1982). The features and effect of friendship in early adolescence. *Child Development, 53*, 1447–1460.

Blos, P. (1970). *The adolescent passage*. New York: International Universities Press.

Blum, R. W. (1988). Developing with disabilities: The early adolescent experience. In M. D. Levine & E. R. McAnarney (Eds.), *Early adolescent transitions* (pp. 177–192). Lexington, MA: Lexington Books.

Blum, R. W., Resnick, M. D., Nelson, R., & St. Germaine, A. (1991). Family and peer relationships among adolescents with spina bifida and cerebral palsy. *Pediatrics, 88*(2), 280–285.

Blyth, D. A., Simmons, R. G., & Carlton-Ford, S. (1983). The adjustment of early adolescents to school transitions. *Journal of Early Adolescence, 3*, 104–120.

Bouissou, M. F. (1983). Androgens, aggressive behavior and social relationships in higher mammals. *Hormone Research, 18*, 43–61.

Brooks-Gunn, J., & Warren, M. (1987, April). *Biological contributions to affective expression in young adolescent girls*. Paper presented at the biennial meeting of the Society for Research on Child Development, Baltimore, MD.

Brown, B. B. (1982). The extent and effects of peer pressure among high school students: A retrospective analysis. *Journal of Youth and Adolescence, 11*, 121–133.

Brown, B. B. (1990). Peer groups and peer cultures. In S. S. Feldman & G. R. Elliott (Eds.), *At the threshold: The developing adolescent* (pp. 171–196). Cambridge, MA: Harvard University Press.

Brown, B. B., Clasen, D., & Eicher, S. (1986). Perception of peer pressure, peer conformity, dispositions, and self-reported behavior among adolescents. *Developmental Psychology, 22*, 521–530.

Brown, B. B., Lohr, M. J., & McClenahan, E. L. (1986). Early adolescent's perceptions of peer pressure. *Journal of Early Adolescence, 6*, 139–154.

Coleman, J. (1978). Current contradictions in adolescent theory. *Journal of Youth and Adolescence, 7*, 1–11.

Collu, R., Gibb, W., & Ducharme, J. R. (1984). Effects of stress on gonadal function. *Journal of Endocrinological Investigations, 7*, 529–537.

Compas, B. E. (1987). Stress and life events during childhood and adolescence. *Clinical Psychology Review, 7*, 275–302.

Crockett, L. J., Losoff, M., & Petersen, A. C. (1984). Perceptions of the peer group and friendship in early adolescence. *Journal of Early Adolescence, 4*, 155–181.

Crockett, L. J., & Petersen, A. C. (1987). Pubertal status and psychosocial development: Findings from the early adolescence study. In R. M. Lerner & T. T. Foch (Eds.), *Biological-psychosocial interactions in early adolescence: A life-span perspective* (pp. 173–188). Hillsdale, NJ: Lawrence Erlbaum Associates.

Crockett, L. J., & Petersen, A. C. (1993). Adolescent development: Health risks and opportunities for health promotion. In S. G. Millstein, A. C. Petersen, & E. O. Nightingale

(Eds.), *Promoting the health of adolescents: New directions for the twenty-first century* (pp. 13–37). New York: Oxford University Press.

Crockett, L. J., Petersen, A. C., Graber, J. A., Schulenberg, J. E., & Ebata, A. (1989). School transitions and adjustment during early adolescence. *Journal of Early Adolescence, 8,* 405–419.

Dornbusch, S. M., Petersen, A. C., & Hetherington, E. M. (1991). Projecting the future of research on adolescence. *Journal of Research on Adolescence, 1,* 7–17.

Douvan, E., & Adelson, J. (1966). *The adolescent experience.* New York: Wiley.

Eccles, J. S., & Midgley, C. (1989). Stage/environment fit: Developmentally appropriate classrooms for early adolescents. In R. E. Ames & C. Ames (Eds.), *Research on motivation in education* (Vol. 3, pp. 139–186). San Diego: Academic Press.

Eichorn, D. H. (1975). Asynchronization in adolescent development. In S. E. Dragastin & G. H. Elder, Jr. (Eds.), *Adolescence in the life cycle: Psychological change and social context* (pp. 81–96). Washington, DC: Hemisphere.

Eleftherious, B. E., & Sprott, R. L. (1975). *Hormonal correlates of behavior: Vol. 1. A lifespan view.* New York: Plenum.

Elliott, D. S. (1993). Health enhancing and health compromising lifestyles. In S. G. Millstein, A. C. Petersen, & E. O. Nightingale (Eds.), *Promoting the health of adolescents: New directions for the twenty-first century* (pp. 119–145). New York: Oxford University Press.

Elliott, G. R., & Feldman, S. S. (1990). Capturing the adolescent experience. In S. S. Feldman & G. R. Elliott (Eds.), *At the threshold: The developing adolescent* (pp. 1–14). Cambridge, MA: Harvard University Press.

Emde, R. N., & Harmon, R. J. (Eds.). (1984). *Continuities and discontinuities in development.* New York: Plenum.

Epstein, J. L., & Karweit, N. L. (Eds.). (1983). *Friends in school.* New York: Academic Press.

Feldman, S. S., & Elliott, G. R. (Eds.). (1990). *At the threshold: The developing adolescent.* Cambridge, MA: Harvard University Press.

Fend, H., & Schrörer, S. (1985). The formation of self-concepts in the context of educational systems. *International Journal of Behavioral Development, 8,* 423–444.

Fenzel, L. M., & Blyth, D. A. (1986). Individual adjustment to school transitions: An exploration of the role of supportive peer relations. *Journal of Early Adolescence, 6,* 315–329.

Freud, A. (1958). Adolescence. *Psychoanalytic Study of the Child, 13,* 255–278.

Furby, L., & Beyth-Marom, R. (1990). *Risk-taking in adolescence: A decision-making perspective.* Washington, DC: Carnegie Council on Adolescent Development, Carnegie Corporation of New York.

Gilligan, G., & Belenky, M. F. (1980). A naturalistic study of abortion decisions. In R. Selman & R. Yando (Eds.), *Clinical-developmental psychology* (Vol. 7, pp. 69–90). San Francisco: Jossey-Bass.

Groner, J. A., Holtzman, N. A., Charney, E., & Mellits, E. D. (1986). A randomized trial of oral iron on tests of short term memory and attention span of young pregnant women. *Journal of Adolescent Health Care, 7,* 44–48.

Hall, G. S. (1904). *Adolescence: Its psychology and its relations to physiology, anthropology, sociology, sex, crime, religion, and education.* New York: Appleton.

Hamburg, B. (1986). Subsets of adolescent mothers: Developmental, biomedical, and psychosocial issues. In B. Lancaster & B. A. Hamburg (Eds.), *School-age pregnancy and parenthood: Biosocial dimensions* (pp. 115–145). New York: Aldine de Gruyter.

Hamp, M. (1984). The diabetic teenager. In R. W. Blum (Ed.), *Chronic illness and disabilities in childhood and adolescence* (pp. 217–238). Orlando, FL: Grune & Stratton.

Hanson, C. L., Harris, M. A., Relyla, G., Cigrang, J. A., Carle, D. L., & Burghen, G. A. (1989). Coping styles in youth with insulin dependent diabetes mellitus. *Journal of Consulting and Clinical Psychology, 57*, 644–651.

Hanson, C. L., Henggeler, S. W., Harris, M. A., Burghen, G. A., & Moore, M. (1989). Family system variables and the health status of adolescents with insulin-dependent diabetes mellitus. *Health Psychology, 8*, 239–253.

Harter, S. (1990). Self and identity development. In S. S. Feldman & G. R. Elliott (Eds.), *At the threshold: The developing adolescent* (pp. 352–387). Cambridge, MA: Harvard University Press.

Hauser, S. T., & Bowlds, M. K. (1990). Stress, coping, and adaptation. In S. S. Feldman & G. R. Elliott (Eds.), *At the threshold: The developing adolescent* (pp. 388–413). Cambridge, MA: Harvard University Press.

Hill, J., Holmbeck, G., Marlow, L., Green, T., & Lynch, M. (1985). Menarcheal status and parent–child relations in families of seventh-grade girls. *Journal of Youth and Adolescence, 14*, 301–316.

Inhelder, B., & Piaget, J. (1958). *The growth of logical thinking from childhood to adolescence*. New York: Basic Books.

Kashani, J. H., Carlson, G. A., Beck, N. C., Hoeper, E. W., Corcoran, C. M., McAllister, J. A., Fallahi, C. , Rosenberg, T. K., & Reid, J. C. (1987). Depression, depressive symptoms, and depressed mood among a community sample of adolescents. *American Journal of Psychiatry, 144*, 931–934.

Keating, D. P., & Clark, L. V. (1980). Development of physical and social reasoning in adolescence. *Developmental Psychology, 16*, 23–30.

Kestenberg, J. (1968). Phase of adolescence with suggestions for correlation of psychic and hormonal organizations. Part III. Puberty, growth, differentiation, and consolidation. *Journal of the American Academy of Child Psychiatry, 6*, 577–614.

Laursen, B., & Collins, W. A. (1994). Interpersonal conflict during adolescence. *Psychological Bulletin, 155*, 197–209.

Leffert, N., Graham, B. L., & Petersen, A. C. (1994, May). Gender-based development of behavioral and emotional problems during early adolescence. In J. A. Graber (Chair), *Methods for studying stress during reproductive transitions*. Symposium conducted at Psychosocial and behavioral factors in women's health: Creating an agenda for the 21st century, Washington, DC.

Leffert, N., Susman, A., & Collins, W. A. (1993, March). Developmental transitions in parent–adolescent relationships in families with an adolescent with chronic illness. In G. N. Holmbeck (Chair), *Family relationships and psychosocial development in physically impaired and chronically ill children*. Symposium at the biennial meetings of the Society for Research on Child Development, New Orleans, LA.

Lewis, C. (1981). How adolescents approach decisions: Changes over grades seven to twelve and policy implications. *Child Development, 52*, 538–544.

Magnusson, D. (1987). *Individual development in an interactional perspective: Vol. 1. Paths through life*. Hillsdale, NJ: Lawrence Erlbaum Associates.

Marshall, W. A., & Tanner, J. M. (1969). Variations in the pattern of pubertal changes in boys. *Archives of Disease in Childhood, 44*, 291–303.

Marshall, W. A., & Tanner, J. M. (1970). Variations in the pattern of pubertal changes in boys. *Archives of Disease in Childhood, 45*, 13–23.

McCarthy, J. D., & Hoge, D. R. (1982). Analysis of age effects in longitudinal studies of adolescent self-esteem. *Developmental Psychology, 18*, 372–379.

Millstein, S. G., Petersen, A. C., & Nightingale, E. O. (Eds.). (1993). *Promoting the health of adolescents: New directions for the twenty-first century*. New York: Oxford University Press.

Montemayor, R. (1983). Parents and adolescents in conflict: All families some of the time and some families most of the time. *Journal of Early Adolescence, 3*, 83–103.

Nottelmann, E. D., Susman, E. J., Inoff-Germain, G., Cutler, G. G., Jr., Loriaux, D. L., & Chrousos, G. P. (1987). Developmental processes in early adolescence: Relations between adolescent adjustment problems and chronological age, pubertal stage, and puberty-related serum hormone levels. *Journal of Pediatrics, 110*, 473–480.

Offer, D., & Offer, J. (1975). *From teenage to young manhood: A psychological study*. New York: Basic Books.

Offer, D., Ostrov, E., & Howard, K. I. (1981). *The adolescent: A psychological self-portrait*. New York: Basic Books.

Olweus, D. (1986). Aggressions and hormones: Behavioral relationships with testosterone and adrenaline. In D. Olweus, J. Block, & M. Radke-Yarrow (Eds.), *Development of antisocial and prosocial behavior: Research theories and issues* (pp. 51–72). Orlando, FL: Academic Press.

Olweus, D., Mattsson, A., Schalling, D., & Low, H. (1980). Testosterone, aggression, physical and personality dimensions in normal adolescent males. *Psychosomatic Medicine, 42*, 253–269.

O'Malley, P. M., & Bachman, J. G. (1983). Self-esteem: Change and stability between ages 13 and 23. *Developmental Psychology, 19*, 257–268.

Oski, F. A., Honig, A. S., Helu, B., & Howanitz, P. (1983). Effect of iron therapy on behavioral performance in nonanemic, iron deficient infants. *Pediatrics, 71*, 877–880.

Petersen, A. C. (1988). Adolescent development. *Annual Review of Psychology, 39*, 583–607.

Petersen, A. C. (1993). Presidential address: Creating adolescents: The role of context and process in developmental trajectories. *Journal of Adolescent Research, 3*(1), 1–18.

Petersen, A. C., Compas, B., Brooks-Gunn, J., Stemmler, M., Ey, S., & Grant, K. (1993). Depression in adolescence. *American Psychologist, 48*(2), 155–168.

Petersen, A. C., Ding, S., Leffert, N., Graham, B. L., & Alwin, J. (1995, March). Improving coping behaviors during adolescence. In J. Schulenberg & J. Maggs (Chairs), *Developmental transitions during adolescence: Health risks, health benefits*. Symposium paper presented at the biennial meetings of the Society for Research on Child Development, Indianapolis, IN.

Petersen, A. C., & Ebata, A. T. (1987). Developmental transitions and adolescent problem behaviors: Implications for prevention and intervention. In K. Hurrelmann, F. X. Kaufmann, & F. Lösel (Eds.), *Social intervention: Potential and constraints* (pp. 167–184). New York: Walter de Gruyter.

Petersen, A. C., Ebata, A. T., & Graber, J. (1987, April). *Responses to developmental and family changes in early adolescence.* Paper presented at the annual meeting of the American Educational Research Association, Washington, DC.

Petersen, A. C., Kennedy, R. E., & Sullivan, P. (1991). Coping with adolescence. In M. E. Colten & S. Gore (Eds.), *Adolescent stress: Causes and consequences* (pp. 93–110). New York: Aldine de Gruyter.

Petersen, A. C., & Leffert, N. (1995). What is special about adolescence? In M. Rutter (Ed.), *Psychosocial disturbances in young people: Challenges for prevention* (pp. 3–36). London: Cambridge University Press.

Petersen, A. C., & Leffert, N. (in press). Developmental issues influencing guidelines for adolescent health research. *Journal of Adolescent Health.*

Petersen, A. C., Leffert, N., Graham, B., Ding, S., & Overbey, T. (1994). Depression and body image disorders in adolescence. *Women's Health Issues, 4*(2), 98–108.

Petersen, A. C., Leffert, N., Miller, K., & Ding, S. (1993, March). The role of community and intrapersonal coping resources in the development of depressed affect and depression in adolescence. In *Depression in childhood and adolescence: Developmental issues.* A symposium presentation at the biennial meetings of the Society for Research in Child Development, New Orleans, LA.

Petersen, A. C., Sarigiani, P. A., Camarena, P., & Leffert, N. (in press). Resilience in adolescence. *International Annals of Adolescent Psychiatry.*

Petersen, A. C., Sarigiani, P. A., & Kennedy, R. E. (1991). Adolescent depression: Why more girls? *Journal of Youth and Adolescence, 20,* 247–271.

Petersen, A. C., Schulenberg, J. F., Abramowitz, R. H., Offer, D., & Jarcho, H. D. (1984). A self-image questionnaire for young adolescents (SIQYA): Reliability and validity studies. *Journal of Youth and Adolescence, 13,* 93–111.

Petersen, A. C., & Spiga, R. (1982). Adolescence and stress. In L. Goldberger & S. Breznitz (Eds.), *Handbooks of stress: Theoretical and clinical aspects* (pp. 515–528). New York: The Free Press.

Petersen, A. C., Susman, E. J., & Beard, J. L. (1989). The development of coping responses during adolescence: Endocrine and behavioral aspects. In D. S. Palermo (Ed.), *Coping with uncertainty: Behavioral and developmental perspectives* (pp. 151–172). Hillsdale, NJ: Lawrence Erlbaum Associates.

Petersen, A. C., & Taylor, B. (1980). The biological approach to adolescence: Biological change and psychosocial adaptation. In J. Adelson (Ed.), *Handbook of adolescent psychology* (pp. 117–155). New York: Wiley.

Pollitt, E. (1986). Nutrition and intellectual performance. *Clinical Nutrition, 5,* 219–225.

Pollitt, E. , Loibel, R. L., & Greenfield, D. B. (1983). Iron deficiency and cognitive test performance in preschool children. *Nutrition and Behavior, 1,* 137–146.

Quadrel, M. J., Fischhoff, B., & Davis, W. (1993). Adolescent (in)vulnerability. *American Psychologist, 48*(2), 102–116.

Richards, M. H., Abell, S., & Petersen, A. C. (1993). Biological development. In P. H. Tolan & B. J. Cohler (Eds.), *Handbook of clinical research and practice with adolescents* (pp. 21–44). New York: Wiley.

Rohde, P., Lewinsohn, P. M., & Seeley, J. R. (1991). Comorbidity of unipolar depression: 2. Comorbidity with other mental disorders in adolescents and adults. *Journal of Abnormal Psychology, 100*, 214–222.

Rutter, M. (1980). *Changing youth in a changing society: Patterns of adolescent development and disorder*. Cambridge, MA: Harvard University Press.

Rutter, M., Graham, P., Chadwick, O., & Yule, W. (1976). Adolescent turmoil: Fact or fiction. *Journal of Child Psychology and Psychiatry, 17*, 35–56.

Simmons, R. G., & Blyth, D. A. (1987). *Moving into adolescence: The impact of pubertal change and school context*. Hawthorne, NY: Aldine de Gruyter.

Simmons, R. G., Burgeson, R., Carlton-Ford, S., & Blyth, D. A. (1987). The impact of cumulative change in early adolescence. *Child Development, 58*, 1220–1234.

Simonds, J. F. (1977). Psychiatric status of diabetic youth matched with a control group. *Diabetes, 26*, 921–925.

Steinberg, L. (1981). Transformation in family relations at puberty. *Developmental Psychology, 17*, 833–838.

Steinberg, L., & Silverberg, S. (1986). The vicissitudes of autonomy in early adolescence. *Child Development, 57*, 841–851.

Susman, E. J., Inoff-Germain, G., Nottelmann, E. D., Loriaux, D. L., Cutler, G. B., & Chrousos, G. P. (1987). Hormones, emotional dispositions, and aggressive attributes in young adolescents. *Child Development, 58*, 1114–1134.

Susman, E. J., Nottelmann, E. D., Inoff-Germain, G., Dorn, L. D., & Chrousos, G. P. (1987). Hormonal influences on aspects of psychological development during adolescence. *Journal of Adolescent Health Care, 8*, 492–504.

Tanner, J. M. (1962). *Growth at adolescence*. Springfield, IL: Thomas.

Tanner, J. M. (1972). Sequence, tempo, and individual variation in growth and development of boys and girls aged twelve to sixteen. In J. Kagan & R. Coles (Eds.), *Twelve to sixteen: Early adolescence* (pp. 1–24). New York: Norton.

Tanner, J. M. (1974). Sequence and tempo in the somatic changes in puberty. In M. M. Grumbach, G. D. Grave, & F. E. Mayer (Eds.), *Control of the onset of puberty* (pp. 448–470). New York: Wiley.

Weiner, I. B., & DelGaudio, A. (1976). Psychopathology in adolescence. *Archives of General Psychiatry, 34*, 98–111.

Weithorn, L. A., & Campbell, S. B. (1982). The competency of children and adolescents to make informed treatment decisions. *Child Development, 53*, 1589–1598.

White, N. R. (1991). Diabetes. In R. M. Lerner, A. C. Petersen, & J. Brooks-Gunn (Eds.), *Encyclopedia of adolescence* (Vol. 1, pp. 232–236). New York: Garland.

Youniss, J., & Smollar, J. (1985). *Adolescents' relations with mothers, fathers, and friends*. Chicago: University of Chicago Press.

8

Commentary: Children's Health and the Development of Social Knowledge

Arthur H. Parmelee, Jr.
University of California

Interdisciplinary exchanges of ideas and concerns are urgently needed for the improvement of children's health care. Included in this book are behavioral studies by both pediatricians and psychologists concerning children from infancy through adolescence. Knowledge about children's behavioral development is important to pediatricians in the care of both sick and well children. In addition, in well-child care, children's minor physical problems and illnesses play an important role in their normal behavioral development, a fact frequently overlooked.

In this chapter I provide a longitudinal view of child development and health care from birth through adolescence, integrating the studies presented. My comments are primarily from the point of view of a medical teacher and clinical health care provider, particularly in well-child care. Traditionally, well-child care involves both the physical and mental hygiene of children and constitutes about 40% of a general pediatrician's practice. Children have many minor injuries and illnesses such as diarrhea and respiratory illnesses (colds). Most of these are managed at home within the family, with telephone calls to the doctor as needed. Much of a well-child visit discussion can be about the child's last illness or injury, and how this altered the child's behavior, straining the parent–child relationship. Pediatricians need to understand the normal development of parent–child social relationships to know how to help parents keep a transient relationship perturbation from becoming a major relationship disturbance or prolonged disorder. When pediatricians succeed, they contribute to the family's mental hygiene and to their preparation for future management of more serious illnesses or injuries (Parmelee, 1986, 1989, 1992, 1993).

It is in the context of the family that children learn how to cope with pain and strange illness feelings such as change in mood and strength loss. They also see their siblings and parents go through similar cycles of illnesses and injuries. Therefore, they have ample opportunity to learn how their family copes with pain and illness. Illness behavior in any family also reflects cultural perspectives on all life experiences (Parmelee, 1986). We know from Zborowski's (1952) and Zola's (1956) studies of adult immigrant medical patients from different ethnic groups that, in families of one cultural group, parents looked on any pain or deviation from a child's normal behavior as a sign of illness, making children prone to be anxious about the meaning and significance of these manifestations. In families from another cultural background, parents expressed a great deal of verbal emotion and sympathy toward the "poor child" who happened to be in discomfort or pain, but parents did not concern themselves unduly with the symptomatic meaning of the child's aches and pains. In a third cultural group, children were told "not to run to mother with every little thing," and boys in particular were told to take pain "like a man" and not to cry. Culturally appropriate illness behavior for children in these families meant not getting emotional but, rather, applying the appropriate first aid and calling a doctor. Not surprisingly, adults reared in these different cultural backgrounds tended to react to pain and communicate about illness in very different ways, and to have different expectations about whether health care providers will be able to help them.

Families define a sick role and the special attention and empathy given the sick person (Parsons, 1958). Each family has its own construct of the appropriate place and time for sick and pain behavior for each family member. When a couple marries, they have to negotiate a sick role concept for their new family. Each partner usually has a different point of view from their own family experiences. Included are the parents' folk knowledge of illnesses and the views of their family's culture toward illness and pain. Illnesses and injuries therefore play a major role in children's learning family and cultural social knowledge from the moment of birth. We all need at times to let others care for us when we are too ill or in too much pain to carry on our daily tasks. This is one of the most important lessons for our adult health care learned during our childhood. Some of us have a hard time giving up our daily tasks and submitting to the care of others, particularly if we are from a culture oriented toward striving for individual independence. It may be easier for those from cultures that focus more on interdependent family relationships (Greenfield, 1994; LeVine, 1988).

I first discuss the Papoušeks' study of persistent crying because it occurs at the beginning of life and strongly influences subtle but important early mother–child interactions. It also illustrates my contention that concerns about possible or real illnesses and injuries are central to children's social development. Persistent crying is a problem of state regulation in which mother and baby influence each other in very primary ways. In my experience, however, persistent crying in the first 2 to 3 months is of different biological origin than that after 3 months (Parmelee, 1977). I mention this because most of the infants seen by the Papoušeks were older than 3 months and few were less than 2 months, the crucial time of brain change toward regulation strong enough to begin to control crying. In their consultation clinic, they were also not in a position to anticipate the problem in time to minimize it. The early mother–infant relationship disturbance sets the stage for the crying to continue beyond 3 months. Because this is not uncommon, as the Papoušeks document, their observations are extremely important and consistent with mother–infant relationships that are already disturbed. The Papoušeks clearly define this process and base their interventions on these observations, providing an important model.

Let me turn to our own efforts to prevent too much disturbance of the mother–infant relationship in the first 3 months to illustrate the mental hygiene aspects of well child care. We know that in the first months, mothers view feeding as their primary role whether they feed by breast or bottle. Because their primary interactions with their infants are when their infants awaken for feedings, much of the crying is considered food related. This creates the almost inevitable maternal view that their breast milk is inadequate or bad, the milk fed by bottle is wrong, or the infant has an abnormal digestive system. At the very beginning of their infant's life, parents are trying to decide if their infant is ill and in pain or just overaroused.

Most pediatricians have found the hard way that discontinuing breast feeding and starting formula or changing formula does not reduce the crying. This maneuver tends to confirm, rather than alleviate a mother's concerns that her infant's digestive system is abnormal. Forsyth and Canny (1991) found that mothers who had formula changes for control of colic in the first 3 months continued to see their child as physically vulnerable 3 years later.

In our teaching well-baby clinic, we have ample time for mothers to express their views fully and for the pediatrician to present other ways of thinking about their concerns without minimizing the mothers' points of view. We indicate that an increasing amount of crying in the first 6 to 8 weeks of life is usual and expected. We point out that in our experience, as infants' nervous systems mature, they become increasingly sensitive to all stimulation, both internal and external. We see this as a good sign of normal brain development. It is a fact that in the first 2 months there is an acceleration of sensory nerve conduction as reflected in visual, auditory, and tactual evoked potentials. It is also a time when infants' capacities to regulate brain arousal are not well developed. We stress that it takes a while longer for infants to be able to control their responses to these stimuli and to use them to energize themselves for play and social interaction. In our studies, we can see the regulation increase during the first 3 months, with increasing organization of quiet and active sleep, and alert awake states (Parmelee, 1977; Parmelee & Stern, 1972; Parmelee, Wenner, & Schulz, 1964). We point out that the stimulation to arousal and crying in the infant results from a summation of all visual, auditory, tactual, movement, temperature, hunger, and bowel activity occurring at one time. In addition, there is an accumulation of arousal from the stimuli throughout the day. This is why there is likely to be the most crying toward the end of a busy day and the least in the after-midnight hours (Brazelton, 1962), assuming the household and neighborhood are generally less active during the nighttime hours. Along with the Papoušeks, we find that in households with infants with persistent crying, the infants are generally overstimulated. This is usually unintentional. For example, sometimes a crying infant does not soothe easily when first approached and patted or held gently; the intensity of the soothing efforts soon crescendos, and the soothing person becomes increasingly tense. The effect is to further stimulate rather than soothe. A mother of an infant with persistent crying also often finds the rare moment of alert quiet wakefulness so enjoyable that she is likely to overstimulate her infant to crying. It is interesting that mothers often observe spontaneously that, on a day when they have had many visitors, all interested in seeing the infant, the price is more infant crying that evening.

Often parents' struggles with their infants' persistent crying have barely settled when the infant has a minor illness causing diarrhea or vomiting and loss of appetite. There follows a disruption of feeding routines and some weight loss, to the parents' great distress. Again they lose confidence in their ability to adequately care for their infant. A month or two later the infant has a cold, clearly not life threatening but disruptive of family interactions. There is more crying and again loss of appetite. It is in this context that parents evolve general social routines as well as those for handling their own and their children's illnesses (Parmelee, 1989).

I have focused on the early infancy period as a reminder that illness and pain are part of the development of social knowledge from the beginning of life. We sometimes forget this when studying older children's adaptations to hospitalization and medical procedures. There is a need to integrate family management of illness and pain into children's understanding of relationships and understanding of prosocial behavior. As a pediatrician, I would like more information on parents' different styles of coping with their children's illness and the type of sick role they have evolved for the family.

As already indicated, life for infants and parents can start with high stress, and some infants and parents cope more successfully than others. The stress is both social and physical for parents and infants. Coping includes a very delicate balance in social interactions of carefully adjusted stimulation and calming. It is not surprising that, by the time of entry into school, there are children who have a harder time coping both behaviorally and physiologically as described by Boyce. In the studies presented, some children are identified as having highly reactive biological systems that predict both injuries sustained and susceptibility to infection. It is difficult to know whether these children have always been this way or evolved to this state due to the complex social interactions, illnesses, and injuries I have described.

Pediatricians and parents are aware that, in the first 3 to 4 weeks of school, illnesses are frequent. This is true of children at all elementary school levels, but more often in kindergarten as we know from school attendance records (Parmelee & Schimmel, 1958). Parents also know that this is more likely to be true of one child in the family than another. Boyce goes a long way toward helping us understand this phenomenon. In addition, parents know that this phenomenon does not limit itself to the stress of beginning school; it also happens with much anticipated happy events, such as going on a vacation trip in the summer or special family events such as Christmas festivities. Apparently, happy and exciting pleasurable events can also be stressful.

The studies by Genevro, Andreassen, and Bornstein and by Kain and Mayes fit into my longitudinal view of illnesses and health care. The study by Genevro and colleagues expands our understanding of the development of children's cognitive ability to cope with medical procedures including surgery. Kain and Mayes' study deals with the anxiety of children about to undergo surgical anesthesia and discusses procedures intended to minimize this. Their particular focus is on the development of better methods of assessing children's anxiety during this process.

The information from both of these studies is urgently needed to aid hospitals in helping children and families cope more successfully. Both studies stress that current efforts to prepare children and families for procedures and surgeries are not universally successful. They indicate that we will need to adapt these procedures more to the individual needs of children and families. Genevro et al. found that higher levels of maternal concern about the child's general health status related to the presence of negative affective content and the number of acts in the children's doctor event interview responses. Kain and Mayes found that the hospital and surgery preparation procedures made some parents and children more anxious, although helping others. Similarly, during anesthesia induction, the parents' presence contributed to child anxiety.

In this regard we too have found that although most mothers would like to be with their child in the hospital, many do not know how to be helpful. In the hospital mothers can no longer play the omnipotent protector, and their usual caregiving roles are taken over by the hospital staff. The important socially supportive role of just being there is not easily comprehensible, particularly when one has limited protective power. In addition, the rigid social structure of hospitals does not recognize or adapt to varying sick role styles. We do not know how children from families with strong interdependent support systems may deal differently with hospitalization than those from families fostering independence and self-sufficiency at an early age. Given the current multicultural nature of most of our cities, we see many variations of family styles (Bornstein, Tal, & Tamis-LeMonda, 1991; Greenfield, 1994; LeVine, 1988).

I think we need to probe more deeply into ways to individualize our intervention procedures. Our social work and child life staffs try to individualize their work with mothers on these issues. We have experimented with having this staff meet with the child and family in their own home before the child's hospitalization. This way the family and staff get to know each other in the home context, and the staff obtains information for individualizing their interventions in the hospital. The same staff then visits the families again after the children are discharged home to express their continued interest and try to determine what was most and least helpful for the family and the child (Brill, Fauvre, Klein, Clark, & Garcia, 1981). These efforts have not been as frequent as we would like, but indicate some ways to extend hospital care studies.

What helps children through most hospitalizations are any social support, activities, or other reminders that there is some continuity to their life, and that they will resume their former activities and continue to be themselves. In the hospital setting, having parents present, visits from friends and siblings, or telephone calls and letters help provide this continuity. Similarly, play activities, in bed if necessary, or in the playroom, help younger children considerably; surprisingly, schoolwork for the older children is appreciated. The ward teacher contacts the children's schools and teachers for current lessons for each hospitalized child. They agree that only the simplest part of these may be completed. Schoolwork gives hospitalized children a common discussion topic when they phone their classmates.

The experience of many minor illnesses and injuries managed at home would hardly prepare a child or family for the treatment of leukemia that includes numerous painful procedures over a long period of time. The usual efforts to provide hospitalized children with some life continuity through people and activities are less successful. It is hard for children and families to anticipate their return to former activities considering the still significant mortality rate of leukemia. As Steward, O'Connor, Acredolo, and Steward state, it is probable that children are most concerned with the numerous recurring procedures, whether very painful or not. Having so many aspects of their life out of control for so long must be overwhelming. When faced with their child's possibly fatal illness, parents also have extreme difficulty coping simultaneously with their child's and their own emotional feelings concerning the procedures. My coworkers tell me that some children are so concerned about their parents' distress that they shield them from their own fears and feelings. This is consistent with Steward and colleagues' report of follow-up interviews with children and their parents in which the children often discussed having had more pain and discomfort than their parents indicate. We need the information Steward and colleagues are providing about this very stressful type of medical care. There are other potentially fatal illnesses in children such as renal, liver, and cardiac failure now treated by transplants. These also often include painful procedures. I have been emphasizing the importance of the development of social knowledge for understanding children's behavior when they are ill or injured. This also applies to understanding their behavior during medical procedures, hospitalization, and surgery. I consider our health and illness behavior a function of our general social competence (Mechanic, 1964, 1979; Pratt, 1973). So far, I have discussed primarily the development of children's understanding of family social relationships during illnesses and injuries. I have emphasized the affective learning of empathy and prosocial behavior toward others who are ill or injured, but these are only part of the development of general social knowledge and competence (Parmelee, 1986, 1989, 1992, 1993).

In this regard I find the work of Turiel (1983; Tisak & Turiel, 1984), Nucci (1994; Nucci, Guerra, & Lee, 1991), and Smetana (1983, 1989, 1994) relevant. They discuss a domain-specific construction of social knowledge. From early in life they find that children differentiate four types of social regulations: moral, social conventional, personal, and prudential. *Moral* issues are defined as acts that are wrong because they affect the rights or welfare of others. Included are harming another person or depriving another person of what is rightfully theirs. Transgressions are consistently evaluated as the most serious offenses and universally wrong even without rules. *Conventional* issues concern daily social interactions in different social systems and require rules. The rules are generally agreed on and depend on context. Examples for a child include not talking in church, table manners, and cleaning one's room. The consequences of transgressing these categories of rules vary with the occasion and within family parenting styles, but are not as serious as for moral transgressions. *Personal* issues are defined as acts that have consequences only to the actor and are viewed as beyond societal regulation and moral concern. With increasing age, children—particularly adolescents—assume more responsibility for these. Included are dress, preferred music, type of friends, and so on. *Prudential* issues pertain to comfort and health, and concern safety and harm to self. The effects are on the actor rather than on other individuals or societal structures. Health risk behaviors fall in this category. Although prudential behavior affects only the actor, it is considered more serious than other personal behavioral decisions and is more regulated by parents. For young children, prudential rules are given to them by their parents; for example, do not go out in the cold without your sweater, do not eat too much candy before dinner, and do not play with knives. Children seem to be able to differentiate the significance of these behavioral categories rather early in life. I have discussed this construct of social knowledge because one of the categories is rather specifically related to health matters, and again emphasizes that health behavior is an integrated part of parenting behavior directed toward general social competence.

I believe this discussion bears on Steward et al.'s study of leukemia patents and Leffert and Petersen's discussion of adolescents. Moral and prudential behavior are particularly relevant; both of these are concerned with harming someone. Moral behavior concerns not hurting others and is always true, whereas prudential behavior concerns hurting only one's self and is more dependent on personal and contextual circumstances. It is possible that young children undergoing painful or frightening medical procedures see these as moral transgressions and as inexplicable adult behavior condoned by their parents. This makes them anxious and fearful. On the other hand, older children might be convinced that, because these procedures are clearly for their own good, they fall into the prudential category. They then can make their own decisions to suffer the pain for their own welfare. The teenage boy, cited by Steward and colleagues, who ran away from home rather than continue to suffer medical procedures, may have felt it was his prerogative to make the prudential decision to risk no more treatment and take the consequences. I believe it will be useful to study in more detail the development of social knowledge in relation to children's coping with medical procedures, hospitalization, and general health care.

In Leffert and Petersen's studies of adolescents, the focus is on the interaction of biological and social development, which is in turn intertwined with the development of social knowledge. It is important for adolescents to assume more and more responsibility for their own decisions rather than to follow parental rules. In the area of personal issues, parents usually concede this, sometimes with reluctance. As indicated, these decisions pertain to dress, choice of friends, music, movies, and television program preferences. Prudential issues, although affecting only the actor, are considered more serious and sometimes are moralized by the parents. Certainly parents would like to continue with some control in this area even with adolescents. Further study of how parents and adolescents define and govern personal and prudential issues may help us better understand and intervene in risk taking that adversely affects health.

The reviews by Tinsley (1992, 1995) point out the numerous and complex interactions between general social developmental processes and health and illness care. A true synthesis of health and illness care and general social development seems almost impossible. I, nevertheless, remain hopeful. The physician-philosopher Kass (1994) wrote a very interesting synthesis of human biology, nutrition, and physical form, and human reflective, rational, and ethical efforts toward the development of social order. However, this is more from an evolutionary than a developmental point of view.

I have tried to weave together some major threads of behavioral development that integrate the studies presented in this volume. These threads are a function of parenting styles and the cultural context in which they take place. They concern children's acquisition of general social knowledge within which are woven health care and health care concerns of parents for their children. Dimensions of general knowledge that children acquire include conventions concerning behavior when ill or in pain, and prudential rules for health behavior. This process starts at birth, as I indicated in the discussion of persistent crying in the first months of life. Health concerns from this beginning become part of parenting style in the form of conventional and prudential social rules. They are also an underlying theme of parent–child relationships, parents' views of their parenting effectiveness, and children's views of themselves. Mental health is an integral part, because children's concepts of self and relationships with others are involved.

An underlying theme of personal interest is that of well-baby and well-child care. A number of intervention programs have been developed for the mental welfare of infants and young children for a variety of risk categories. On the other hand, the intervention potential of well-baby and well-child care programs has been overlooked. These programs are administratively in place and are socially accepted. Furthermore, they are not categorically targeted, and start at birth. Such programs potentially could aid all children and parents in dealing with all of the issues we have discussed. I am hopeful that more interdisciplinary consideration will be given to the expansion of these services.

REFERENCES

Bornstein, M. H., Tal, J., & Tamis-LeMonda, C. (1991). Parenting in cross-cultural perspective: The United States, France, and Japan. In M. H. Bornstein (Ed.), *Cultural approaches to parenting* (pp. 69–90). Hillsdale, NJ: Lawrence Erlbaum Associates.

Brazelton, T. B. (1962). Crying in infancy. *Pediatrics, 4,* 579–588.

Brill, N. S., Fauvre, M., Klein, N., Clark, S., & Garcia, L. (1981). Caring for chronically ill children: An innovative approach to children's health care. *Chronic Illness, 16,* 105–113.

Forsyth, B. W., & Canny, P. F. (1991). Perceptions of vulnerability 3½ years after problems of feeding and crying behavior in early infancy. *Pediatrics, 88,* 757–763.

Greenfield, P. M. (1994). Independence and interdependence as developmental scripts: Implications for theory, research and practice. In P. M. Greenfield & R. R. Cocking (Eds.), *Cross-cultural roots of minority development* (pp. 1–37). Hillsdale, NJ: Lawrence Erlbaum Associates.

Kass, L. R. (1994). *The hungry soul: Eating and the perfecting of our nature.* New York: The Free Press.

LeVine, R. A. (1988). Human parental care: Universal goals, cultural strategies, individual behavior. In R. A. LeVine, P. M. Miller, & A. M. West (Eds.), *Parent behavior in diverse societies* (pp. 3–12). San Francisco: Jossey-Bass.

Mechanic, D. (1964). The influence of mothers on their children's health attitudes and behaviors. *Pediatrics, 33,* 444–453.

Mechanic, D. (1979). The stability of health and illness behavior: Results from a 16-year follow-up. *American Journal of Public Health, 69,* 1142–1145.

Nucci, L. P. (1994). Mothers' beliefs regarding the personal domain of children. In J. G. Smetana (Ed.), *Beliefs about parenting: Origins and developmental implications* (pp. 81–97). San Francisco: Jossey-Bass.

Nucci, L. P., Guerra, N., & Lee, J. Y. (1991). Adolescent judgments of personal, prudential, and normative aspects of drug usage. *Developmental Psychology, 27,* 841–848.

Parmelee, A. H. (1977). Aldrich Award Remarks—The first three months. *Pediatrics, 59,* 389–395.

Parmelee, A. H. (1986). Children's illnesses: Their beneficial effects on behavioral development. *Child Development, 57,* 1–10.

Parmelee, A. H. (1989). The child's physical health and the development of relationships. In A. J. Sameroff & R. N. Emde (Eds.), *Relationship disturbances in early childhood: A developmental approach* (pp. 145–162). New York: Basic Books.

Parmelee, A. H. (1992). Wellness, illness, health, disease concepts. In E. J. Susman, L. V. Feagans, & W. J. Ray (Eds.), *Emotion, cognition, health, and development* (pp. 165–187). New York: Basic Books.

Parmelee, A. H. (1993). Children's illness and normal behavioral development: the role of caregivers. *Zero to Three, 13*(4), 1–9.

Parmelee, A. H., & Schimmel, B. F. (1958). Absence from school: Its relation to illness in the community. *California Medicine, 88,* 144–148.

Parmelee, A. H., & Stern, E. (1972). Development of states in infants. In C. Clemente, D. Purpura, & F. Meyer (Eds.). *Sleep and the maturing nervous system* (pp. 199–304). New York: Academic Press.

Parmelee, A. H., Wenner, W. H., & Schulz, H. R. (1964). Infant sleep patterns from birth to 16 weeks of age. *Journal of Pediatrics, 65,* 576–582.

Parsons, T. (1958). Definitions of health and illness in light of American values and social structure. In E. G. Jaco (Ed.), *Patients, physicians, and illness: Sourcebook in behavioral science and medicine* (pp. 165–187). New York: The Free Press.

Pratt, L. (1973). Child rearing methods and children's health behavior. *Journal of Health and Social Behavior, 14,* 61–69.

Smetana, J. G. (1983). Social-cognitive development: Domain distinctions and coordinations. *Developmental Review, 3,* 131–147.

Smetana, J. G. (1989). Toddlers' social interactions in the context of moral and conventional transgressions in the home. *Developmental Psychology, 25,* 499–508.

Smetana, J. G. (1994). Parenting styles and beliefs about parental authority. In J. G. Smetana (Ed.), *Beliefs about parenting: Origins and developmental implications* (pp. 21–36). San Francisco: Jossey-Bass.

Tinsley, B. J. (1992). Multiple influences on the acquisition and socialization of children's health attitudes and behavior: An integrative review. *Child Development, 63,* 1043–1069.

Tinsley, B. J. (1995). Health behavior of mothers. In D. S. Gochman (Ed.), *Handbook of health behavior research* (Vol. 1, pp.) New York: Plenum.

Tisak, M., & Turiel, E. (1984). Children's conceptions of moral and prudential rules. *Child Development, 55,* 1030–1039.

Turiel, E. (1983). *The development of social knowledge: Morality and convention.* New York: Cambridge University Press.

Zborowski, M. (1952). Cultural components in responses to pain. *Journal of Social Issues, 8,* 16–30.

Zola, I. K. (1956). Culture and symptoms—An analysis of patients' presenting complaints. In R. E. Spector (Ed.), *Cultural diversity in health and illness* (pp. 84–105). New York: Appleton-Century Crofts.

About the Authors

CURT ACREDOLO is Associate Adjunct Professor in the Department of Human and Community Development at the University of California, Davis. Educated at the Institute of Child Development at the University of Minnesota, his research focuses on middle childhood cognition. Acredolo is Principal Investigator on a project examining the role of uncertainty as the motivating force underlying linguistic and cognitive development.

* * *

CAROL J. ANDREASSEN is a Postdoctoral Research Fellow in the Child and Family Research Section of the National Institute of Child Health and Human Development, where she has held a National Research Council Neuroscience Fellowship and currently holds an NIH Intramural Research Training Award. She received her PhD in developmental psychology from the State University of New York at Stony Brook. Her principal research interests are in cognitive development, broadly defined to include the effects of mother–child interaction on children's cognitive and social-cognitive development. She is a member of the American Psychological Association, the Society for Research in Child Development, and the International Society for Infancy Studies.

* * *

MARC H. BORNSTEIN is Senior Research Scientist and Head of Child and Family Research at the National Institute of Child Health and Human Development. He holds a BA from Columbia College and MS and PhD degrees from Yale University. Bornstein was a J. S. Guggenheim Foundation Fellow, and he received a Research Career Development Award from the National Institute of Child Health and Human Development.

He was recipient of the C. S. Ford Cross-Cultural Research Award from the Human Relations Area Files and the B. R. McCandless Young Scientist Award from the American Psychological Association. Bornstein has held faculty positions at Princeton University and New York University as well as academic appointments in Munich, London, Paris, New York, and Tokyo. Bornstein is coauthor of Development in Infancy and Perceiving Similarity and Comprehending Metaphor. He is general editor of The Crosscurrents in Contemporary Psychology Series, including Psychological Development From Infancy, Comparative Methods in Psychology, Psychology and Its Allied Disciplines (Vols. I–III), Sensitive Periods in Development, Interaction in Human Development, and Cultural Approaches to Parenting. He also edited Maternal Responsiveness: Characteristics and Consequences and the Handbook of Parenting (Vols. I–IV), and he coedited Developmental Psychology: An Advanced Textbook, Stability and Continuity in Mental Development, Contemporary Constructions of the Child, Early Child Development in the French Tradition, and The Role of Play in the Development of Thought. He is author of several children's books and puzzles in The Child's World series. Bornstein is Editor of Child Development, and has contributed scientific papers in the areas of human experimental, methodological, comparative, developmental, cross-cultural, pediatric, and aesthetic psychology.

* * *

W. THOMAS BOYCE is Professor of Epidemiology and Child Development at the University of California, Berkeley, and Professor of Pediatrics at the University of California, San Francisco. He received a BA in psychology and philosophy from Stanford University and an MD from Baylor College of Medicine. Following a residency in pediatrics at UCSF, Boyce completed fellowship training as a Robert Wood Johnson Foundation Clinical Scholar at the University of North Carolina, Chapel Hill. As a member of the pediatrics faculties at the University of Arizona and UCSF, Boyce headed the development of research programs in behavioral and developmental pediatrics and now serves as Director of the Division of Health and Medical Sciences, School of Public Health, University of California, Berkeley. He is a member of the Society for Pediatric Research, the American Pediatric Society, the American Psychosomatic Society, and the Academy of Behavioral Medicine Research. He has served on the American Academy of Pediatrics' Council on Pediatric Research and the Executive Council of the Society for Behavioral Pediatrics. Boyce is a member of the Core Scientific Group of the MacArthur Foundation Research Network on Psychopathology and Development and the Board of Editors of *Child Development*.

JANICE L. GENEVRO is a Postdoctoral Research Fellow in the Child and Family Research Section, Laboratory of Comparative Ethology, National Institute of Child Health and Human Development. She is currently the recipient of an NIH Intramural Research Training Award and was previously awarded a Research Associateship from the National Research Council of the National Academy of Sciences. She received a baccalaureate degree with a special project major in Child Development from the University of California, San Diego, a Master's degree in social work from San Diego State University, and a PhD in health psychology from the University of California, San Francisco. Genevro has worked extensively in interdisciplinary community-based and university medical center-affiliated programs designed to promote the health and well-being of children and their families. Her primary research interests include the interplay between development and health, and cross-generational influences on health attitudes and behaviors. Since coming to the National Institutes of Health, Genevro has focused on examining the contributions of development, experience, and individual differences to children's understanding of and coping with distressing medical experiences. She is a member of the American Psychological Association, the American Public Health Association, the Association for the Care of Children's Health, and the Society for Research in Child Development.

* * *

ZEEV N. KAIN is Assistant Professor of Anesthesiology and Pediatrics at Yale University School of Medicine. Kain did his pediatric residency at Schneider Children's Hospital and his anesthesia residency at Yale. Following training in anesthesiology, Kain completed both a fellowship in Pediatric-Anesthesia at the Boston Children's Hospital and a Robert Wood Johnson fellowship at Yale. Kain is the principal investigator of multiple studies involving perioperative anxiety in young children. His other research interests include anesthetic implications of cocaine abuse.

* * *

NANCY LEFFERT is a Research Scientist at Search Institute in Minneapolis, Minnesota. She received her BA and MSW from San Diego State University and PhD in child psychology at the Institute of Child Development, University of Minnesota. She was a Postdoctoral Fellow in a joint appointment of the Institute on Community Integration (College of Education, University of Minnesota) and the Center for Children with Chronic Illness and Disabilities (Department of Pediatrics, University of Minnesota). Leffert is a member of the American Psychological Association, National Association of Social Work, Society for Research on Adolescence, and Society for Research in Child Development.

* * *

LINDA C. MAYES is the Arnold Gesell Associate Professor of Child Development, Psychology, and Pediatrics in the Yale Child Study Center. Mayes earned her undergraduate degree from the University of the South and her medical degree from Vanderbilt University. She did her pediatric residency at Vanderbilt as well as a postdoctoral fellowship in neonatology. Mayes came to the Yale Department of Pediatrics as a Robert Wood Johnson General Academic Pediatrics Fellow. She joined the faculty of the Yale Child Study Center as an Assistant Professor. Mayes is the principal investigator of a longitudinal study of the effects of prenatal cocaine exposure on early development. Her other research interests include the developmental outcome of medically compromised infants and young children.

* * *

JACQUELINE O'CONNOR is a Lecturer in the Department of Human and Community Development at the University of California, Davis. O'Connor received her PhD in Human Development from the University of California, Davis. Her research interests have focused on the role of uncertainty and ambivalence in human development throughout the life span, with emphasis on the implications for mental and physical health and psychological well-being. She is Principal Investigator on a project evaluating women's cancer preventive behaviors following benign breast biopsy.

* * *

HANUŠ PAPOUŠEK is consulting Professor of Developmental Psychobiology at the Research and Intervention Program for Early Development and Parenting, Institute for Social Pediatrics, University of Munich, Germany. Papoušek earned his medical degree at Masaryk University in Brno, Czechoslovakia. After postdoctoral training in pediatrics, he led a research lying-in unit for interdisciplinary research on behavioral development and immunological resistance at the Research Institute for Mother and Child Care in Prague. He received the DSC degree at Charles University in Prague. He was Chief of the Developmental Psychobiology Unit at the Max-Planck Institute for Research in Psychiatry in Munich, Germany, and Professor of Developmental Psychobiology at the Ludwig-Maximilian

University of Munich. Papoušek was visiting Professor of Developmental Psychology at the University of Denver and of Developmental Psychobiology at Harvard University; honorary Harvard scientist in the Center for Cognitive Studies, the Department of Psychology and Social Relations, and the Medical Center of Children's Hospital; visiting senior scientist in the Laboratory of Comparative Ethology of the National Institute of Child Health and Human Development; and Special Professor of Developmental Psychology at the Free University of Amsterdam, The Netherlands. Papoušek's research has focused on early development of learning and cognitive abilities, early social and communicative development, and on intuitive forms of parental support to these abilities.

* * *

MECHTHILD PAPOUŠEK is Chief of the Research and Intervention Program for Early Development and Parenting, Institute for Social Pediatrics, University of Munich, Germany. Papoušek was promoted to MD at the University of Tübingen, Germany, and was habilitated as Associate Professor in Developmental Psychobiology at the University of Munich. She was a fellow of the Foundation's Fund for Research in Psychiatry at Harvard University, Research Child Psychiatrist at the Max-Planck Institute for Research in Psychiatry in Munich, and research fellow of the Hughes Foundation in the Laboratory of Comparative Ethology of the National Institute of Child Health and Human Development. Papoušek's interests are in preverbal communication between infants and caregivers, cross-cultural comparisons of preverbal communication, musical elements in early communication, persistent crying, and interactional and communicative disorders in infants.

* * *

ARTHUR H. PARMELEE, JR. received BS and MD degrees from the University of Chicago, and spent 4 years in the U.S. Navy Medical Corps. He undertook specialty training in pediatrics at the Yale University Medical School and at the Los Angeles Children's Hospital. Parmelee joined the faculty of the Department of Pediatrics at the University of California, Los Angeles School of Medicine, remaining there until his retirement. He was named Head of the Division of Child Development within the Department of Pediatrics, and throughout his career at UCLA maintained formal ties to the schools of education, social work, and public health. Parmelee was Commonwealth Fellow at the Centre de Recherches Biologique Neonatales, Clinique Obstericale Baudeloque, Paris; Research Professor of

Pediatrics, Göttingen, Germany; and Fellow at the Center for the Advanced Study in the Behavioral Sciences, Stanford, California. He was elected a member of the American Pediatric Society and the Society for Pediatric Research. Parmelee also served on the National Research Council Committee on Child Development and Public Policy, and as Chairman of the Section on Child Development of the American Academy of Pediatrics, Examiner of the American Board of Pediatrics, and President of the Society for Pediatric Research. He received the *Folke Bernadotte* Award for Services for the Handicapped (Sweden), the C. Anderson Aldrich Award in Child Development from the American Academy of Pediatrics, and the Society for Research in Child Development Award for Distinguished Scientific Contributions to Child Development. Parmelee has published on medical education, the development of handicapped children, the neurological and physiological development of preterm and full-term infants in the neonatal period, and long-term behavioral follow-up studies.

* * *

ANNE C. PETERSEN is Professor of Adolescent Development and Pediatrics, University of Minnesota. She received her BA in mathematics, MS in statistics, and PhD in measurement, evaluation, and statistical analysis at the University of Chicago. Petersen was Vice President for Research and Dean of the Graduate School at the University of Minnesota. She was previously associated with the Pennsylvania State University where she was Dean of the College of Health and Human Development and Head of the Department of Individual and Family Studies. Petersen is a founding member and past president of the Society for Research on Adolescence. She is past president, Developmental Psychology Division of the American Psychological Association, and is a fellow of the American Association for the Advancement of Science, the American Psychological Association, and the American Psychological Society. She serves on the Executive Council of the International Society for the Study of Behavioral Development. Petersen is the author of numerous books, including *Promoting the Health of Adolescents: New Directions for the Twenty-First Century* and *Youth Employment and Society.*

* * *

DAVID S. STEWARD is Professor Emeritus of Religious Education at Pacific School of Religion and the Graduate Theological Union in Berkeley, CA. Steward received his PhD from Yale University. His theoretical and teaching interests have focused on the experience that children and their families have of limiting conditions such as illness, pain, and death. Steward has collaborated extensively on empirical research focused on patterns of interaction between teacher and learner and on factors that impact the memories of early childhood experiences.

*　*　*

MARGARET S. STEWARD is a Professor and Associate Dean for Women's Affairs in the School of Medicine, University of California, Davis. Steward received her PhD from Yale University, and she holds a Diplomate in Clinical Psychology from the American Board of Professional Psychology. Her research, teaching, and clinical work has focused on children and families at risk as a result of prematurity, illness, divorce, and abuse.

*　*　*

Author Index

Subject Index

A

Abdominal pain, persistent crying in infants, 12

Academic performance, in adolescence, 138

Active sleep state, definition and characterization in infants, 14, *see also* Sleep, wake cycles

Acute lymphocytic leukemia (ALL), incidence in children, 107

Adaptive approach strategy, children's understanding of stressful medical experiences, 74, 76, 78

Adjustment, hormone relation during adolescence, 143, *see also* Behavior

Adolescence

    childhood trauma

        health behavior/development, 116–118

        modeling the link, 118–121

    developmental transition

        biological changes, 132–136

        characterization and overview, 130–132

        cognitive changes, 136–137

        secondary changes, 140–141

        social changes, 137–140

        summary, 141

    physical/mental health

        biology, challenge, coping effects overview, 129–130

        coping, 145–147

        health factors, 144

        stress, 142–144

    risk-taking behavior and childhood injuries, 41

Adolescent Perceived Events Scale, injury relations in adolescents, 48

Adolescent Risk Behavior Survey, injury relations in adolescents, 48–49

Adrenal hormones, adjustment problems during adolescence, 143

Adrenocortical response, children's anxiety over surgery, 89, 97, 98–99

Adults, cancer treatment in children, 106, *see also* Parents

Adverse outcomes, children's anxiety over surgery, 86

Affect regulation, capacity and children's anxiety over surgery, 88, 96

Affective responses, children's understanding of routine medical care, 65–66, 69, 70

African-Americans, childhood injuries, 37

Age, *see* Chronological age

Aggression

    childhood injuries, 41

    hormonal effects during adolescence, 142–143

Alert activity, development in infants, 16

Alert inactivity, development in infants, 15–16

Alert waking state, *see also* Sleep, wake cycles

    development in infants, 16

    integration processes in infants, 16–17

    persistent crying relation in infants, 24

ALL, *see* Acute lymphocytic leukemia

Androgens, effects during adolescence, 143

Androstenedione, aggressive behavior during adolescence, 143

Anesthesia, *see also* Perioperative period

    methods of induction and children's anxiety over surgery, 87–93

    risk, 86

Anxiety

185